PAT BROWN, MBA

Tech Business Founders

"The Financial Literacy Playbook for Startup Founders"

ABRAM 47 BROWN

First published by AbramBrown47 2025

First edition

ISBN: 978-1-967737-42-0

This book was professionally typeset on Reedsy.
Find out more at reedsy.com

Contents

Preface

Tech Business Founders

If you are holding this book, chances are you already understand something fundamental: being a tech founder requires a different kind of thinking. You've spent years building, scaling, failing, pivoting, iterating. You've seen ideas turn into products, products turn into companies, and companies turn into ecosystems. But when it comes to wealth—the kind that equity grants, successful funding rounds, or liquidity events bring—you're navigating a world for which no one gave you a manual. And make no mistake: the wealth management world wasn't built for you. It was built for salaried professionals, not for visionaries playing at the edges of innovation.

Imagine you're sitting across from me. You've got Series B shares that could be worth tens of millions if all goes well. Or maybe you've just exited and wired eight or nine figures to your bank account. Maybe you're still grinding, head down, building product-market fit, wondering if your equity will ever translate into real wealth. Wherever you are in your journey, you are living in a reality where traditional financial advice breaks down. And that's exactly why this book exists.

The wealth management industry assumes predictability. It assumes stable W-2 incomes, diversified portfolios, steady contributions to 401(k) plans, and slow, cautious wealth accumulation. Your life doesn't look like that. Your wealth is likely concentrated in one volatile, illiquid asset: your company. Your income is likely uncertain or deferred. Your financial future is not a straight line—it's a roller coaster. And that roller coaster demands a different playbook. This chapter—and this book—is that playbook.

Let's talk first about concentrated wealth. When your net worth is tied up in your company, you face a unique kind of risk. One product launch gone wrong, one competitor surge, one funding round delay—and your paper fortune can evaporate. Diversification is a classic principle, but diversifying when you are sitting on pre-IPO shares, when liquidity is locked up by restrictions and blackout periods, is far from straightforward. Most advisors will tell you to "diversify"—but few know how to navigate tender offers, secondary markets, or structured liquidity solutions tailored for founders.

Liquidity is not just an accounting issue—it's a freedom issue. Without liquidity, you can't fund your lifestyle, your next venture, or your philanthropic goals. Worse, without liquidity planning, you risk facing a massive tax bill you can't pay if and when you finally liquidate your shares. Smart liquidity planning—whether through 10b5-1 plans, secondary market sales, pre-liquidity wealth planning, or even hedging strategies—becomes vital. Wealth without liquidity is just an accounting mirage.

And then there's the tax trap. You've probably heard about AMT—the Alternative Minimum Tax—lurking when you exercise ISOs. You may have heard whispers about QSBS—Qualified Small Business Stock—that could shield you from millions in capital gains taxes if properly structured. But knowing these terms and using them effectively are two different things. A single misstep in the timing of stock option exercises, or failing to file an 83(b) election within the 30-day window, can cost you millions. The tax code is not founder-friendly unless you know how to navigate it like a chessboard, planning ten moves ahead.

Let's also talk about what happens post-exit. Imagine a wire transfer lands, and you are suddenly staring at $50 million in your bank account. The world assumes that's the end of your worries—but you and I know it's just the beginning. Now, the problem is not how to build wealth, but how to protect it, grow it wisely, and ensure it becomes a foundation, not a burden, for your family. Family governance, multi-generational estate planning, asset protection, and legacy building become the new frontier. Without structure, windfalls often become wastelands.

And then there's the emotional side of the exit—the part no one talks about. You spent years being "the founder." Your identity was tied to your company. What happens when the company is gone, but you remain? Post-exit depression is real. So is decision fatigue. So is aimlessness. True wealth mastery is about creating not just financial structures, but life structures that give you purpose beyond your company. Wealth without purpose is just a gilded cage.

Now, let's be clear: building a financial life post-exit is not just about hiring more advisors. It's about building the right team and knowing how to lead it. You need wealth managers who understand equity comp, not just asset allocation. You need estate attorneys who know dynasty trust design, not just boilerplate wills. You need tax strategists who think globally and creatively. Most importantly, you need an integrated team that communicates—a wealth command center you quarterback.

Real founders don't micromanage—but they don't abdicate either. You have to lead your financial life with the same clarity, intensity, and intentionality that you brought to your company. You have to understand that delegation without oversight leads to disaster. Your financial team should be your boardroom now—accountable, transparent, and world-class.

Here's the real opportunity: tech founders, with the right financial architecture, can do more than preserve wealth. They can amplify it. They can leverage it to build venture portfolios, launch philanthropic foundations, invest in future founders, and create lasting legacies. You have the tools, the capital, and the vision. What you need now is the playbook for mastery.

If you learn nothing else from this chapter, learn this: what got you here—grit, vision, risk tolerance—won't automatically get you to the next level. Post-liquidity, the game changes. The moves that built your wealth must give way to the moves that preserve it, protect it, and grow it quietly, wisely, intentionally.

The path to wealth mastery for tech founders is not paved with luck. It's paved with structure. With strategy. With stewardship.

Your next company is your financial life. Your next legacy is what you build after the exit. It's time to architect both with the same brilliance you brought to your startup.

The Unique Financial Journey of a Tech Founder

The Financial Life of a Tech Founder: What No One Tells You

Let's begin with the truth: the financial life of a tech founder does not look like anyone else's. It doesn't follow the neat, predictable arc that traditional financial planning assumes—the one built around steady salaries, gradual promotions, 30-year careers, and retirement at 65 with a gold watch and a diversified portfolio. No, founders live differently. And because you live differently, you must plan differently. This chapter is your introduction to the real financial journey of a tech founder—the volatility, the concentration, the complexity, and the extraordinary potential.

Volatile Wealth: The Roller Coaster Ride

When you're a founder, your wealth doesn't trickle in steadily. It rides waves of valuation events, investor sentiment, product-market fit—or lack thereof. One year you're raising a seed round at $5 million post-money. The next you're a Series A darling at $50 million. Six months later, the market shifts, and you're renegotiating down rounds or strategizing layoffs. The truth is stark: your net worth is volatile, and because it's based on private equity, it's not just volatile—it's opaque, hard to value, hard to liquidate. Founders must learn to live with these waves. You can't predict or prevent volatility, but you can plan for it, insulating your personal life from your professional roller coaster.

Concentrated Risk: All Your Eggs in One Basket

Diversification is the classic financial advice for the masses: 60% stocks, 40% bonds. A little real estate, maybe some alternative assets. But you? You're a founder. You have everything in one place: your company.

Concentration is a double-edged sword. It's the reason founders are the richest cohort in wealth studies—but it's also why many flame out without a parachute. The key isn't panic-diversifying. It's strategic risk management: pre-planned liquidity, asset protection structures, and having an off-ramp in mind long before you need it.

Illiquidity: Rich on Paper, Cash Poor in Reality

Many founders are "wealthy" in theory, broke in practice. Paper valuations can look impressive, but without liquidity, you're stuck. You can't sell, you can't borrow cheaply, and you can't de-risk. Worse, illiquidity pressures founders into poor decisions—raising rounds on unfavorable terms, cashing out early, or taking risks they otherwise wouldn't. Liquidity planning—secondary sales, tender offers, structured exits—is an art form at this level, and without it, your financial life is a fragile house of cards.

Irregular Income: Feast or Famine

Founders live in extremes: high highs, low lows. Some months, it's tight salaries—if you're drawing one at all. Other months, a secondary offering puts millions in your account overnight. But in between, there can be years of drought. Traditional budgeting doesn't work here. You need dynamic cash flow management: larger reserves, flexible investing strategies, disciplined spending, and proactive tax planning that assumes erratic inflows, not consistent bi-weekly paychecks.

Asymmetric Opportunity: The High Stakes Game

Founders don't just face volatility; they face asymmetry. You can work for a decade, scraping by, only to hit a $200 million payday—or end with nothing but experience and scars. The risk is disproportionate to the potential reward. Your financial plan must be equally asymmetric: aggressive enough to capture opportunity, but resilient enough to weather years of zero cash flow, dilution, or failed ventures. You're playing a different game. Your wealth management strategy should reflect that.

Taxes: The Silent Wealth Killer

Few founders realize how tax-inefficient exits can be—until it's too late. A mistimed ISO exercise triggers AMT. A missed 83(b) election costs millions. A move to a high-tax state pre-IPO results in an unnecessary 13% haircut.

The IRS, the state tax boards—they're your silent, ever-present partners. Good tax planning isn't an afterthought; it's an ongoing strategy. Founders must structure for QSBS eligibility, understand timing strategies around liquidity events, and know when to relocate for maximum tax efficiency. The difference isn't small—it's life-changing.

Emotional Complexity: Wealth Changes You

Beyond spreadsheets and trusts lies the most complex variable: you. Money changes relationships, alters self-perception, challenges identities. After a liquidity event, many founders struggle with guilt, imposter syndrome, or a sudden loss of purpose. The company was your identity. The hustle was your heartbeat. Now what? Managing wealth isn't just financial—it's psychological. The most successful founders build not just financial plans, but life plans. They create purpose beyond business. They define new metrics for success: impact, legacy, family, personal growth.

The Founder's Financial Journey: Not Linear, But Worth It

There's nothing straightforward about the founder's path. It's volatile, concentrated, illiquid, unpredictable. And yet, for those who master it, it offers not just wealth, but freedom. Freedom to create. Freedom to give. Freedom to live on your terms.

Imagine a founder—call her Elena. She built a fintech company, bootstrapped it, fought tooth and nail for market share. After nine brutal years, she exited for $150 million. But she didn't wait until the end to plan. She exercised ISOs strategically, filed 83(b) elections, structured a QSBS-eligible sale, and moved to a no-income-tax state two years before the exit. Post-exit, she diversified wisely, built a family office, and established a donor-advised fund to formalize her philanthropy. Today, Elena isn't just wealthy. She's free. She's purposeful. She's at peace.

Contrast her with a founder who ignored the warning signs. No pre-exit planning. AMT triggered without liquidity to pay it. Moved to California right before the exit. Half the proceeds lost to taxes. Poor diversification decisions post-exit. Depression followed, then lawsuits. The difference wasn't luck. It was preparation.

Action Steps

- Conduct a volatility audit: How exposed are you to valuation swings?
- Build a liquidity map: When and how can you unlock cash?
- Structure for taxes today—not tomorrow.
- Engage in emotional due diligence: What will life look like post-exit?
- Assemble a founder-friendly financial team: tax strategists, estate planners, liquidity specialists—not just stockbrokers.
- Start now. The biggest cost is waiting.

You are already a founder. You know how to build. Now it's time to build something even more enduring: financial mastery. The journey is complex, but so is the life you've already chosen. You've built extraordinary companies. Now build extraordinary wealth—and an extraordinary legacy.

Why Founders Need Specialized Financial Planning

Founders Need a Different Financial Playbook

Let's start with a truth most of the financial world won't tell you: most financial advice wasn't built for people like you. It was built for people with steady jobs, predictable salaries, gradual wealth accumulation, and retirement timelines. It wasn't designed for founders who live in a world of volatility, concentrated risk, unpredictable liquidity events, and extraordinary potential. You don't fit that mold—and you shouldn't try to. Your journey requires a different map. Let's break down why.

Your Wealth is Highly Concentrated

Let's be honest: most founders have their net worth tied to one thing—their company. You're not holding a neat 60/40 stock-bond portfolio. You're holding equity in the business you built. You're not diversified, and traditional advice that says "just diversify" misses the point. Diversification isn't easy when 90% of your net worth is in a private company. You need strategies that recognize this reality—secondary sales, pre-planned liquidity events, strategic exit timing. Holding onto your equity isn't just a financial move; it's an emotional investment in your life's work. Specialized planning respects both the math and the meaning behind your concentration.

Your Income is Irregular and Unpredictable

Traditional financial plans assume a regular, predictable paycheck. Yours looks nothing like that. Early on, you may not even pay yourself. Later, your income is feast or famine—small salary now, potential windfall later. This income pattern creates enormous planning complexity. How do you structure your expenses during lean years? How do you prepare for the tax tsunami during liquidity years? How do you smooth the ride? Standard plans can't answer these questions. Founder-focused financial strategies do—building resilience into your cash flow, tax strategy, and personal risk management.

Your Taxes Are Wildly Complicated

The tax landscape for founders is a minefield. ISOs trigger AMT issues. QSBS rules can save you millions—if you know how to qualify. An 83(b) election can be the difference between life-changing tax savings and costly surprises. Your residency can shift your effective tax rate dramatically. And it's not just this year's tax return—it's a multi-year strategy, tied to liquidity events you can't afford to mishandle. Specialized advisors ensure you navigate AMT, QSBS, 83(b), and pre-exit planning with surgical precision.

Liquidity Events Are High-Stakes, One-Time Deals

Founders build wealth in moments—an acquisition, an IPO, a secondary sale. These moments are high-stakes. There are no do-overs. If you're not prepared, you could lose millions to taxes, bad structuring, or poor post-exit planning. Planning needs to begin long before you're in the room negotiating terms. Liquidity planning ensures you know where the cash will go, how it will be protected, how it will be invested, and how your life changes after the wire hits. A missed opportunity here could alter the next 30 years of your life.

Your Wealth Carries Emotional Weight

Wealth is not just about dollars—it's about identity. Your wealth is tied to something deeply personal: your company. When you exit, the emotional aftermath can be disorienting. Who are you without your business card? What now? Some founders experience anxiety, others feel an odd hollowness. Financial planning for founders must address more than just assets; it must help navigate the shift in purpose, identity, and legacy. Building a next chapter that's as intentional as the company you built is essential.

You Need a Personal Board of Advisors

You wouldn't run your company without a great board. Why would you manage your financial life without one? A founder's financial world needs a quarterback—someone who coordinates tax strategists, estate attorneys, investment managers, insurance professionals, and family governance experts. A good advisor manages money. A great advisor orchestrates your entire financial life, ensuring everything works in concert toward your bigger vision.

Your Goals Are Bigger Than Just "Retirement"

The average financial plan leads toward one goal: retirement. But you aren't average. Founders dream of more than just retiring on a beach. You want to build, invest, give back, mentor, create impact. Your wealth isn't a finish line—it's fuel for your next venture. Founder-focused planning recognizes this. It doesn't just ask, "When do you want to retire?" It asks, "What do you want your life to look like after the exit—and how do we build it?"

Founders Need Flexibility, Not Just Security

Startups move fast. Markets pivot. Opportunities emerge suddenly. Your financial life must be just as agile. You don't need a rigid retirement plan—you need liquidity, optionality, adaptability. Plans must allow for new investments, opportunistic moves, and evolving dreams. Founder wealth management is about optionality—keeping your future open, not boxed in.

Your Legacy Matters

True founders don't just think about today. They think about tomorrow—and beyond. You're not just building wealth for yourself. You're thinking about family, community, philanthropy, industry. You want to leave more than an inheritance; you want to leave impact. Specialized planning helps you transition from wealth builder to legacy architect—ensuring that what you create lasts far beyond your own lifetime.

The Cost of Bad Advice is Enormous

For founders, mistakes aren't just costly—they're catastrophic. Bad tax advice could cost millions. Poor liquidity planning could blow your only chance at generational wealth. Missed QSBS eligibility could vaporize 100% tax exclusions. Inexperienced advisors don't understand the stakes—and you don't have the luxury of a learning curve. Founder-specific financial planning isn't a luxury—it's a necessity. Because in your world, the cost of getting it wrong is too high to ignore.

Closing Thought

You've already built something extraordinary. Now, it's time to protect it, grow it, and extend it into a legacy that reflects everything you've worked for. Specialized financial planning is not about restriction—it's about freedom. Freedom to live, build, and give on your terms. Freedom to step into the next chapter of your life with clarity, confidence, and calm.

You're not just managing money. You're mastering legacy. Let's build a financial life worthy of the company—and the future—you've created.

How to Use This Book

How to Use This Book: A Founder's Guide to Financial Mastery

Let's start with a simple truth: this is not a book you need to read from front to back in one sitting. It's not a linear path, not a story with a beginning and end you have to follow sequentially. This is a toolkit—built to meet you where you are, whether you're just launching your founder journey, staring down the realities of a liquidity event, or already thinking about how to transform your success into a lasting legacy. You don't need to be patient with this book. You need to be intentional.

1. Find Your Starting Point

Where are you today? Are you a first-time founder, fueled mostly by ambition and optimism, still living lean and focusing on product-market fit? Are you later-stage, wrestling with term sheets, valuation swings, and the sudden realization that real money could be around the corner? Are you post-exit, looking at an entirely new life and wondering, "What's next?" Each of these stages demands different financial muscles. That's why this book is divided by the stage of your journey:

- Early-stage founders: Focus on cash flow resilience, basic estate planning, risk management.
- Growth-stage founders: Dive into liquidity planning, pre-exit tax strategies, secondary market opportunities.
- Post-exit founders: Explore legacy planning, multi-generational wealth strategies, family governance, and philanthropy.
- Start where you are. Flip to the chapters that feel urgent. Your journey is unique—your roadmap should be too.

2. Don't Rush—Digest and Reflect

This isn't a race. Ultra-affluent financial mastery isn't built by rushing through pages—it's built by absorbing wisdom and applying it deliberately. After each chapter, pause. Reflect. Ask yourself: *What does this mean for me right now?* Write down one action you could take immediately. Schedule time to move on it this month—not someday. Big financial wins are not built in a sprint; they're built in consistent, strategic steps, just like building a great company.

3. Use the Action Steps

Every chapter ends with real, founder-specific action steps. Not theory. Not vague encouragement. Actual moves you can make. Things like:

- Filing your 83(b) election before the IRS deadline.
- Setting your personal liquidity timeline ahead of a secondary or IPO.
- Calculating your "Work Optional" number so you know when enough is enough.
- Meeting with a CPA who understands startup stock tax implications.
- Even one step per chapter will put you miles ahead of most founders, many of whom delay this kind of thinking until it's too late. Action compounds.

4. Bring Your Team Into It

You don't have to, and shouldn't, do this alone. The best founders are not soloists—they're orchestrators. You already know how to build a team around your company. Now it's time to build a team around your financial life. Bring your:

- CPA
- Estate planning attorney
- Investment advisor
- Insurance specialist
- Family office or philanthropic consultant
- Highlight the sections that resonate most. Use them as conversation

starters. Challenge your advisors. Ask better questions. Great wealth is not just built; it's stewarded. And it's always a team effort.

5. Return to It Often

Your financial life will evolve as your business and life evolve. You'll move through funding rounds, grants of equity, tender offers, exits, and post-exit realities. Each chapter of your journey will raise new, higher-stakes questions. When that happens, come back here:

- When you close your next funding round.
- When you update your cap table.
- When you're staring down an exit offer.
- When you're thinking about your next company—or the life after company-building.
- Financial mastery is not a one-time achievement. It's a continuous recalibration. Think of this book as your financial companion, ready whenever the terrain shifts.

6. Apply the Founder Mindset

Founders are visionaries. Builders. Problem-solvers. Apply that same founder mentality to your personal finances:

- Creativity when structuring deals and liquidity events.
- Persistence in pursuing tax optimization and risk management.
- Vision when designing a lasting legacy for your family, your causes, and your community.
- Managing your personal wealth is not different from managing your startup: both require intention, resilience, and a long view. Treat your financial life like the next great company you're building—only this time, the IPO is freedom.

7. Stay Humble. Stay Hungry. Stay Teachable.

Wealth does not eliminate uncertainty—it magnifies it. Markets will shift.

Laws will change. New risks and opportunities will appear. Stay humble enough to know you don't have all the answers. Stay hungry enough to keep growing and refining your strategy. Stay teachable enough to seek out and listen to real expertise. The founders who build wealth that lasts beyond their lifetime are the ones who stay curious and committed long after the big checks clear.

Final Thought

This book is not about just having money. It's about having dignity, freedom, and agency. It's about designing a financial life that supports not just bigger bank accounts but a bigger life. A life that allows you to:

- Build without fear.
- Step back without regret.
- Give back with impact.
- Pass on not just wealth but wisdom.
- So don't rush. Don't skip steps. But most importantly, don't wait. Start where you are. Use what you have. Move forward today. Read a chapter. Take an action. Build a future.

Your future self—and the future generations who follow you—will thank you.

Overview: From Illiquidity to Liquidity to Legacy

The Founder's Financial Cycle: From Illiquidity to Liquidity to Legacy

There's a cycle most tech founders will live through if they're fortunate enough to build something successful. It's a journey from illiquidity—where most of your wealth is tied up in your company—to liquidity, when that paper wealth becomes real, to legacy, when you start thinking about what happens to that wealth after you. It's not a simple path. It's not clean. It's not quick. And it's rarely obvious which phase you're in at any given moment. But make no mistake: understanding this journey is essential. Because if you navigate it wisely, you can do more than just get rich—you can create real, lasting impact.

1. Illiquidity: Where Founders Begin

Almost every founder starts here. Illiquidity is the default state of a startup founder's wealth. Your company is private. Your shares aren't publicly tradable. The value is theoretical—dependent on the latest funding round, not a willing buyer in a public market. You may look wealthy on a cap table, but in real life, you're managing cash flow cautiously, carefully, sometimes precariously. You may live modestly even as others perceive you as ultra-wealthy based on paper valuations.

Illiquidity means financial vulnerability in disguise. You can't easily unlock wealth to buy a house, diversify, or hedge against downturns. It demands humility and discipline. Some founders fall into the trap of early overconfidence—borrowing against future success, inflating their lifestyle, or assuming paper wealth equals real power. The wiser ones recognize that surviving the illiquidity phase is about staying lean, managing downside risks (with proper insurance, estate planning, and liquidity contingency plans), and preparing for the moment opportunity truly strikes.

2. Liquidity: When Theory Becomes Reality

Liquidity is when the theoretical becomes tangible. The moment of a secondary sale, a tender offer, an acquisition, or an IPO. Suddenly, wealth crystallizes. What was once uncertain is now concrete—and in your bank account. For founders, it feels like the world tilting on its axis: you wake up the same person but with life-altering financial resources at your disposal.

But liquidity is dangerous if unprepared. The psychological whiplash can cause poor decision-making. Sudden wealth invites a flood of advisors, investment opportunities, and well-intentioned (or not) friends and relatives. Taxes loom large. A poorly structured sale or ill-timed liquidity event can erase half of your gains overnight through taxes and fees.

The key during this phase is preparation. Smart founders work months—sometimes years—in advance to align their equity, optimize tax strategies (QSBS, 83(b) elections, state residency considerations), and plan post-liquidity asset allocations. They build a personal balance sheet just as carefully as they built their company's. Liquidity is not a destination. It's a launchpad—for a new, vastly more complex financial life.

3. Legacy: Building Something That Outlives You

After the shock and awe of liquidity wears off, the deeper question surfaces: What now? For most founders, the answer is not endless consumption. It's contribution. It's the beginning of legacy planning—not just writing checks to heirs or charities, but creating structures that ensure your wealth continues to have purpose beyond your lifetime.

Legacy planning involves more than technical estate documents and tax efficiency. It demands clarity of vision. Who do you want to become now that you no longer have to work for money? What causes, communities, or industries do you want to uplift? How do you pass down not just money but values, wisdom, and opportunity to the next generation?

Family foundations, donor-advised funds, dynasty trusts, and thoughtful governance structures all become tools of legacy. They are the instruments by which wealth is stewarded, not squandered. Founders who view their wealth as fuel for generational empowerment, not just personal lifestyle elevation, are the ones who truly master this phase.

4. Real-Life Scenarios: When It Works—and When It Doesn't

Consider Sarah, a founder who exited her fintech startup with $75 million. She had already built her personal liquidity plan: she timed her move to a low-tax state, filed her 83(b) election years earlier, and held her shares long enough to qualify for QSBS exclusions. Upon exit, she diversified quickly but cautiously—allocating across real estate, public equities, private investments, and municipal bonds. She spent the next year working with her advisors to create a family foundation aimed at improving financial literacy in underserved communities—a cause aligned with her company's mission. Today, her wealth is not just intact—it's growing—and her impact is visible and measurable.

Contrast that with another founder, Mike, who rushed into his liquidity event without planning. He ignored tax advice, assumed his QSBS qualification was automatic, and made large purchases immediately post-exit: a $10M home, speculative investments, multiple luxury cars. Within five years, between taxes, market downturns, and lifestyle bloat, half his liquidity was gone. He's now scrambling for purpose—and financial stability.

The difference wasn't just market timing. It was preparation. It was mindset.

5. The Founder's Cycle: A Different Wealth Arc

Founders live a different financial arc:

- **Illiquidity**: Building value without immediate access.
- **Liquidity**: Capturing and crystallizing that value.
- **Legacy**: Directing that value toward long-term impact.

This cycle can—and often does—repeat. Serial founders move through these phases multiple times, compounding not just wealth but wisdom with each iteration. The key is recognizing which phase you're in—and what strategies serve you best at that stage.

6. The Risks of Neglecting the Cycle

Without intentional planning, founders risk:

- Overconfidence during illiquidity.
- Poor tax strategies during liquidity.
- Entitlement and decay during legacy transfer.
- Families lose wealth not because of bad luck but because of bad stewardship. Taxes, lawsuits, poor investments, and generational mismanagement are silent killers of unprotected wealth. Founders who understand that the journey does not end with liquidity—but truly begins—are the ones who safeguard their success against these risks.

7. **Key Planning Pillars for Each Stage**

- **Illiquidity**:
- Maintain personal financial discipline.
- File 83(b) elections properly.
- Insure against major life risks (disability, life, liability).
- Keep valuations realistic and avoid borrowing against private stock unless necessary.
- **Liquidity**:
- Engage tax professionals before a liquidity event.
- Diversify carefully and with discipline.
- Set a "sleep well at night" number—know what portion of wealth guarantees lifelong security before chasing higher returns.
- Avoid major lifestyle inflation in the first 24 months.
- **Legacy**:
- Draft multi-generational estate plans (dynasty trusts, charitable trusts).
- Build family governance structures.
- Educate heirs gradually on wealth stewardship.
- Focus on impact giving strategies—DAFs, foundations, mission-driven

investments.

8. Why Many Founders Struggle with the Transition

Success in startups is often about controlling chaos, taking risks, and betting big. But wealth stewardship is about discipline, patience, and risk management—nearly the opposite skill set. The traits that make you an outstanding entrepreneur can be the same traits that sabotage your financial life post-exit. Recognizing this mismatch is crucial. Building a great company was act one. Building a great financial legacy is act two. And it requires a different mindset, a different team, and a different set of habits.

9. Action Steps to Begin Mastering the Cycle

Wherever you are today:

- Conduct a full audit of your current financial life—personal cash flow, equity positions, estate documents.
- If you're pre-liquidity, build a liquidity-readiness plan with clear tax strategies.
- If you're nearing liquidity, assemble your "after" team—CPA, estate attorney, investment advisor.
- If you've exited, block time to draft a personal mission statement for your wealth: what you want it to achieve beyond your lifestyle.
- Start family conversations early about wealth, responsibility, and values.

10. Final Thought: Wealth as a Force for Good

Money is a magnifier. It doesn't change who you are—it reveals who you are. As a founder, you already have a rare set of skills: vision, courage, resilience. Apply those same skills to your financial life. Build not just companies, but a legacy. Create not just wealth, but impact. Navigate the cycle of illiquidity, liquidity, and legacy with the same intentionality you brought to your startup. You built a company against the odds. Now, build a future that honors that effort.

Section 1: The Financial Blueprint for Founders

Building a company is hard — but building personal wealth as a founder is a different challenge entirely. Most founders are experts at raising capital, scaling products, and navigating competition. Yet, few are prepared for the complex financial realities that come with living on equity, surviving on irregular income, and managing concentrated, illiquid wealth.

Section 1 lays the foundation for understanding how different your financial life is compared to the average professional — and why generic financial advice doesn't fit.

We start by unpacking the unique financial journey of a founder: the volatility, the concentration of risk, the illusions of wealth on paper, and the silent tax traps waiting at every stage. From there, we explain why founders must have specialized financial planning that adapts to their non-linear careers and liquidity events.

Next, we walk through the founder lifecycle: from early-stage illiquidity, where survival and discipline matter most, to the critical transition of unlocking liquidity during a sale, IPO, or secondary offering. And finally, we introduce the concept of legacy — because true success isn't just about the first exit, it's about what you build with the wealth you create.

You'll learn why standard financial advice can actually put founders at risk, why waiting until after an exit to plan is a recipe for regret, and why intentional, proactive strategies are the key to turning startup success into lasting financial independence.

This section frames everything that follows — giving you a clear blueprint to understand where you are in your founder journey, what financial challenges are ahead, and how to start thinking like the CEO of your personal wealth.

Chapter 1: The Financial Reality for Founders

Understanding the Founder's Financial Reality

Let's start here: the financial life of a tech founder does not look like anyone else's. You are not a traditional W-2 employee with a stable salary, a 401(k), and a neat, predictable career arc. You're not climbing a corporate ladder. You're building the ladder yourself, hammering it together with your own hands, hoping it holds long enough to reach the sky. Because of that, the personal financial blueprint that works for most people doesn't work for you.

Founders live in a world of volatility, concentration, and illiquidity. You can be worth millions on paper but not have the cash to cover next month's mortgage. You can look wealthy on LinkedIn but feel poor in real life. This chapter is about helping you understand that reality — and giving you the framework to navigate it. No judgment. No guilt. No financial shame. Just a clear, respectful conversation about where you are, what you're facing, and how to take control. Let's get into it.

1. Your Wealth is Volatile

Founders' wealth is not a steady drip; it's a high-pressure firehose that turns on — or doesn't — depending on thousands of variables, many of them beyond your control. Your wealth is tied to your company's valuation. One good funding round and you're the next great hope. One bad quarter, and you're another cautionary tale. Your company's value can swing based on investor sentiment, market conditions, competitive threats, team turnover, and product missteps. And your personal net worth swings right along with it.

This kind of volatility is emotionally exhausting and financially dangerous. You have to build a plan that acknowledges this reality. A plan that assumes there will be ups and downs. A plan that doesn't crumble the first time the market does. A plan that lets you survive the volatility long enough to enjoy the upside.

2. Your Wealth is Concentrated

Most people are taught from an early age to diversify. Spread your bets. Don't put all your eggs in one basket. But you? You're a founder. You have one basket: your company. This isn't bad. Concentration is how massive wealth is built. Every household-name founder — Bezos, Zuckerberg, Musk — got rich because they bet everything on one company.

But concentration creates risk: If your company fails, your wealth evaporates. If your company thrives, you're rich beyond your wildest dreams. The challenge is managing that risk intelligently. Hedging when you can. Liquidity planning when opportunities arise. Diversifying after you've captured your upside. You don't need to abandon concentration. You need to respect its power — and its danger.

3. Your Wealth is Illiquid

Illiquidity means you own something valuable — but you can't easily sell it. Founders' wealth is trapped in private company stock. Until you go public, get acquired, or find a secondary buyer, your wealth is paper wealth. You can't borrow against it easily. You can't sell it when you need cash. You can't diversify out of it.

This is why many founders delay major life purchases, take lower salaries, and live much "poorer" than their net worth suggests. Planning for illiquidity means keeping personal expenses low, building cash reserves, and preparing for eventual liquidity events before they happen.

4. Traditional Financial Planning Doesn't Work for You

Most financial planning advice is built for steady, predictable income. Save 10% of your salary. Max out your 401(k). Dollar-cost average into index funds. You're playing a different game. You need founder-specific financial planning — plans that account for long periods of low salary, strategies that maximize once-in-a-lifetime liquidity events, tax planning for complex equity compensation, and risk management that addresses concentration and illiquidity. You don't need a cookie-cutter plan. You need a custom blueprint.

5. You Need a Founder-Specific Financial Blueprint

Here's what that looks like: Liquidity Timeline — map out when you realistically expect to access cash from your equity. Tax Strategy — plan for AMT, QSBS exclusions, and capital gains taxes before they become a crisis. Risk Management — hedge where you can; insure where you must. Investment Strategy — diversify intelligently after liquidity. Legacy Planning — think beyond wealth accumulation to wealth stewardship. This blueprint isn't static. It evolves as your company grows, as funding rounds close, as exit windows open and shut. It's not just about wealth creation. It's about wealth preservation — and ultimately, wealth liberation.

6. Real-Life Scenarios

Scenario 1: You Just Raised $5M

Congratulations. You closed your seed round. But here's the hard truth: That $5M doesn't belong to you. Your personal cash flow is still tight. Your company's valuation is not liquid wealth. What should you do? Pay yourself a reasonable salary — enough to live, not to splurge. Build a personal emergency fund separate from the company. Resist the urge to inflate your lifestyle.

Scenario 2: You're Post-Series B, Worth Millions on Paper

Your paper net worth looks incredible. But you're still illiquid. This is the danger zone. You feel rich but can't access your wealth. Banks may lend against your shares — but at brutal terms. What should you do? Explore secondary sales cautiously. Set up a 10b5-1 plan if you're nearing an IPO. Start pre-liquidity tax planning now.

Scenario 3: You've Exited. You're Sitting on $10M

The check cleared. Now what? Taxes are looming. Every friend, cousin, and investment pitch finds its way to you. What should you do? Park cash safely while you assemble your advisory team. Hire a tax strategist immediately. Build a liquidity management and investment plan before you start spending.

Scenario 4: You're a Serial Entrepreneur

You've built and exited. Maybe more than once. Now you have personal wealth and experience — a new kind of responsibility. What should you do? Create a family office structure. Formalize legacy and philanthropy plans. Become intentional about mentoring and investing.

7. Plain-Language Breakdowns

AMT: Alternative Minimum Tax

When you exercise ISOs, you might trigger AMT — a parallel tax system calculated differently than regular income tax. Early exercises can trigger a huge AMT bill. Plan ahead. Model your AMT exposure before exercising. Time exercises to minimize AMT. Explore AMT credits in future years.

QSBS: Qualified Small Business Stock

QSBS can exempt up to $10M (or more) in gains from federal taxes. The company must be a "qualified" small business. Shares must be held for at least five years. Must acquire stock directly from the company. Plan early. Confirm QSBS eligibility with your legal counsel. Track when your holding periods begin.

10b5-1 Plans

If your company is public or nearing IPO, insider trading rules apply. A 10b5-1 plan lets you pre-schedule stock sales. It protects you legally and avoids the appearance of insider trading. Set it up early. Work with a lawyer familiar with SEC regulations. Structure it to align with your cash flow needs.

8. Pros and Cons

Raising VC Funding vs. Bootstrapping

VC Funding Pros: Access to capital, faster growth.

VC Funding Cons: Dilution, pressure to exit.

Bootstrapping Pros: Maintain control, build profitably.

Bootstrapping Cons: Slower growth, higher personal financial risk.

Holding vs. Selling Stock Post-Exit

Holding Pros: Potential for further upside.

Holding Cons: Market risk, opportunity cost.

Selling Pros: Lock in gains, diversify.

Selling Cons: Capital gains taxes, potential regret if stock continues to climb.

Renting vs. Buying

Renting Pros: Flexibility, less cash tied up.

Renting Cons: No equity build-up.

Buying Pros: Build equity, potential appreciation.

Buying Cons: Ties up cash, less flexibility.

DIY Wealth Management vs. Hiring Professionals

DIY Pros: Save fees, total control.

DIY Cons: Risk of costly mistakes.

Professional Pros: Expertise, coordination.

Professional Cons: Advisory fees.

Investing in Next Venture vs. Diversifying

Investing Pros: High upside, founder's expertise advantage.

Investing Cons: Concentrated risk.

Diversifying Pros: Risk reduction.

Diversifying Cons: Lower potential returns.

9. Action Steps

- Build a Liquidity Timeline: Map out key funding rounds, secondary opportunities, IPO windows.
- Review Your Tax Exposure: Model AMT, QSBS, and capital gains exposure before your next round or exit.
- Automate Post-Liquidity Investment: Pre-commit to allocating liquidity event proceeds into diversified portfolios.
- Assemble Your Financial Team: Wealth advisor, CPA, estate planner — schedule meetings now.
- Create a "Work Optional" Plan: Calculate your "enough" number. Build your plan around freedom, not just wealth.

10. Final Thought

This isn't just about managing money. It's about managing freedom. It's about protecting the life you're building — not just the company. You didn't risk everything to build a company just to end up feeling trapped by your own success. You built it to create options. To create impact. To create peace.

This chapter is the foundation. Everything that follows will build on it — deeper strategies, sharper tools, bigger visions. But first: Make one money move before you go to bed tonight. Just one. And then do another next week. Your future self will thank you. So will your bank account. So will your peace of mind. Welcome to the journey.

Chapter 2: Understanding Equity Compensation

If there's one thing that defines the financial life of a tech founder, it's equity. Equity is your currency. It's your paycheck when salaries are low. It's your retirement plan when 401(k)s aren't even in the conversation. It's your "maybe" fortune. But most founders don't truly understand it. They get caught up in valuations, share prices, and headlines, but they miss the fine print. They sign stock option agreements without reading the terms. They assume more shares equal more wealth. They treat all equity the same. It's not. And if you want to build, protect, and grow the wealth your hard work is creating, you need to really understand what you're holding.

Let's start by talking about the three main types of equity compensation: ISOs, NSOs, and RSUs. Each one has its rules, its traps, and its opportunities. ISOs, or Incentive Stock Options, are often considered the golden ticket if managed well. They offer favorable tax treatment if you satisfy the two-year grant and one-year exercise holding periods. Done correctly, your profits can be taxed as long-term capital gains rather than ordinary income. The catch? The Alternative Minimum Tax (AMT) can turn your smart strategy into a cash-flow nightmare if you're not careful. NSOs, or Non-Qualified Stock Options, are simpler—no AMT issues, but the spread between strike price and fair market value at exercise is taxed as ordinary income. Straightforward, but often more expensive in tax terms. RSUs, or Restricted Stock Units, are different altogether. You don't have to purchase anything; they are granted and taxed as ordinary income when they vest. They're simple to understand but can create liquidity issues since taxes are due even if you haven't sold the shares.

Vesting schedules are more than fine print; they are your roadmap to ownership. Most equity grants follow a four-year vesting schedule with a one-year cliff. That first year is critical—you have to stick around to earn that initial 25%. After that, shares typically vest monthly. If you leave before the cliff, you walk away empty-handed. Afterward, you leave with whatever's vested. Pay close attention to acceleration clauses in your contract. Single-trigger acceleration could vest your equity if the company is acquired. Double-trigger requires both acquisition and termination without cause. These details can turn a good deal into a life-changing one—or a bitter pill.

Taxes are the silent killer of equity dreams. Many founders are blindsided by tax bills they didn't anticipate. Exercising ISOs can subject you to AMT, which requires careful planning and often a liquidity event to cover. NSOs will hit you with ordinary income tax at exercise, and RSUs at vesting. Special rules like Qualified Small Business Stock (QSBS) allow for up to $10 million in tax-free gains—but only if you meet very specific criteria and hold your shares for five years. The IRS is unforgiving. Ignorance is not an excuse. The most successful founders integrate tax planning into their equity strategy from day one, not the day after the term sheet.

Equity is not just about building wealth; it's about structuring your financial life for longevity and impact. Managed wisely, it funds new ventures, builds a "work-optional" life, fuels philanthropic endeavors, and supports generational wealth. Managed poorly, it leads to massive tax bills, forced stock sales at bad times, and eroded net worth. Equity is not a lottery ticket; it's a sophisticated business asset. Diversifying after a liquidity event isn't weakness—it's discipline. Risk management isn't a hedge against your success—it's a reinforcement of it. Use your equity to build a stable platform, not a rollercoaster.

Consider a few real-life scenarios. An early exercise strategy on your ISOs can start the long-term capital gains clock sooner and reduce AMT exposure. But it also means tying up cash in something illiquid and risky. A founder facing an IPO might find their RSUs vesting at a sky-high valuation, creating a massive tax bill on paper wealth that could vanish if the stock price drops. Setting up a 10b5-1 plan to sell shares in a structured, pre-approved way protects against volatility and insider trading accusations. Another founder might face a secondary market opportunity to sell some shares—tempting for immediate liquidity but costly in ordinary income tax. Thoughtful modeling and planning are key. Finally, selling a company for $50 million opens the door to family trusts, donor-advised funds, and legacy planning—but only if you start before the deal closes.

Let's demystify two essential tools: the 83(b) election and the 10b5-1 plan. The 83(b) election allows you to pay taxes upfront on restricted shares based on their current, likely low value. If the shares skyrocket later, your future gain is taxed more favorably. But you must file within 30 days of the grant. Miss the window, miss the benefit—and there's no fixing it later. The 10b5-1 plan lets you schedule stock sales in advance, insulating you from insider trading accusations and enabling disciplined diversification.

Early exercising ISOs comes with pros and cons. Pros include a lower AMT hit and an earlier start to the long-term capital gains clock. Cons include tying up cash and the risk of the company failing. Holding versus selling post-liquidity is a classic conundrum. Holding offers potential upside but concentrates risk; selling locks in gains but triggers taxes and the regret if the stock later soars. Investing in a new venture is thrilling and could deliver high returns but also carries enormous risk. Diversifying reduces risk but tempers potential upside. There's no universal right answer—only the right answer for your specific goals and risk tolerance.

Here are the action steps you should take. First, audit your equity grants. Understand exactly what you have—ISOs, NSOs, RSUs—and their terms. Second, model your tax scenarios. Run projections for AMT, QSBS eligibility, and capital gains exposure. Third, create a liquidity plan. Think through secondary sales, IPOs, and acquisition outcomes. Fourth, assemble your financial team. You need a wealth advisor who understands founders, a CPA who can handle complex tax scenarios, and an estate planner who can map out legacy structures. Fifth, draft your "work-optional" number—the amount you need to achieve financial freedom. Finally, explore legacy structures now. Trusts, foundations, donor-advised funds—these aren't just for billionaires. They are tools for founders who think long-term.

Equity is the fuel that powers your financial future. But fuel without a destination is just stored energy. You didn't build your company without a plan. Don't build your financial life without one. Respect your equity. Understand it deeply. Plan for its risks. Equity can change your life—if you manage it wisely. The goals you set today will shape your financial freedom tomorrow. Ask yourself: Are you equipped to steer this ship alone, or is it time to bring in seasoned navigators to help you cross to the other side?

Chapter 3: ISOs vs. NSOs Deep Dive

Equity is one of the most powerful wealth-creation tools available to founders. But not all equity is created equal. You've probably heard of ISOs and NSOs. You might even have a stack of paperwork with those words splashed across the top. Yet if you're like most founders, the difference between them is still a little fuzzy. You might know that ISOs are "better for taxes" and NSOs are "less complicated." But beyond that, you're guessing. It's time to stop guessing. Because the type of options you hold — and how you manage them — can mean the difference between building life-changing wealth and handing half your gains to the IRS. This chapter is about clarity. About empowerment. About giving you the knowledge and confidence to handle your equity with the same strategic vision you bring to your company. Let's get into it.

What are ISOs and NSOs, really? At their core, ISOs and NSOs are both stock options. A stock option is the right (but not the obligation) to purchase shares of your company's stock at a predetermined price (called the strike price) within a certain period. The difference between ISOs and NSOs isn't about what you're getting — it's about how the IRS treats it. ISOs get preferential tax treatment. NSOs don't. That's the headline. But let's break it down further. ISOs, or Incentive Stock Options, are offered only to employees. They offer special tax treatment if certain holding periods are met, giving potential for long-term capital gains tax rates instead of ordinary income tax, but with potential Alternative Minimum Tax (AMT) exposure when exercised. With ISOs, there's no tax at grant, no tax at vesting, and no regular tax at exercise. However, the spread (difference between strike price and fair market value) at exercise can trigger AMT. If you hold shares for two years after grant and one year after exercise, gains are taxed at long-term capital gains rates.

ISOs are like fine wine: they reward patience but come with hidden risks if you don't understand the timing. NSOs, or Non-Qualified Stock Options, can be granted to employees, contractors, board members, and advisors. They have simpler tax treatment but less favorable terms. There's no AMT exposure, but at exercise, the spread is taxed as ordinary income. Any additional gain between exercise and sale is taxed as capital gains. In short, NSOs are simpler but hit you with a higher immediate tax bill. Think of NSOs as a blunt instrument: easy to understand, but potentially costly.

Let's compare ISOs and NSOs side-by-side. ISOs are only available to employees, while NSOs can be granted more broadly. ISOs have no regular tax at exercise but pose an AMT risk; NSOs are taxed as ordinary income at exercise with no AMT. ISOs, if handled properly, offer favorable long-term capital gains rates, whereas NSOs do not. ISOs are more complex but can be more tax-efficient; NSOs are simpler but may cost more in taxes.

The AMT trap is one of the biggest dangers for founders exercising ISOs. AMT is a parallel tax system designed to ensure high-income earners pay a minimum tax. When you exercise ISOs, the IRS adds the spread (fair market value minus strike price) to your income for AMT purposes. If your AMT calculation is higher than your regular tax, you owe the difference. For example, if your strike price is $1 per share and the fair market value is $10, exercising 100,000 shares means an AMT income of $900,000. Even if you're cash-poor, you could owe AMT on phantom income. Early exercise when FMV is low is attractive. Exercising in small batches can also help manage AMT exposure. But careful modeling with a tax advisor is critical.

So, what's the tax playbook for ISOs? Step one: model AMT exposure before exercising. Step two: exercise early if possible, when FMV is low. Step three: start the holding period clock early to qualify for long-term capital gains. Step four: monitor FMV valuations each year. Step five: plan liquidity events carefully to avoid triggering disqualifying dispositions. ISOs reward those who plan ahead. If you're reactive, you'll pay more. If you're proactive, you'll keep more.

For NSOs, the tax playbook is different. Step one: be ready for a tax bill at exercise. Step two: if possible, exercise early when FMV is lower to minimize the spread. Step three: understand the ordinary income tax impact and plan cash reserves accordingly. Step four: hold shares post-exercise to qualify for long-term capital gains on additional gains. Step five: if secondary markets are available, consider selling to cover taxes. NSOs are about simplicity and speed, but they are less forgiving on taxes.

Choosing the right strategy is about your situation and priorities. There is no universal "best" option. If you prioritize tax efficiency and can handle the complexity, ISOs are attractive. If you prioritize simplicity and ease, NSOs might be better. If you expect big upside and can stomach risk, ISOs with early exercise can be life-changing. If you're more conservative or later-stage, NSOs might be safer and simpler.

Let's consider some real-life scenarios. Scenario one: an early-stage founder with ISOs, a strike price of $0.50, and a fair market value of $0.55, with 500,000 ISOs. Early exercise is attractive because there's minimal AMT risk and you start the capital gains clock early. The right action: exercise all shares now, file an 83(b) election within 30 days, and lock in minimal tax exposure. Scenario two: a growth-stage executive with 100,000 NSOs at a $10 strike price and $15 FMV. Exercising triggers $500,000 of ordinary income. The strategy: exercise in smaller batches, plan tax payments in advance, and use post-IPO liquidity to diversify. Scenario three: a post-exit founder who exercised ISOs years ago and paid a big AMT bill. After selling shares, you can claim AMT credit to offset future regular taxes. The action: file tax returns carefully and use AMT credits. Scenario four: a serial entrepreneur with ISOs from Company A and NSOs from Company B. Exercise ISOs early, exercise NSOs closer to liquidity, and diversify after exits.

Let's break down some plain-language terms. AMT credit allows you to apply AMT payments made in prior years as a credit against future regular income taxes. It can take years to fully recover but requires careful tracking. The 83(b) election allows you to elect to be taxed on the value of your equity at the time of grant or early exercise, locking in a low valuation and starting the capital gains clock early. It must be filed within 30 days without exception.

Pros and cons are important to weigh. ISOs offer favorable tax treatment, potential long-term capital gains, and lower initial tax costs, but they come with AMT risk and more complex planning. NSOs are simpler and have no AMT risk but come with an immediate ordinary income tax hit and a higher overall tax burden. Early exercising minimizes AMT and starts the capital gains clock but ties up cash and exposes you to company risk.

Your action steps are clear. Inventory your options and list ISOs and NSOs separately. Model AMT exposure with a tax advisor. Plan early exercises strategically. File 83(b) elections promptly within the 30-day window. Set aside tax reserves so you're not caught short. Build a diversification plan for post-liquidity. Most importantly, work with equity-savvy advisors. Not all CPAs understand startup equity intricacies.

ISOs and NSOs are powerful tools. But power without understanding is dangerous. You're not just a founder; you're the CFO of your personal financial life. Master your equity. Plan your moves. Protect your upside. The difference between a lucky break and a lasting fortune is knowledge and execution. Make one money move before you go to bed tonight. Just one. And then do another next week. You've got this. Your future self will thank you. So will your bank account. So will your peace of mind. Welcome to founder financial mastery.

Chapter 4: RSUs: Taxation and Planning

If ISOs and NSOs are the high-wire acts of startup equity, RSUs are the steady, no-frills option. But steady doesn't mean simple — not when the IRS is involved. Restricted Stock Units (RSUs) are one of the most common ways founders and key employees get compensated in growth-stage companies, especially as companies prepare for IPOs. They're straightforward to understand on the surface: you're granted shares, they vest over time, and once vested, they're yours. Sounds easy, right? But the real complexity — and the real wealth-building opportunity — lies beneath the surface. RSUs come with significant tax implications, and what you do after your shares vest can determine whether you build lasting wealth or leave millions on the table. This chapter is your deep dive into RSUs: how they're taxed, how to plan around vesting events, and how to diversify after you finally hold those long-awaited shares. Let's break it down.

An RSU is a promise. The company promises to give you shares. You have to earn them by staying employed or meeting performance milestones. Once vested, they're yours. You don't have to pay anything to get them. You don't have to exercise anything. You just have to wait. The typical RSU vesting schedule runs over four years with a one-year cliff (25% after 12 months) and monthly or quarterly vesting thereafter. Some companies accelerate vesting at IPO or acquisition. But in most cases, you're earning your shares slowly over time. The key point: Until RSUs vest, they are just a promise. You don't own anything.

RSUs are taxed as ordinary income when they vest. Not when granted. Not when sold. When they vest. What's taxed? The fair market value of the shares on the vesting date. For example, if 1,000 RSUs vest and the stock price on vesting day is $50, the taxable income is $50,000. That $50,000 gets reported as W-2 income if you're an employee. Your company will usually withhold taxes at vesting, often at the IRS minimum withholding rate of 22% federal. But — and this is critical — the actual taxes you owe may be higher based on your total income. If you're a high-earner (as many founders are), your real tax rate could be 35% or 37% federal — plus state taxes. Bottom line: RSU vesting equals a tax bill, whether or not you sell the shares.

Because companies often withhold at a flat 22% federal rate, but your real tax rate might be 35%+, many founders end up under-withheld. Suppose RSU vesting generates $500,000 of taxable income. The company withholds 22% or $110,000. But your real tax liability is 37%, totaling $185,000. As a result, you owe an additional $75,000 come tax time. Many founders get burned because they don't set aside cash to cover this gap. The action here is to work with a tax advisor, estimate your real tax bill, and set aside extra cash or sell some shares to cover it.

Because vesting equals a taxable event, smart planning around vesting dates can reduce your tax burden. Some strategies include bunching vesting in a lower-income year if your company allows negotiation of vesting schedules. If eligible, consider the 83(i) Election for certain private companies, which allows deferring tax on RSUs for up to five years. Another simple tactic is to sell to cover—selling just enough shares at vesting to cover taxes. Advanced planning is critical. If you're near an exit (IPO or acquisition), model the potential tax impact of vesting post-event. Pre-IPO, stock is usually valued lower, leading to lower taxes; post-IPO, higher valuations can result in bigger tax bills. Timing matters. Model scenarios. Plan ahead.

At IPO, two things happen: RSUs often vest ("double trigger"), and shares become liquid (after the lock-up period). The problem is tax is due at vesting, not when you sell. You might not be able to sell right away due to the lock-up period. If the stock price tanks during lock-up, you could owe tax on a high value but sell for much less later. For example, RSUs vest at $50/share, and the lock-up ends six months later with the stock at $25/share. You pay tax on $50/share but can only sell at $25/share. Brutal. Mitigation strategies include negotiating for longer lock-ups or structured selling windows, pre-arranging liquidity through secondary sales (if available), and setting aside cash to cover taxes regardless of the share price.

Once RSUs vest, you face a decision: hold the shares or sell some or all immediately. Holding allows you to participate in future upside and pay capital gains tax on future appreciation. However, it also exposes you to concentration and market risk, not to mention the psychological risk of watching the stock price swing. Selling allows you to lock in gains, diversify, and reduce risk but also means giving up potential future upside. Reality check: You already took a huge risk building the company. It's okay—in fact, it's smart—to de-risk your personal balance sheet.

Once you've sold RSUs and have cash, you need a plan. Key diversification strategies include building a core portfolio with index funds and diversified ETFs, exploring alternatives like real estate, private equity, and venture funds, maintaining defensive assets like bonds and cash reserves, and engaging in philanthropy through donor-advised funds or private foundations. Family wealth planning, including setting up trusts and governance structures, is essential. Your action plan is to allocate proceeds intentionally, build a portfolio aligned with your long-term goals, and avoid "founder FOMO." You're no longer betting on one stock; you're building a financial life.

Consider these real-life scenarios. Scenario one: pre-IPO RSU vesting. Your company goes public, your RSUs vest at $40/share, but the lock-up period is six months, and the stock drops to $25/share by the time you can sell. Lesson: plan for taxes at $40/share and prepare psychologically for volatility. Scenario two: windfall sale post-vesting. RSUs vest, you sell immediately at $60/share, locking in $3 million. Lesson: pay estimated taxes promptly, diversify, and build a "Work Optional" plan. Scenario three: holding too long. RSUs vest at $70/share, but you hold, and the stock slides to $30/share over 18 months. Lesson: concentration risk is real, and emotional attachment to stock is dangerous. Scenario four: tax surprise. RSUs vest, the company withholds 22% for taxes, but your real tax rate is 37%. Lesson: estimate real tax liability and save extra.

Let's break it down in plain language. RSU tax summary: no tax at grant, taxable as ordinary income at vesting, and capital gains tax if sold for more than the value at vest. The 83(i) Election is for private companies, deferring tax for up to five years under certain conditions. Sell to cover means the company sells enough shares to cover tax withholding. Lock-up periods, typically six months post-IPO, mean no selling allowed during that time. Prepare emotionally and financially.

Pros and cons matter. RSUs have no upfront cost, are simple to understand, and provide immediate ownership post-vesting. But they come with ordinary income tax, a tax bill regardless of liquidity, and market risk post-vesting. Selling immediately locks in value and reduces concentration risk but means potential upside is lost. Holding long-term allows for future growth participation but exposes you to concentration risk and volatility.

Your action steps are clear. Know your vesting dates and calendar them. Model your tax exposure with a tax advisor. Plan for under-withholding and set aside extra cash. Decide on a hold vs. sell strategy based on personal goals, not emotions. Diversify post-vesting by building a real financial plan. Work with a professional team including a tax advisor, wealth manager, and estate planner.

RSUs are a gift, but gifts come with responsibility. You've already taken extraordinary risks to build your company. You don't need to gamble again with your personal wealth. Understand the tax rules. Plan for the cash flow needs. Diversify smartly. You didn't come this far just to stay on the startup rollercoaster forever. Make one money move before you go to bed tonight. Just one. And then do another next week. You've got this. Your future self will thank you. So will your bank account. So will your peace of mind. Welcome to the next level of founder financial mastery.

Chapter 5: Early Exercise and 83(b) Elections

When it comes to building real wealth from your startup equity, the right move at the right time can make the difference between retiring early and watching half your gains evaporate into taxes. One of the most powerful moves — and least understood — is the early exercise of stock options combined with the 83(b) election. This isn't Financial Literacy 101. This is founder-level strategy. If you're serious about maximizing what you've built, you need to know how these tools work, why they matter, and how to execute them flawlessly. This chapter is your real-world, no-nonsense guide. Let's get into it.

Early exercise means buying your stock options before they vest. Normally, you earn options gradually over time and exercise them as they vest. With early exercise, you buy the shares immediately, even though they're not fully vested. They remain subject to the vesting schedule—if you leave early, the company can repurchase unvested shares, often at the lower price you paid. Why early exercise? Lock in a low exercise price, start the capital gains clock sooner, and potentially minimize or avoid AMT. Early exercise is about timing. It's about front-loading your ownership at the lowest possible valuation.

The 83(b) election is a little-known IRS form that can save you millions. When you early exercise, your shares are still restricted (subject to vesting). Without an 83(b) election, you get taxed when the shares vest, based on their value at that time. With an 83(b) election, you elect to be taxed now, based on the value at exercise, and you start the long-term capital gains holding period immediately. The key is if the value of the shares is low when you exercise, the immediate tax hit is small—sometimes zero. If the shares increase in value over time, all that growth could be taxed at the much lower long-term capital gains rate. Critical: You must file the 83(b) election within 30 days of the exercise. No extensions. No exceptions.

If you early exercise and file an 83(b), you pay minimal or no taxes upfront, lock in a low basis for capital gains, and start the capital gains clock immediately. When you eventually sell, you potentially pay long-term capital gains tax instead of ordinary income tax. For example, if your strike price is $0.01 per share and the fair market value at exercise is $0.01, exercising 1 million shares means taxable income at exercise is $0. Later, the company goes public and the stock is worth $10/share. Your gain is $9.99/share, taxed at long-term capital gains rate (15%-20%), not ordinary income tax rate (up to 37%). You've saved millions.

No strategy is perfect. Risks of Early Exercise + 83(b) include having to pay for shares upfront, losing your investment if the company fails, losing unvested shares if you leave early, and the necessity to file the 83(b) within 30 days without any second chances. Key considerations: Can you afford to lose the upfront cost? Are you confident in the company's prospects? Are you planning to stick around long enough to vest? Early exercise is a bet. But if you believe in the company—and yourself—it's often a bet worth making.

Filing an 83(b) election isn't hard but must be done precisely. Complete IRS Form 83(b), mail it to the IRS within 30 days of early exercise, send a copy to your employer, and keep a copy for your records. Important tips include sending via certified mail with a return receipt and getting confirmation from the IRS. No electronic filing is allowed. This is one piece of paper that can change your financial future. Treat it with respect.

Consider real-life scenarios. Scenario 1: Early-stage founder early exercises. You co-found a company with a strike price of $0.01 and early exercise 1 million shares at a cost of $10,000, filing the 83(b) election. Years later, the company IPOs, stock is worth $50/share, and your gain is

$49.99/share, taxed at 20% long-term capital gains, saving you millions. Scenario 2: Missed 83(b) election. You early exercise but forget to file the 83(b). Four years later, shares vest when the stock is worth $10/share, resulting in $10 million of ordinary income taxed at the top rate of 37%. Scenario 3: Early exercise before big valuation jump. You early exercise when the company is valued low. Within two years, the valuation jumps, and you're fully vested, positioned for long-term capital gains treatment. Scenario 4: Early exercise, company fails. You early exercise, but the company folds. You lose the upfront cost—a risk of entrepreneurship, but better to risk small money early than big money later.

Early Exercise vs. Waiting has pros and cons. Early Exercise pros: lock in low tax basis, start capital gains clock, minimize AMT exposure. Cons: requires upfront cash, risk of losing investment, requires discipline and paperwork. Waiting pros: no upfront cash needed, see how the company progresses. Cons: higher future tax bill, miss capital gains benefits, greater AMT exposure. There's no one-size-fits-all answer, but for founders and early employees, early exercise + 83(b) is often the smart play.

One huge benefit of early exercise is minimizing or eliminating AMT. When FMV is low, the "spread" is tiny, resulting in a small AMT adjustment. If you exercise later when FMV is high, the big spread results in a big AMT bill. Model AMT exposure carefully. Use a tax advisor who understands startup equity. This is specialized knowledge.

Can you file an 83(b) election for RSUs? No. 83(b) applies to restricted stock and early-exercised options. RSUs have no option to early exercise and are taxed at vesting. However, if you're granted restricted stock (common for very early employees/founders), 83(b) is still a powerful tool.

Early exercise works best when the company's valuation is low, FMV is close to the strike price, and liquidity is far off. Market timing matters. If you believe an IPO or acquisition is imminent, the clock is ticking. Early exercise before valuation jumps can save fortunes.

Let's break it down in plain language. 83(b) in one sentence: File an 83(b) election to pay minimal taxes now and maximize capital gains later. Early exercise in one sentence: Buy your shares early, when they're cheap, to start the clock on lower taxes. Why 30 days matter: Miss the 30-day window? No 83(b), no do-overs. 30 days from exercise—period. No forgiveness. No second chances. Mark the date.

Your action steps are clear. Review your equity grants to see if early exercise is allowed. Model early exercise costs by multiplying strike price times number of shares. Evaluate your risk tolerance. Can you afford to lose this money? Plan cash flow and set aside funds. Complete and file the 83(b) election within 30 days. Work with a tax advisor specialized in startup equity. Track holding periods: two years from grant and one year from exercise. Prepare for liquidity events: IPOs, acquisitions, secondaries. Stay organized with records of exercise, filing, and confirmations. Revisit as the company evolves—early exercise isn't a one-time decision. Review each new grant.

You didn't build your company without a plan. Don't build your financial future without one either. Early exercise and 83(b) elections are founder-level moves. They're strategic, deliberate, and powerful. Handled right, they turn paper promises into real wealth. Handled wrong, they turn into missed opportunities and massive tax bills. Make one money move before you go to bed tonight. Just one. And then do another next week. File the 83(b). Start the clock. Own your future. You've got this. Your future self will thank you. So will your bank account. So will your peace of mind. Welcome to the financial freedom you've been building all along.

Section 2: Equity, Taxes, and Liquidity – Building and Unlocking Founder Wealth

For tech founders, wealth isn't built in steady, predictable paychecks – it's built in concentrated, high-risk, high-reward equity. But owning equity is only half the equation. The real challenge lies in understanding how to manage it, when to unlock it, and how to protect it from the hidden costs of taxes and poor planning.

Section 2 dives deep into the most critical – and misunderstood – areas of founder finance: equity compensation, liquidity events, and tax strategy.

We break down the confusing alphabet soup of startup equity – **ISOs**, **NSOs**, **RSUs** – and explain how to think about each piece of your compensation from both a risk and opportunity perspective. We cover the all-important **83(b) election**, a simple form that could save you millions in taxes if handled correctly – and cost you the same if ignored.

Next, we tackle the mechanics of **liquidity**: how to navigate **secondary sales**, **tender offers**, and prepare for an **IPO** or **acquisition**. Liquidity is often a once-in-a-lifetime opportunity – but only if approached strategically, with tax efficiency and risk management top of mind.

And because taxes can quietly erode even the largest exit windfalls, we show you how to plan ahead for **AMT**, **QSBS exclusions**, and how your **state residency** at the time of a liquidity event can swing your tax bill by millions.

This section isn't just about technical strategies – it's about protecting what you've built. You'll learn how to move from theoretical, paper wealth to real, lasting financial security — without letting avoidable mistakes, hidden tax traps, or emotional decision-making get in your way.

By the end of Section 2, you'll understand how to maximize your upside, minimize your risks, and convert startup success into financial freedom.

Chapter 6: Secondary Sales Explained

You've built something real. On paper, you might be a millionaire. But here's the truth every founder eventually bumps into: being "paper rich" doesn't pay the mortgage. Your wealth is trapped in private shares. An IPO might be years away. An acquisition might not happen. You're sitting on value you can't touch. Or can you? Enter secondary sales. Secondary sales are a way to unlock liquidity before your company goes public or gets acquired. They're powerful. They're risky. They're misunderstood. And for founders, they're an increasingly essential part of the wealth strategy. This chapter is about cutting through the noise. No fluff. No hype. Just a clear, founder-focused guide to understanding secondary sales: what they are, how they work, when they make sense, and how to execute them intelligently. Let's dive in.

In a traditional startup journey, you raise rounds, you grow, you IPO or get acquired. Early shareholders get liquidity at exit. But what if you want (or need) liquidity before then? A secondary sale is when a shareholder—a founder, employee, or early investor—sells their shares in a private transaction to a third party. Key point: the company doesn't issue new shares. You're selling existing shares. Secondary sales let you turn illiquid stock into real cash before a formal exit.

Secondary sales aren't about cashing out and quitting. They're about de-risking. Concentrated wealth in one stock is dangerous. They're about liquidity. Life doesn't wait for IPOs. They're about optionality. Freedom to invest, save, breathe. Common reasons founders sell early include buying a home, paying off debt, funding children's education, diversifying personal assets, and reducing financial stress. You've taken enough risk building the company. It's okay—smart, even—to de-risk your personal balance sheet.

Secondary sales come in a few flavors: Private Transactions, where you find a buyer, negotiate terms, and the company must approve the transfer. Organized Secondary Offerings, where the company facilitates a sale, often part of a larger financing round—cleaner, but you might get less favorable terms. Tender Offers, where the company offers to repurchase shares, often tied to new funding rounds. Each method has different levels of company involvement, pricing efficiency, and restrictions. Important: check your shareholder agreements. Some companies have a right of first refusal (ROFR). Some restrict secondary sales until specific events.

The mechanics of secondary sales are straightforward but must be handled carefully. Identify a buyer or platform—individual investors, private equity, or secondary market platforms like Forge or EquityZen. Negotiate terms—price per share, volume, rights transfer (if any). Seek company approval—submit transfer request and wait for approval or exercise of ROFR. Execute the sale—handle legal documents and fund transfers. Report taxes—capital gains tax event, reportable on your personal tax return. Secondary sales are legal, common, and growing, but must be done carefully.

Secondary sales are taxable events. If you've held the stock for over one year, you pay long-term capital gains (15%-20% federal). If less than one year, you pay short-term capital gains (ordinary income rates, up to 37% federal). Also consider state income taxes and the Net Investment Income Tax (NIIT) of 3.8% on high earners. QSBS (Qualified Small Business Stock) exemptions can also come into play—if eligible, the first $10M (or 10x basis) may be tax-free, provided you meet the five-year holding period. Action: work with a tax advisor to model tax exposure before selling.

Pros of secondary sales include liquidity, diversification, reduced personal financial stress, funding life goals, and reduced concentration risk. Cons include potential signaling risk ("Why is the founder selling?"), pricing discounts versus public markets, legal and compliance complexity, and the potential to miss upside. The key: secondary sales aren't about giving up.

They're about smart risk management.

When should you consider selling? Best times include post-Series C/D+ rounds when valuations are higher and more buyers are available, the pre-IPO window when liquidity appetite grows, and during company-organized secondary offerings—cleaner processes. Risky times include early-stage (low valuations, few buyers) and pre-major milestones (you could miss a huge value jump). Timing is part science, part art. You can't time it perfectly. But: sell a portion, leave some for the upside, and balance risk and reward.

Consider real-life scenarios. Scenario 1: Early secondary for de-risking. A founder at a Series C company has a paper net worth of $5M but zero liquidity. They sell $1M in a secondary sale, pay off the mortgage, create an emergency fund, and still hold $4M+ in equity upside. Smart. Scenario 2: Missed secondary opportunity. A company organizes a secondary at $10/share. The founder declines to sell. The market turns; the next round is at $5/share. Paper wealth is cut in half with no liquidity—opportunity cost. Scenario 3: Signaling risk. A founder sells a large block early, raising concerns with investors. The company's reputation suffers, and later funding struggles. Lesson: sell modest amounts and manage optics. Scenario 4: QSBS optimization. A founder holds shares for five years and then conducts a secondary sale, with the first $10M in gains tax-free—huge savings. Plan for it.

If you don't have personal buyers, use platforms like Forge, EquityZen, CartaX, or SharesPost. They match buyers and sellers, handle legal paperwork, and provide pricing benchmarks. They are convenient, but fees apply. Know the trade-offs.

Insider tips for smart secondary sales: Know your company's policies. Work with professionals—lawyer and tax advisor. Sell gradually—avoid big, flashy sales. Use proceeds wisely—don't blow it. Diversify intelligently. Keep some upside—don't sell everything. Model tax scenarios—no surprises. Think about life goals—align sales to your personal needs.

Let's break it down in plain language. Secondary Sale: selling your private shares to a third party before an IPO or acquisition. Tender Offer: company buys back your shares at a set price. ROFR: Right of First Refusal, where the company can match your sale. QSBS: Qualified Small Business Stock, with potential $10M+ tax-free gains. Capital Gains: tax on the profit when you sell stock—short-term (<1 year) at ordinary income rates, long-term (>1 year) at lower tax rates.

Your action steps are clear. Inventory your equity holdings. Review company secondary policies. Model tax implications. Evaluate personal liquidity needs. Consider diversification goals. Engage with secondary platforms if needed. Negotiate terms carefully. Coordinate with legal and tax advisors. Strategize sale timing. Execute transactions professionally.

Secondary sales aren't a betrayal of your company. They're a smart, strategic step toward personal financial independence. You've taken huge risks to build something valuable. It's okay to harvest some of that value early. It's okay to protect your family, your future, your sanity. But do it with a plan. Make one money move before you go to bed tonight. Just one. And then do another next week. Build liquidity. Build freedom. Build your life. You've got this. Your future self will thank you. So will your bank account. So will your peace of mind. Welcome to the founder's financial toolkit.

Chapter 7: Tender Offers, Company-Driven Liquidity

Building a company means building value. But sometimes, the value you've created stays locked up in private stock, untouchable for years. You've worked for it. You've earned it. So how do you access it — without waiting for an IPO or acquisition that could be years away? Enter tender offers. If secondary sales are the "wild west" of liquidity, tender offers are the organized, company-led alternative. They're clean. They're structured. They're increasingly common in high-growth companies. But they're not risk-free. Tender offers come with complexities, trade-offs, and consequences you need to understand if you want to navigate them wisely. This chapter is your founder's guide to tender offers: what they are, how they work, how to evaluate them, and how to plan your liquidity strategy around them. Let's dive in.

A tender offer is a company-organized event where shareholders are offered the opportunity to sell their stock. Often tied to a funding round. Typically backed by new or existing investors. Offers are made at a set price. Shareholders can choose to participate (or not). The key difference: in a secondary sale, you find your own buyer. In a tender offer, the company facilitates the buyer. Tender offers are clean—one set of documents, one price, company blessing. But they require careful thought.

Companies aren't offering tender offers out of charity. They're strategic. Common reasons include attracting and retaining talent, managing the cap table by bringing in strategic investors, setting a valuation benchmark for future rounds, and rewarding early employees and founders. Liquidity can be a powerful retention tool. It shows the company cares about more than just the top-line valuation. It shows it cares about you. But remember: the company's goals and your goals might not always align.

Here's how tender offers work step-by-step. First, the company's board approves a tender offer. Next, the offer terms are finalized: price per share, volume allowed, eligibility criteria. The offer is made to shareholders, with legal documents sent and a time window to decide (often 20 business days). As a shareholder, you must decide to accept all, part, or none. Finally, shares are transferred, cash is paid, and tax reporting obligations arise. Simple in theory, messy in practice if you're not prepared.

Key terms to evaluate include price per share—is it fair? Discounted from the last round? A premium? Volume limits—how many shares can you sell? Is there a cap on the total amount offered? Eligibility—are employees included, founders, only vested shares? Lock-up or restrictions—are you restricted from selling again for a period? Tax withholding—will the company withhold taxes, and how will it report the sale? Read the tender offer carefully. Work with a lawyer if needed.

Pros and cons of participating need careful weighing. Pros: liquidity, turning paper wealth into real cash; reduced risk by diversifying away from one stock; cash for life goals like buying a house, paying debt, or building savings; and a cleaner process thanks to company involvement. Cons: cap on volume sold; missed future upside by selling early; signaling risk to investors; and potential big tax bills. There's no perfect answer, but there's a right answer for you.

Planning liquidity around tender offers is critical. Tender offers are opportunities, but smart founders don't just jump—they plan. Steps include defining goals—how much cash do you really need and what are you funding? Conduct tax modeling to understand your capital gains exposure and model federal, state, and NIIT. Have a diversification strategy—where will you deploy proceeds? Build a portfolio; don't just stockpile cash. Set a liquidity timeline—think long-term and plan for future tender offers or exit events. Build a professional team—tax advisor, wealth manager, estate planner. Your first tender offer won't be your last. Build a process now.

Consider these real-life scenarios. Scenario 1: first tender, first liquidity. The company does a Series D tender offer. A founder sells 10% of holdings, pays off student loans, sets up a diversified investment portfolio, and keeps 90% of shares for future upside. Smart. Balanced. Scenario 2: all-in, all-out. An employee sells 100% of vested shares. The company IPOs a year later; the stock 5x's. Missed out on millions. Lesson: sell some, keep some. Scenario 3: tax surprise. A founder sells $2M worth of shares but makes no estimated tax payments. Result: a $700K tax bill the following year and a cash crunch. Lesson: plan tax payments now, not later. Scenario 4: lock-up burn. A tender offer restricts further sales for 12 months. The market crashes. The founder can't sell. Lesson: understand lock-up risks.

Insider tips for tender offers: start planning early—as soon as you hear rumors of a tender. Negotiate if possible—some founders can negotiate better terms. Watch for hidden fees—transaction fees, legal fees. Balance today versus tomorrow—sell enough to de-risk but leave upside. Protect optics—don't dump huge volumes. Review the tax lot—match sales to longest-held shares if possible. Liquidity is power, but only if used wisely.

Let's break it down in plain language. Tender Offer: company-backed opportunity to sell private shares. Lock-up: period during which you can't sell shares after the tender. Capital Gains Tax: tax on profit from sale of shares—short-term (under one year) taxed at ordinary income rates, long-term (over one year) at lower rates. Tax Withholding: the company may or may not withhold taxes from the sale—you're still responsible for the final bill. Diversification: spreading investments to reduce risk.

Action steps: get the tender documents early. Read every line. Model the tax impact before selling. Decide how much to sell. Plan where proceeds will go. Coordinate with advisors. Confirm lock-up restrictions. Set aside cash for taxes. Diversify proceeds prudently. Track holding periods for remaining shares.

Tender offers aren't a lifeboat. They're an opportunity. An opportunity to take some chips off the table. To turn years of work into freedom. To shift from survival mode to strategic wealth-building. Handled well, a tender offer can be a game-changer. Handled poorly, it can be a regret. Make one money move before you go to bed tonight. Just one. And then do another next week. Plan for the tender. Execute with clarity. Protect your upside. You've got this. Your future self will thank you. So will your bank account. So will your peace of mind. Welcome to the liquidity phase of your founder journey.

Chapter 8: Pre-IPO Liquidity Strategies

You've built the company. You've raised the rounds. You've climbed the mountain. Your IPO is on the horizon. On paper, you're wealthy. In reality, your wealth is locked up in private shares. And even if the IPO is six, twelve, or eighteen months away, life doesn't stop. You might want to buy a home. You might want to diversify. You might just want the peace of mind that comes from having real, liquid assets. The challenge? Getting liquidity before an IPO isn't easy. But it's possible—if you understand the landscape. This chapter is your real-world guide to pre-IPO liquidity strategies: structured loans, risks, and alternatives to selling shares early. Because if you're smart about it, you can build liquidity without selling your future short. Let's get into it.

When you're a founder, employee, or early investor, your wealth often looks like this: huge on paper, illiquid in reality. Pre-IPO shares are private, have transfer restrictions, and often can't be sold without company approval. But life happens now. Common needs for pre-IPO liquidity include buying a primary residence, diversifying assets, paying taxes on exercised options, and funding personal obligations like family and medical needs. The key is getting liquidity without giving up too much future upside.

One option? Borrow against your shares instead of selling them. How it works: lenders, often specialty firms, use your private shares as collateral. You get a loan—cash you can use immediately. You don't sell the shares. When liquidity comes (IPO or acquisition), you repay the loan. Types of loans include non-recourse loans—if you default, the lender only recovers the shares, not your other assets—and recourse loans—if you default, the lender can go after other personal assets. Key features: loan-to-value (LTV) ratios are conservative, often 20%-50%; interest rates are higher than traditional loans; lenders may charge fees and require specific covenants. The big appeal? You get cash now. You still own the shares. No tax event (yet). The big risk? If the stock price falls, you could lose your shares. If the IPO is delayed, interest keeps accruing. Borrowing against shares is a powerful tool—but only if you manage the risk.

Pros of structured loans include no immediate tax event, liquidity without selling, potential to keep full upside, and flexible use of funds. Cons include higher interest rates, risk of share forfeiture, complex loan terms, and pressure if IPO timelines slip.

Liquidity before an IPO is tempting. But it's risky. Risks to consider include valuation risk: if the IPO valuation is lower than expected, your shares might not cover the loan. Timeline risk: IPO delays mean longer loan terms and more interest. Market risk: a public market downturn could crater your stock price post-IPO. Tax risk: loans might be considered "constructive sales" by the IRS if not structured carefully. And of course: concentration risk—even with a loan, you're still heavily exposed to one stock. Pre-IPO liquidity is about balancing current needs against future possibilities.

Selling your shares outright isn't the only way. Here are strategies to consider. Secondary sales (company approved): private transactions to sell shares before IPO, requiring company consent, often part of a broader secondary event. Pros: clean liquidity; cons: taxable event, may have to sell at a discount. Forward contracts: contracts to sell shares at a future date for a set price. Pros: immediate liquidity; cons: complex, risk of "constructive sale." 10b5-1 pre-planning: set up a plan to sell shares automatically post-IPO. Pros: reduces risk of insider trading claims; cons: no liquidity until IPO. Personal loans or lines of credit: use other assets as collateral. Pros: avoids entangling company equity; cons: requires other substantial assets. No one strategy fits everyone. Choose what fits your risk tolerance and life needs.

Consider real-life scenarios. Scenario 1: borrowing to buy a house. A founder wants to buy a house, with an IPO expected in nine months. Takes a non-recourse loan against private shares—40% LTV, 8% interest rate, no personal liability beyond the shares. IPO goes smoothly. Founder repays the loan. Keeps remaining shares. Scenario 2: loan goes bad. An early employee borrows against shares. The company delays the IPO by two years. The stock price dips. Loan collateral falls below the threshold. Forced to surrender shares. No cash left. Scenario 3: pre-IPO secondary. The company offers a tender to employees. A founder sells 20% of holdings. Locks in cash. Pays capital gains. Holds 80% for IPO. Balanced approach. Scenario 4: diversifying with a forward contract. An executive enters a forward contract, locking in $40/share. Gets 70% of the value upfront. Transfers shares post-IPO. Complex but provides cash and upside exposure.

Insider tips for pre-IPO liquidity: start planning early. Pre-IPO windows are short and chaotic. Know your shareholder agreements. Many restrict private transfers. Use reputable lenders. Predatory terms are common. Model worst-case scenarios. Can you survive if the IPO delays 24 months? Think about taxes. Loans structured poorly could be taxable. Don't bet the house. Never borrow to the max. Diversify after liquidity. Don't just sit on cash. Coordinate with your company. Keep legal and HR in the loop. Pre-IPO liquidity is a tool. Use it wisely.

Let's break it down in plain language. Structured loan: borrowing cash using your private company shares as collateral. Non-recourse loan: if you default, the lender takes shares but can't pursue personal assets. Constructive sale: IRS may treat some loans or contracts as if you sold your shares, triggering tax. Secondary sale: selling private shares to a buyer before IPO. Forward contract: agreeing today to sell shares at a future date and price.

Action steps: assess your liquidity needs. Understand your shareholder restrictions. Research pre-IPO lenders carefully. Model cash flow and loan terms. Consult tax and legal advisors. Review alternative strategies. Plan for IPO timing risks. Build a diversification strategy. Negotiate terms if possible. Execute and monitor closely.

Pre-IPO liquidity isn't about bailing out. It's about building flexibility. It's about reducing financial stress. It's about turning part of your paper wealth into real-world security—while keeping the door open for future upside. Handled right, structured loans and pre-IPO strategies can be rocket fuel for your personal financial life. Handled wrong, they can become a trap. Make one money move before you go to bed tonight. Just one. And then do another next week. Plan. Execute. Balance today and tomorrow. You've got this. Your future self will thank you. So will your bank account. So will your peace of mind. Welcome to the founder's liquidity playbook.

Chapter 9: Tax Planning for Founders

You can't build wealth if you don't understand taxes. It's that simple. As a tech founder, your tax life isn't normal. You're not a W-2 employee with a single paycheck and a predictable refund at the end of the year. Your income is irregular. Your wealth is concentrated. Your equity is complicated. And when you finally unlock it—through a secondary sale, IPO, or acquisition—the tax bill can be staggering if you're not ready. Here's the good news: Taxes are not just a cost. They're a game. And when you know the rules, you can play it better than 99% of other founders. This chapter is your deep dive into tax planning for tech founders: why proactive planning matters, key deadlines and strategies to keep you ahead, and how to build a dream team of tax professionals. No fluff. No jargon. No shame. Just clarity, confidence, and control. Let's get into it.

Taxes are one of the biggest destroyers of wealth, especially for founders. Why you're different: concentrated equity—most of your wealth is tied up in a single company; liquidity events—when you finally cash out, the numbers are big; irregular income—salary, bonuses, equity—all over the map; complex structures—ISOs, NSOs, RSUs, QSBS, AMT—alphabet soup. Without planning, taxes can wipe out 40% or more of your liquidity event, trigger penalties and interest, and miss opportunities for tax breaks like QSBS. With planning, taxes become a manageable expense, a strategic advantage, and a lever to maximize your net worth. Proactive tax planning equals financial power.

Key tax concepts every founder must understand include capital gains—profit from selling assets like stock, with short-term gains (<1 year) taxed as ordinary income and long-term gains (>1 year) taxed at lower rates (15%-20%). Alternative Minimum Tax (AMT)—a parallel tax system designed to ensure high earners pay "enough," with ISOs potentially triggering huge AMT bills. Qualified Small Business Stock (QSBS)—potential for $10M+ in tax-free gains if shares are held for five years and the company qualifies. Estimated taxes—the IRS expects you to pay as you earn, and large tax bills without withholding can trigger penalties. 83(b) elections—accelerate tax recognition to lock in low valuations, must be filed within 30 days of stock grant or early exercise. Understanding these basics puts you ahead of most founders.

Key tax deadlines for founders include 83(b) election deadlines (30 days after stock grant or early exercise—miss it, lose the benefit forever), quarterly estimated taxes (due April 15, June 15, September 15, January 15 of the next year—applies if you expect to owe $1,000+ in taxes), tax filing (individual returns due April 15 or October 15 with extension, LLCs/partnerships due March 15, C-corps due April 15), other deadlines (gift tax returns due April 15 if gifting stock, annual 409A valuations usually annually or after major funding). Mark your calendar—or better yet, have your tax team do it for you.

Tax strategies for founders include early exercise and 83(b) elections—exercise stock options early when value is low, file 83(b) to lock in a low tax basis, start long-term capital gains clock. QSBS planning—ensure your shares qualify, hold for five years, consider gifting QSBS shares to family members to multiply the exclusion. Charitable giving—donate appreciated stock, not cash; set up a Donor-Advised Fund (DAF) to get immediate deduction and give over time. Installment sales—spread tax liability over multiple years. Tax loss harvesting—sell losing investments to offset gains and reduce the overall tax bill. Retirement accounts—Solo 401(k), SEP-IRA—defer income and reduce current-year tax. Gifting strategies—use the annual gift exclusion ($17,000 per recipient in 2024) and the lifetime exemption (~$13 million in 2024) to reduce future estate taxes. AMT planning—model AMT exposure before exercising ISOs and exercise in low-income years. Advanced moves with huge impact.

Consider real-life scenarios. Scenario 1: missed 83(b). A founder forgets to file 83(b). Four years later, RSUs vest at $50/share. Huge ordinary income tax. Missed opportunity. Scenario 2: perfect QSBS planning. An early employee holds shares for 5+ years, sells $12M, and the first $10M is tax-free. Massive tax savings. Scenario 3: no estimated payments. A founder sells $3M in a secondary sale but doesn't make estimated tax payments. Faces penalties and a massive tax bill. Avoidable with better planning. Scenario 4: DAF + IPO windfall. An executive sets up a Donor-Advised Fund pre-IPO, donates shares, gets a big charitable deduction, and funds philanthropy for years—strategic and impactful.

Working with tax professionals is key. You don't need to become a tax expert. You need to hire one. What to look for: experience with founders, understanding of equity compensation, proactive communication, and willingness to model multiple scenarios. Types of tax pros include CPA (Certified Public Accountant—prepares returns, gives tax advice), EA (Enrolled Agent—IRS-certified tax advisor), and tax attorney (handles complex structuring and estate planning). Pro tips: work with a CPA who understands equity compensation; meet quarterly, not just at tax time; pay for planning, not just filing. Your tax team can save you millions, protect you from mistakes, and help you sleep better at night.

Let's break it down in plain language. Capital gains: profit from selling investments. 83(b) election: tax yourself early at a low valuation to save big later. QSBS: potential $10M tax-free gain on startup stock. AMT: alternative tax system that catches ISO holders off guard. Estimated taxes: quarterly payments to avoid penalties. Donor-Advised Fund (DAF): charitable giving account with an upfront tax deduction.

Action steps: inventory your equity. Review 83(b) filing deadlines. Model AMT exposure. Check QSBS eligibility. Plan estimated tax payments. Consider a DAF for charitable giving. Schedule quarterly tax check-ins. Hire a founder-savvy CPA. Review gifting opportunities. Prepare for liquidity events.

Chapter: Tax Planning for Tech Founders — Turning Smart Moves into Lasting Wealth

You can't build wealth if you don't understand taxes. It's that simple. As a tech founder, your tax life isn't normal. You're not a W-2 employee with a single paycheck and a predictable refund at the end of the year. Your income is irregular. Your wealth is concentrated. Your equity is complicated. And when you finally unlock it—through a secondary sale, IPO, or acquisition—the tax bill can be staggering if you're not ready. Here's the good news: Taxes are not just a cost. They're a game. And when you know the rules, you can play it better than 99% of other founders. This chapter is your deep dive into tax planning for tech founders: why proactive planning matters, key deadlines and strategies to keep you ahead, and how to build a dream team of tax professionals. No fluff. No jargon. No shame. Just clarity, confidence, and control. Let's get into it.

Taxes are one of the biggest destroyers of wealth, especially for founders. Why you're different: concentrated equity—most of your wealth is tied up in a single company; liquidity events—when you finally cash out, the numbers are big; irregular income—salary, bonuses, equity—all over the map; complex structures—ISOs, NSOs, RSUs, QSBS, AMT—alphabet soup. Without planning, taxes can wipe out 40% or more of your liquidity event, trigger penalties and interest, and miss opportunities for tax breaks like QSBS. With planning, taxes become a manageable expense, a strategic advantage, and a lever to maximize your net worth. Proactive tax planning equals financial power.

Key tax concepts every founder must understand include capital gains—profit from selling assets like stock, with short-term gains (<1 year) taxed as ordinary income and long-term gains (>1 year) taxed at lower rates (15%-20%). Alternative Minimum Tax (AMT)—a parallel tax system designed to ensure high earners pay "enough," with ISOs potentially triggering huge AMT bills. Qualified Small Business Stock (QSBS)—potential for $10M+ in tax-free gains if shares are held for five years and the company qualifies. Estimated taxes—the IRS expects you to pay as you earn, and large tax bills without withholding can trigger penalties. 83(b) elections—accelerate tax recognition to lock in low valuations, must be filed within 30 days of stock grant or early exercise. Understanding these basics puts you ahead of most founders.

Key tax deadlines for founders include 83(b) election deadlines (30 days after stock grant or early exercise—miss it, lose the benefit forever), quarterly estimated taxes (due April 15, June 15, September 15, January 15 of the next year—applies if you expect to owe $1,000+ in taxes), tax filing (individual returns due April 15 or October 15 with extension, LLCs/partnerships due March 15, C-corps due April 15), other deadlines (gift tax returns due April 15 if gifting stock, annual 409A valuations usually annually or after major funding). Mark your calendar—or better yet, have your tax team do it for you.

Tax strategies for founders include early exercise and 83(b) elections—exercise stock options early when value is low, file 83(b) to lock in a low tax basis, start long-term capital gains clock. QSBS planning—ensure your shares qualify, hold for five years, consider gifting QSBS shares to family members to multiply the exclusion. Charitable giving—donate appreciated stock, not cash; set up a Donor-Advised Fund (DAF) to get immediate deduction and give over time. Installment sales—spread tax liability over multiple years. Tax loss harvesting—sell losing investments to offset gains and reduce the overall tax bill. Retirement accounts—Solo 401(k), SEP-IRA—defer income and reduce current-year tax. Gifting strategies—use the annual gift exclusion ($17,000 per recipient in 2024) and the lifetime exemption (~$13 million in 2024) to reduce future estate taxes. AMT planning—model AMT exposure before exercising ISOs and exercise in low-income years. Advanced moves with huge impact.

For ultra-affluent founders, estate planning becomes a powerful tool. Gifting pre-IPO shares can freeze the value of the gift at today's low valuation. Strategies include:

Grantor Retained Annuity Trusts (GRATs)—transfer appreciating assets to heirs while minimizing gift tax. Set up a GRAT pre-IPO to transfer shares at low valuation. If shares appreciate, excess growth passes to heirs tax-free.

Intentionally Defective Grantor Trusts (IDGTs)—transfer shares into a trust; you pay the income taxes, allowing the trust to grow unencumbered.

An IDGT locks in valuation pre-IPO and shifts future growth out of your estate.

Spousal Lifetime Access Trusts (SLATs)—gift assets to a trust benefiting your spouse, retaining indirect access to assets while removing them from your estate.

Charitable Remainder Trusts (CRTs)—transfer shares to a CRT before IPO; you get a charitable deduction, income stream for life, and diversify shares tax-efficiently.

Dynasty Trusts—gifting shares to a dynasty trust ensures assets stay out of your estate and can provide for multiple generations without being subject to future estate taxes.

Real-life scenarios illustrate these strategies. Scenario 1: missed 83(b). A founder forgets to file 83(b). Four years later, RSUs vest at $50/share. Huge ordinary income tax. Missed opportunity. Scenario 2: perfect QSBS planning. An early employee holds shares for 5+ years, sells $12M, and the first $10M is tax-free. Massive tax savings. Scenario 3: no estimated payments. A founder sells $3M in a secondary sale but doesn't make estimated tax payments. Faces penalties and a massive tax bill. Avoidable with better planning. Scenario 4: DAF + IPO windfall. An executive sets up a Donor-Advised Fund pre-IPO, donates shares, gets a big charitable deduction, and funds philanthropy for years—strategic and impactful. Scenario 5: pre-IPO GRAT. A founder transfers $5M worth of shares into a GRAT pre-IPO. After the IPO, shares are worth $50M—only the initial $5M gift is subject to gift tax, and $45M passes to heirs tax-free.

Working with tax professionals is key. You don't need to become a tax expert. You need to hire one. What to look for: experience with founders, understanding of equity compensation, proactive communication, and willingness to model multiple scenarios. Types of tax pros include CPA (Certified Public Accountant—prepares returns, gives tax advice), EA (Enrolled Agent—IRS-certified tax advisor), and tax attorney (handles complex structuring and estate planning). Pro tips: work with a CPA who understands equity compensation; meet quarterly, not just at tax time; pay for planning, not just filing. Your tax team can save you millions, protect you from mistakes, and help you sleep better at night.

Let's break it down in plain language. Capital gains: profit from selling investments. 83(b) election: tax yourself early at a low valuation to save big later. QSBS: potential $10M tax-free gain on startup stock. AMT: alternative tax system that catches ISO holders off guard. Estimated taxes: quarterly payments to avoid penalties. Donor-Advised Fund (DAF): charitable giving account with an upfront tax deduction. GRAT: trust to transfer appreciating assets to heirs at low cost. IDGT: trust that allows growth outside of estate tax system. SLAT: trust benefiting spouse but removing assets from estate. CRT: trust providing income stream and charitable deduction.

Action steps: inventory your equity. Review 83(b) filing deadlines. Model AMT exposure. Check QSBS eligibility. Plan estimated tax payments. Consider a DAF for charitable giving. Schedule quarterly tax check-ins. Hire a founder-savvy CPA. Review gifting opportunities, especially pre-IPO. Explore GRATs, IDGTs, SLATs, and CRTs for estate and tax efficiency. Prepare for liquidity events.

Tax planning isn't sexy. But it's how you turn a big exit into lasting wealth. You didn't build a startup just to hand half your earnings to the IRS. You didn't sacrifice weekends, vacations, and paychecks just to get crushed by taxes. You've done the hard part. Now do the smart part. Proactive tax planning. Smart strategies. The right team. Make one money move before you go to bed tonight. Just one. And then do another next week. Plan for taxes. Protect your wealth. Play the long game. You've got this. Your future self will thank you. So will your bank account. So will your peace of mind. Welcome to the founder's guide to financial mastery.

Chapter 10: AMT, What Founders Must Know

There's a tax lurking in the shadows. One that catches founders by surprise. One that can turn a victory into a financial nightmare. It's called the Alternative Minimum Tax (AMT). And if you have Incentive Stock Options (ISOs), it's not optional. Here's the truth: If you don't understand AMT, it can crush you. If you do understand it, you can sidestep the landmines and keep more of what you've earned. This chapter is your founder's guide to AMT: what it is, how it impacts ISO holders, strategies to mitigate your liability, and how to plan around exercise timing. No jargon. No panic. Just the information you need to stay in control. Let's get into it.

The Alternative Minimum Tax (AMT) is a parallel tax system. It was designed to ensure high earners pay "enough" taxes. Instead of just calculating your regular income tax, the IRS also calculates your AMT. You owe the higher of the two. How it works is deceptively simple. You start with your taxable income, add back certain "preferences" and "adjustments," subtract the AMT exemption, and apply the AMT rates—26% and 28%. If AMT is higher than your regular tax, you pay AMT. Simple in theory. Devastating in practice—especially if you're exercising ISOs.

Incentive Stock Options (ISOs) have a hidden tax trap. When you exercise ISOs, the "spread" between the strike price (what you pay) and the fair market value (FMV) on exercise day is considered an AMT adjustment. Let's look at a quick example: Your strike price is $1/share, the FMV on exercise day is $50/share, and you exercise 10,000 shares. Your adjustment is (50 - 1) x 10,000 = $490,000. This $490,000 gets added to your AMT income. Even if you haven't sold the shares. Even if they're illiquid. You owe tax now. This is what catches founders—you're rich on paper, but you're paying taxes with real cash.

So how exactly is AMT calculated for ISOs? Start with your regular taxable income—salaries, bonuses, and other compensation. Add the ISO spread—FMV minus strike price at exercise. Subtract the AMT exemption—$85,700 for single filers and $133,300 for married couples (2024 numbers). Then apply the AMT rates: 26% up to about $232,600 and 28% above that. The bottom line: large ISO exercises equal massive AMT adjustments, which means big tax bills. And if your shares aren't liquid yet? You're facing a cash crunch with no easy escape.

Here's a real-life founder horror story. A founder exercises ISOs: 100,000 shares at $1 strike, FMV at exercise is $40/share. The spread? $39 x 100,000 = $3.9 million. AMT liability? Roughly $1 million. But here's the catch—no liquidity and no cash. Worse, after the IPO, the stock crashes to $10/share. Now the founder is stuck with a massive tax bill on wealth that's evaporated. Completely avoidable—with better planning.

What strategies exist to mitigate AMT liability? First, early exercise. Exercise when FMV is close to the strike price to minimize the spread—and minimize AMT adjustments. Second, spread your exercises over multiple years to keep under the AMT exemption threshold each year. Third, exercise in low-income years to reduce overall taxable income. Fourth, monitor your 409A valuations. If your company's 409A valuation dips, it might be the right time to exercise. Fifth, if needed, trigger a disqualifying disposition—sell shares within one year of exercise. It means you lose capital gains tax treatment but avoid AMT. Sixth, if you pay AMT now, you can claim the AMT credit against future regular taxes, though it may take years. Seventh, offset AMT income with charitable donations. Finally, wait until after the IPO to exercise and sell quickly (same-day sale). It turns ISO treatment into NSO treatment but eliminates AMT risk.

Planning around exercise timing is crucial. Early exercise when the FMV is low, late exercise if liquidity is near, exercising in batches over multiple years, and targeting low-income years can each significantly reduce risk. Coordinate with a tax advisor and financial planner. Model different scenarios. Choose the strategy that fits your risk tolerance, liquidity timeline, and tax situation.

Real-life scenarios illustrate the importance of strategy. Scenario 1: A founder early exercises at seed stage—strike price is $0.01, FMV is $0.01. No spread. No AMT. Years later, IPO at $50/share—long-term capital gains treatment. Perfect. Scenario 2: An executive waits until the IPO filing. FMV is $75/share. Massive spread. Huge AMT liability. Forced to sell shares immediately, leaving money on the table. Scenario 3: An employee exercises ISOs and sells within a year. Pays ordinary income tax but avoids AMT—a less optimal path but better than a cash crunch. Scenario 4: A founder pays AMT and recovers through AMT credit over five years—slow, but not a total loss.

Let's break it down in plain language. AMT: a parallel tax system that catches ISO holders by taxing the spread at exercise. ISO spread: the difference between the fair market value and the strike price. 409A valuation: the independent valuation of private company stock. Disqualifying disposition: selling ISO shares before one year triggers ordinary income tax but avoids AMT. AMT credit: a future tax credit for AMT paid today.

Action steps? First, inventory your ISOs. Know your strike prices and vesting schedules. Track 409A valuations closely. Model AMT scenarios with a qualified CPA. Consider early exercises. Plan exercise batches strategically. Exercise in low-income years if possible. Set aside cash for AMT if exercising later. Understand disqualifying dispositions and how they can be used as a safety valve. Monitor AMT credit carryforwards to reclaim taxes paid.

AMT-Friendly Liquidity Planning Post-IPO

Once the IPO window opens and you finally have liquidity, the AMT challenges don't disappear. In fact, managing the tax consequences of unlocking your wealth becomes even more delicate. Smart liquidity planning can turn a tax burden into a strategic advantage. The goal post-IPO is not just to sell — it's to *harvest, optimize,* and *preserve* what you've built.

Strategic Tranching

One of the most powerful tools post-IPO is tranching your sales. Rather than selling all your stock at once — which spikes your taxable income and triggers the highest marginal rates — you sell in measured, deliberate increments over time.

Why tranch?

- It smooths out your income.
- It allows you to utilize lower marginal tax brackets each year.
- It keeps you from flooding the market and potentially depressing your company's stock price.

Typical Post-IPO Tranch Plan:

- Year 1: Sell enough to cover taxes, lifestyle cash needs, and create a safety net.
- Years 2-5: Gradually sell additional shares to fund investments, philanthropy, or diversify.

Key: Pair each tranche with a strategic goal — not just cashing out, but redeploying thoughtfully.

Harvesting Losses

Another post-IPO tactic? Tax loss harvesting. It sounds strange — selling investments at a loss — but here's why it matters.

Let's say you've diversified into public equities post-IPO. If some of those investments underperform, you can *sell* them to realize losses. Those losses can offset gains from selling your company stock, dollar-for-dollar.

Rules of thumb:

- Short-term losses offset short-term gains (higher tax impact).
- Long-term losses offset long-term gains (lower rates, but still helpful).
- Up to $3,000 of losses can offset *ordinary income* each year beyond capital gains.

If you plan carefully, you can trim your overall tax liability dramatically by systematically harvesting losses alongside tranching gains.

Timing Gifts to Foundations or DAFs

For ultra-high-net-worth founders, charitable giving isn't just about generosity — it's a tax strategy. By contributing appreciated stock to a Donor-Advised Fund (DAF) or a private foundation, you can:

- Avoid paying capital gains tax on the appreciation.
- Get an immediate charitable deduction (up to 30% of AGI for appreciated stock).
- Retain control over when and how the funds are distributed to charities.

Post-IPO is the perfect time to consider funding a DAF:

- Your stock is highly appreciated.
- Your income is temporarily high (maximizing the value of the deduction).

- You're likely looking for ways to minimize this year's taxable income.

Advanced Move: Combine a large DAF contribution with a tranche sale in the same year to offset gains with a charitable deduction, potentially eliminating millions from your taxable income.

Gifting During Low Valuation Windows

If your company's stock price declines post-IPO — whether temporarily or due to a market correction — that's not always a bad thing. A lower valuation creates a unique opportunity to gift shares into family trusts (GRATs, IDGTs, SLATs).

Why gift when the stock is down?

- You use less of your lifetime gift exemption ($13M+ in 2024).
- Future appreciation happens outside your taxable estate.
- It's like locking in a discount on your estate plan.

Tip: Coordinate this move with your estate attorney and tax advisor to ensure compliance with IRS valuation rules and minimize audit risk.

Hedging Concentrated Stock

If you don't want to sell — maybe you're bullish on the long-term prospects — but you want protection, consider hedging strategies like:

- Collars: Sell call options and buy puts to lock in a trading range.
- Prepaid Variable Forward Contracts: Monetize shares now without an immediate sale.

These allow you to protect against downside without triggering an immediate tax event.

Important: Complex hedging strategies are considered "constructive sales" by the IRS in some cases. Make sure your tax team signs off before execution.

Managing the AMT Credit Carryforward

If you paid AMT in the past (from pre-IPO exercises), you can reclaim it over time as a credit against your regular tax. But there's a catch: it's not automatic.

The IRS allows you to claim the AMT credit in years when your regular tax liability exceeds your AMT liability — meaning, you need to have enough ordinary taxable income to utilize it.

Strategy:

- Monitor your AMT credit annually.
- Prioritize liquidity events (tranche sales) that create enough regular tax to absorb the credit.
- Work closely with your CPA to avoid letting credits expire unused.

Large liquidity years are prime for using up the AMT credit — don't leave that money on the table.

Real-World Founder Case Study

Let's take an example: Sarah, a founder of a SaaS company, finally sees her company IPO after seven years. She has:

- $20M in company stock.
- $1.5M AMT paid in the past.
- A goal to fund a family foundation and diversify her wealth.

Sarah's strategy:

1. **Year 1**: Sells $4M worth of stock.

- Funds a $2M Donor-Advised Fund.
- Claims a $2M charitable deduction.
- Offsets $2M of her $4M gain.

1. **Year 2**: Markets cool; her remaining stock value dips.

- Gifts 500,000 shares to an IDGT while valuation is lower.
- Locks in future appreciation outside her estate.

1. **Year 3**: Gradual sales.

- Harvests $300,000 in investment losses from diversified portfolio.
- Offsets gains from stock sales.

Over five years, Sarah builds:

- A diversified $25M portfolio.
- A $10M family foundation.
- An estate plan shielding $30M+ from future estate taxes.
- Full recovery of her AMT credits.

She didn't just cash out — she transformed wealth into legacy.

Final Action Steps

- Build a Tranche Plan Before IPO
- Pair Charitable Contributions With Liquidity Events
- Monitor and Harvest Investment Losses Annually
- Gift Shares During Market Lows
- Explore Hedging to Protect Without Selling
- Track and Use Your AMT Credits
- Coordinate All Moves With Your Tax Attorney and CPA
- Think in Decades, Not Years

Final Thought (Extended)

You didn't build this company just for the headline number on IPO day. You built it for freedom, for impact, for the future. AMT, taxes, liquidity events — they're not threats. They're tools. Tools to master if you want to convert *paper wealth* into *real-world wealth* that lasts generations.

Make one money move before you go to bed tonight. Just one. And then another next week. Map your AMT exposure. Draft your post-IPO tranche plan. Run your AMT credit recovery strategy. Fund your foundation.

Build a tax plan as sophisticated as the business you built.

You've got this. And your future self — and your heirs — will thank you.

Welcome to the tax-savvy founder's journey, now with the legacy tools built in.

Section 3: Protecting Your Future — Risk Management and Wealth Defense

Wealth creation is only part of the equation. The bigger — and often overlooked — part is wealth protection.

Founders operate in one of the riskiest ecosystems in the world: startups are volatile, public scrutiny increases after success, and personal financial threats multiply once wealth becomes visible. Without a plan to manage these risks, even the most impressive exit can be undone by poor preparation or a single misstep.

Section 3 focuses on the critical but often ignored side of the financial equation — risk management and wealth defense.

We start with the challenge of **concentrated stock** positions and explain strategies to manage risk without completely giving up upside. You'll learn how to protect against major losses while still holding onto the vision that built your company.

Next, we dig into **10b5-1 plans** — essential tools for pre-scheduling stock sales and avoiding insider trading accusations, especially in the high-stakes public market phase. You'll learn how to structure a plan that works with your long-term goals and protects your reputation.

Then we move into broader **insurance essentials** that founders need but often ignore — including **D&O coverage**, **umbrella policies**, and personal **cybersecurity**. As your profile and wealth grow, so does your exposure. Protection needs to scale alongside success.

Finally, we address **estate planning** for entrepreneurs: creating trusts, protecting assets, preparing your family, and thinking about succession not just for your company but for your life's work and wealth.

This section is about more than defense. It's about resilience.

It's about ensuring that the wealth you work so hard to build survives the volatility of markets, legal challenges, and life itself.

Because real wealth isn't just about making money — it's about keeping it, protecting it, and ensuring it lasts long after the last term sheet is signed.

Chapter 11: QSBS and $10M Tax-Free Gains

Imagine building a company from scratch. Years of sweat. Late nights. Hard choices. Then, one day, you finally cash out. $10 million. And guess what? You don't owe a dime in federal taxes on it. Sounds too good to be true. But it's not. It's called Qualified Small Business Stock (QSBS). If you qualify, it can be the single greatest tax break available to founders. This chapter is your deep dive into QSBS: what it is, how to qualify, how to maximize the benefit, and what timing traps to avoid. If you get this right, it's not just wealth. It's tax-free wealth. Let's dive in.

QSBS stands for Qualified Small Business Stock. It's a tax provision—Section 1202 of the IRS Code—that allows up to $10 million, or 10 times your original investment (whichever is greater), in capital gains to be completely excluded from federal taxes. Translation: you sell your startup shares, and the first $10 million is tax-free. Or, if you invested $2 million, up to $20 million could be tax-free. It's one of the few truly founder-friendly tax breaks out there. But only if you play by the rules.

Not every company—or every founder—qualifies. Here's what's required. First, Company Qualifications: It must be a domestic C-Corporation, not an LLC or S-Corp. The company must have gross assets of less than $50 million at all times before and immediately after stock issuance. It must be in a Qualified Business—no personal services businesses (like law, accounting, finance, or consulting), banking, farming, mining, hotels, or restaurants. Second, Stock Issuance: You must acquire the stock directly from the company—in exchange for money, property (not stock), or services. Third, Holding Period: You must hold the stock for more than 5 years. Fourth, Active Business Requirement: At least 80% of the company's assets must be used in an active trade or business. Mess up any of these, and you're out.

So how do you maximize the $10M capital gains exclusion? Start early. The 5-year clock starts at issuance—early exercises mean the clock starts ticking sooner. Spread across family: each individual gets their own $10M exclusion. Gifting QSBS to a spouse or children multiplies the benefit. Trust Planning: Establish non-grantor trusts—each trust gets its own $10M exclusion. Rollover under Section 1045: If you sell QSBS before the 5-year holding period is up, you can roll over proceeds into new QSBS and continue deferral. Stacking exclusions through strategic gifting and trust planning can multiply the $10M benefit several times over. Advanced, but powerful.

Timing considerations are critical for QSBS eligibility. Early exercise ISOs: exercise options early and file an 83(b) election—the clock starts sooner. Vesting schedules don't matter; for QSBS, it's the exercise date that matters. Watch for down rounds: New stock issuances during down rounds might reset QSBS eligibility. Beware of mergers and acquisitions: stock-for-stock mergers can disrupt QSBS status, whereas cash acquisitions preserve it. Also, asset sales typically don't qualify for QSBS treatment—always push for stock sales. Planning ahead could mean the difference between a $10M tax-free gain and a hefty tax bill.

Let's consider some real-life scenarios. Scenario 1: A founder exercises ISOs early, holds for six years, and sells the company. A $12M gain—first $10M tax-free, only $2M taxed. Scenario 2: An executive waits until the IPO to exercise. Exercises just before IPO—5-year clock just starts, and no QSBS benefit on the immediate sale. Scenario 3: A founder gifts shares to three non-grantor trusts pre-exit. Each trust holds for 5 years, then sells. $10M exclusion x 4 (founder + 3 trusts) = $40M tax-free. Scenario 4: A company sells assets instead of stock. No QSBS treatment; full tax bill. Ouch.

Common pitfalls to avoid? Electing S-corp status. QSBS only applies to C-corporations—electing S-corp disqualifies you. Late exercises: Waiting to exercise options delays the 5-year clock—exercise early. No 83(b) election: If you early exercise restricted shares and don't file an 83(b), the IRS doesn't recognize it for QSBS. Improper stock transfers: Transferring stock incorrectly can blow your QSBS status. Asset sales: Always push for stock sales in exit negotiations.

Let's simplify. QSBS: Qualified Small Business Stock. Section 1202: the IRS code provision governing QSBS. 83(b) Election: Informs the IRS you're starting your ownership clock early. 409A Valuation: Independent valuation of your private company's stock. Section 1045 Rollover: Allows you to reinvest QSBS proceeds into another QSBS to continue tax deferral.

Here's your action plan. Confirm your company's QSBS eligibility. Exercise ISOs early. File your 83(b) election within 30 days. Hold your shares for 5 years. Avoid disqualifying activities like S-corp elections or asset sales. Consult tax and legal advisors to ensure QSBS compliance. Explore gifting and trust planning—non-grantor trusts can multiply your exclusions. Negotiate for stock sales in exit events. Document everything meticulously. Model tax outcomes before selling.

Advanced QSBS Stacking Strategies

For the ultra-affluent founder who is serious about not just preserving but exponentially growing tax-free wealth, QSBS stacking is where sophistication meets strategy. Think of stacking not as loophole hunting, but as elegant, fully compliant use of the tax code's most generous provisions.

What exactly is stacking? It's the art of multiplying your $10M QSBS exemption across multiple taxpayers — legally. By spreading ownership among family members or trusts, each with their own $10M cap, you can scale the QSBS benefit far beyond a single exclusion.

Here's how it works:

Individual Gifting

Each individual — spouse, children, even parents — can claim their own $10M exemption if they hold QSBS and meet the requirements. By gifting QSBS shares early (before major value appreciation), you effectively assign future gains to different taxpayers.

Important:

- Gifts must be made outright, not held jointly.
- Gifting while the company is still private and valuations are low maximizes the leverage.

Non-Grantor Trusts

Non-grantor trusts are the real engine of QSBS stacking. Each independent trust — if structured properly — gets its own $10M exclusion.

Key guidelines:

- Trust must be irrevocable.
- Trustee must have real, independent control.
- Beneficiaries must be bona fide.

By setting up multiple trusts (children, grandchildren, dynasty trusts), you can multiply the QSBS shield many times over.

Example: A founder sets up five non-grantor trusts for five family members. Each trust qualifies for $10M. Founder retains their own $10M exemption. End result: $60M total gains — entirely tax-free.

Timing Matters

Stacking must happen before value appreciates significantly. Post-growth gifting can trigger gift tax or eat into your lifetime exemption. Early stage = best stage.

Pro Tip: Freeze the value at gift time via a grantor retained annuity trust (GRAT) or other estate-freezing strategies to minimize gift tax exposure.

Pitfalls to Avoid

- Improperly administered trusts (IRS can "collapse" them).

- Failing to start the 5-year holding period with the new owner.
- Gifting too close to a liquidity event (scrutiny risk).

Bottom Line: Done right, QSBS stacking isn't gaming the system — it's strategic planning at the highest level.

10. Post-Sale Wealth Deployment: Protecting the Tax-Free Windfall

Winning the QSBS game is just the beginning. The next step is protecting and multiplying the tax-free capital you've built.

Here's a framework for ultra-affluent founders post-liquidity:

Immediate Actions (0-6 months post-sale)

- **Rebalance Risk**: You've just transitioned from an illiquid single-stock position to liquid cash. Don't rush. Preserve first. Resist the temptation to immediately chase yield or hot investments.
- **Build a Core Portfolio**: Think boring first — global diversification, asset allocation aligned with your risk tolerance.
- **Tax-Efficient Vehicles**: Max out tax-deferred or tax-free options like IRAs, 529s for kids' education, health savings accounts.
- **Debt Paydown**: Pay off high-interest personal debts.
- **Liquidity Reserve**: Set aside 2-3 years of lifestyle costs in cash or ultra-safe short-term investments.

Medium-Term Moves (6-24 months)

- **Philanthropy**: Revisit or establish a family foundation or Donor-Advised Fund (DAF) strategy. Tax-free money has its greatest leverage when matched with purpose.
- **Alternative Investments**: Allocate a portion (not majority) into private equity, venture funds, or real estate. Think 10-20%, not 50%.
- **Second Act**: If you're launching a new venture, use post-QSBS

proceeds to fund your next startup (and set up new QSBS eligibility!).

Long-Term Wealth Structure (2+ years)

- **Family Governance**: Formalize wealth management with family meetings, education for next-gen, and clear succession planning.
- **Asset Protection**: Consider domestic asset protection trusts or offshore trusts (with compliant structures) to shield wealth from future risks.
- **Dynasty Planning**: For those truly thinking multi-generationally, establish dynasty trusts that can preserve wealth beyond your grandchildren's lifetimes.

Key Mindset Shift: Your first company was about growing wealth. Post-sale life is about *preserving, protecting, and thoughtfully deploying* wealth for impact and legacy.

11. Real-World Ultra-Affluent Founder Playbook

Let's walk through a real-world founder scenario:

Emily, a founder of a fintech platform, sold her shares after seven years. She had:

- $10M in her own QSBS exclusion.
- $30M gifted across three non-grantor trusts.
- $40M total tax-free.

Her post-sale playbook:

- 50% of proceeds went into a globally diversified core portfolio.
- 15% went into a series of venture funds and direct startup investments.
- 10% seeded a family foundation, allowing for charitable initiatives.
- 25% held in ultra-safe cash equivalents and short-term municipals for

opportunistic moves.

She scheduled annual family wealth meetings, established trusts for future generations, and laid out a philanthropic roadmap. Net result? She didn't just sell a company — she laid the groundwork for a dynasty.

12. Final Action Steps

- Confirm QSBS eligibility early.
- Set up and fund non-grantor trusts if appropriate.
- Exercise stock options early and file 83(b) elections.
- Map a five-year exit and gifting timeline.
- Use professional trustees and tax advisors — this isn't DIY territory.
- Build a deliberate post-sale investment and philanthropic plan.
- Hold family governance sessions to create shared vision and responsibility.

Building a business was never just about money. It was about freedom. Impact. Legacy. The QSBS code gives you a once-in-a-lifetime chance to turn entrepreneurial risk into tax-free generational wealth.

But no one hands you this win automatically. It's earned — through foresight, structure, and disciplined execution.

You've already done the hardest part — creating something from nothing.

Now it's time to finish well. Plan early. Stack wisely. Deploy intentionally.

Make one move tonight — review your eligibility, start your family trust structure, sketch your five-year deployment plan.

Your future self, your family, and generations you'll never meet — they'll all thank you.

Welcome to not just tax-free millions — welcome to lasting wealth mastery.

Chapter 12: State vs. Federal Tax Planning

You've built the company. You've sweated every round. You've sacrificed. Now the payoff is near. Maybe it's an IPO. Maybe it's an acquisition. Maybe it's a tender offer. Whatever the form, there's real money coming your way. But here's what most founders forget: it's not just the IRS that wants a cut. Your state wants a slice, too. And depending on where you live when you exit, that slice can be brutal. This chapter is your no-nonsense guide to state vs. federal tax planning: how state taxes impact your exit proceeds, how domicile strategies can reduce (or eliminate) state tax, and how to time relocation to make it count. Let's dive in.

Why do state taxes matter? At the federal level, you're paying capital gains taxes—0%, 15%, or 20% depending on your income—plus a 3.8% Net Investment Income Tax (NIIT). But at the state level? It varies wildly. Some examples for 2024: California at 13.3% top marginal rate, New York at 10.9% (plus 3.876% NYC tax if you live in the city), Massachusetts at 5%, and Texas and Florida at 0%. If you're in California and cash out $10M, federal tax at 23.8% plus state tax at 13.3% means a total of 37.1%. That's $3.71M gone. Move to Texas first? Save $1.33M. Serious money.

So how exactly do state taxes work at exit? Most states tax residents on all income, no matter where it's earned. The key concept: it's where you live on the date of the taxable event that matters. Sold your shares while living in California? California wants its 13.3%. Even if you move to Texas a month later. Exit Day = Tax Day. Residency is everything.

But what is domicile, really? Domicile is your true, permanent home. It's where you vote, have your driver's license, register your car, own or rent your primary residence, work, and maintain family ties. States have their own tests. California focuses on intent and facts—where you spend the most time and where your closest connections are. New York has a statutory residency test: 183 days or more plus a permanent place of abode. The point: you can't just say you live in Texas. You have to actually live in Texas.

So what are the key domicile strategies to reduce state taxes? First, move early. Relocate well before the liquidity event—ideally 6 to 12 months minimum. Second, cut ties: sell or rent out your old home, give up your old driver's license, deregister to vote, cancel gym memberships, and sever ties to old clubs. Third, establish new ties: buy or rent a home in your new state, get a new driver's license, register to vote, move your primary bank accounts, and join local organizations. Fourth, spend time wisely: spend the majority of your days in your new state—track it with cell phone records, apps, and calendars. Finally, document everything. Changing domicile isn't just paperwork; it's a lifestyle shift. And you must be ready to prove it.

Timing and considerations are critical. When should you move? Before any taxable event. Before exercising options (if that triggers tax). Before selling shares. Before a tender offer closes. Timing is everything. Miss it, and you're stuck paying. How long should you stay? At least 6 months plus 1 day, but ideally 12 months or more to be safe. What about remote work? If your company is based in California but you live in Texas, California may still want a cut if you're deemed to work in California. Remote work rules vary—plan carefully. A prudent exit planning timeline looks like this: Year 1, relocate; Year 2, establish domicile fully; Year 3+, liquidity event. Longer timelines mean a stronger case.

Let's talk real-life scenarios. Scenario 1: A California founder moves to Texas 12 months before the IPO, sells shares post-IPO, and pays no California tax—saving millions. Scenario 2: Another founder moves to

Florida 3 months before acquisition. California audits. Still "domiciled" in California. Pays full California taxes. Scenario 3: An executive maintains apartments in New York and Florida but spends 185 days in New York. New York claims residency and taxes the entire gain. Scenario 4: A founder moves, sells their home, relocates their entire family, and lives 14 months in the new state before liquidity. No state tax. A clean win.

Let's break it down in plain language. Domicile is your primary, true home for tax purposes. Statutory residency occurs when you spend enough days in a state to be taxed as a resident, even if it's not your domicile. Liquidity event means IPO, acquisition, tender offer, or major secondary sale. Taxable event is when you sell shares and trigger capital gains tax. Exit Day is the day you sell—sets your state tax liability.

What are your action steps? Evaluate your state tax exposure. Decide if relocation makes sense. Choose a no-income-tax state—Texas, Florida, Nevada, Washington, etc. Relocate well before your exit. Sell or rent out your old residence. Get a new driver's license and voter registration. Spend the majority of your days in your new state. Document residency diligently. Consult tax and legal advisors. Stay put until after the liquidity event.

Beware: High-Tax States Fight Hard to Keep You

You might think leaving California or New York is enough to dodge the tax hit, but here's the hard truth: high-tax states don't let go easily. They have aggressive residency audits. They have complex, founder-specific tax traps. They have resources — and incentives — to pursue high-profile exits like yours.

If you're planning a move to reduce or eliminate state taxes, you need to know how these states really operate — and what you're up against.

California's Residency Playbook

California's Franchise Tax Board (FTB) is infamous for auditing wealthy individuals who leave the state before a liquidity event. Why? Because every founder that exits from California costs them millions in lost revenue.

Here's how California approaches it:

- **Domicile Test**: Where is your true, fixed, permanent home?
- **Closest Connections Test**: Where are your most significant ties — business, social, family, and financial?
- **Time Test**: Where do you spend the majority of your time? (But time alone isn't dispositive.)

California residency audits are brutal:

- They'll subpoena your phone records, credit card statements, and flight itineraries.
- They'll scrutinize where your family lives.
- They'll look at where your advisors (lawyers, accountants, wealth managers) are based.
- They'll analyze where your kids go to school.

Key: **California cares about facts, not just paperwork.** Changing your voter registration won't save you if they can prove your life is still in California.

New York's Statutory Residence Trap

New York is even trickier. They have a **Statutory Residency Test**:

- If you maintain a "permanent place of abode" in New York *and* spend more than 183 days there in a year, you are taxed as a New York resident — period.

A "permanent place of abode" is broadly defined. Even a small apartment you keep for occasional business trips can qualify.

Worse: partial days count. Fly in at 11 p.m. for a meeting the next morning? That's a day. Doctor's appointments, theater trips, board meetings — they all count.

New York residency audits are notorious for being:

- Detailed (cell phone towers, EZ-pass records, social media).

- Time-consuming (often 2-3 years of documentation).
- Expensive (state and city taxes combined can approach 14%).

States that Tax Based on Where Work Was Performed

Other states are getting more creative:

- **Massachusetts** and **New York** sometimes argue that stock options or RSUs were earned while you worked in the state — so they claim the right to tax the portion of the gain based on your "workdays" allocation.
- If you spent years working in Boston or Manhattan, they might argue that the value accrued while you were there, regardless of where you live at exit.

It's a murky and aggressive area of tax law — one where founders often find themselves blindsided post-liquidity.

10. Special Considerations for Founders

Founders have unique challenges when it comes to state taxation:

- **Vesting Schedules**: If your shares vest over time, some states claim the right to tax based on the vesting period tied to your work history.
- **Option Exercises**: Exercising ISOs or NSOs while a resident creates a tax footprint. Some states will try to tax even years later at liquidity.
- **Grant Date vs. Sale Date**: Some states look at when you were granted stock or options and attempt to apportion gain accordingly.
- **Secondaries Before Exit**: If you sell shares in a secondary market before an IPO, the timing of that sale and your state of residency on that date are crucial.

Bottom Line: It's not enough to think about where you are on IPO day — you need to think about where you were when value was created and when key stock milestones occurred.

Ultra-Affluent Best Practices: Domicile Defense Blueprint

If you're serious about protecting your wealth, you must treat domicile planning like a pre-emptive legal defense.

Here's the blueprint:

- **Move Early**: Ideally 12–24 months before exit.
- **Sell or Sever**: Sell your old home or rent it to an unrelated third party.
- **New Driver's License**: Immediately upon moving.
- **Register to Vote**: New state, immediately.
- **Banking and Professional Ties**: Move your primary banking, law firm, wealth management relationships to your new state.
- **Social Ties**: New clubs, new gym memberships, new religious or civic affiliations.
- **Mail Forwarding**: Close old P.O. boxes. Update your address with IRS, banks, brokers, and service providers.
- **No "Permanent Place of Abode"**: If dealing with New York, don't maintain even a tiny apartment.
- **Flight and Cell Records**: Be ready to produce them in an audit. Meticulously track travel.
- **Family Relocation**: If married, spouse and kids must move too — otherwise, the state may argue your true domicile hasn't changed.
- **Intent Documentation**: Journals, emails, memos about your relocation — prove it wasn't just tax motivated.

This isn't paranoia — it's proactive. Losing a residency audit could cost you 10%–13%+ of your exit proceeds. On $100M, that's $10M–$13M gone unnecessarily.

Real-World Founder Audits: Cautionary Tales

Case 1: The CEO Who Moved Too Late

A CEO of a biotech firm moved to Texas three months before his IPO. Despite changing his driver's license and voter registration, California successfully argued he maintained a home, family ties, and significant business activities in San Francisco. Verdict: $8M in California taxes.

Case 2: The VC Who Tried to Hedge Bets

A venture capitalist split time between a New York apartment and a Florida home. Even though he spent 184 nights a year in Florida, the New York apartment was fully furnished and available for his use year-round. New York claimed residency. Verdict: taxed on $25M gain.

Case 3: The Founder Who Moved Early and Clean

A founder moved her entire family to Florida 18 months before her company's tender offer. She sold her home in Palo Alto, enrolled her kids in Miami schools, joined local charities, and severed all ties to California. California attempted an audit but dropped the case after reviewing her evidence. Verdict: $0 state tax.

Action Steps: Your Founder's Tax-Optimized Relocation Plan

- Conduct a Pre-Move State Tax Exposure Audit
- Choose a Tax-Friendly State (TX, FL, NV, WA — no state income tax)
- Relocate 12–24 Months Before Liquidity Event
- Cut Ties With Old State (Home, Voting, Driver's License)
- Build New Ties (Home, Voting, Driver's License, Community Engagement)
- Track Travel Days Meticulously
- Shut Down "Permanent Place of Abode" in High-Tax State
- Align Financial and Professional Advisors to New State
- Document Your Move With Paper Trails and Intent Evidence
- Engage a Tax Attorney Who Specializes in State Residency Audits

You spent a decade building your company — the late nights, the missed holidays, the risk, the roller coaster. Don't let a failure to plan your domicile hand millions back to the state you tried to leave behind.

This is not a game of paperwork. It's a game of evidence.

Start early. Move intentionally. Document aggressively.

Make one money move before you go to bed tonight. Just one. Then another next week. Sketch out your relocation timeline. Audit your existing state ties. Build your defense before the battle begins.

Your future self will thank you. So will your heirs. So will your peace of mind.

Chapter 13: Managing Concentrated Wealth

You did it. You built something from nothing. You created real value. You lived the founder journey — messy, unpredictable, exhilarating. And now you have wealth. But — and this is where most founders find themselves quietly uneasy — your wealth is concentrated. Maybe it's all in your company stock. Maybe it's in a narrow basket of tech startups you advised or invested in along the way. Whatever the details, you face one undeniable financial risk: lack of diversification.

This chapter isn't about guilt. You took the right risks. You deserve the upside. But it's about this moment — right now — where risk shifts from what built your fortune to what could undo it. This is about managing concentrated wealth: why it's dangerous, how to diversify intelligently, and how your mind — yes, even yours — might sabotage you if you're not careful. We're not here to scare you. We're here to seduce you into financial security. Let's dive in.

The risks of concentrated stock positions are real. Most founders think, "I built this company. I know it better than anyone. Why would I diversify away from it?" It's an understandable instinct. But even great companies fall. Enron, Lehman Brothers, Bear Stearns — these weren't poorly managed mom-and-pop shops. They were titans. And yet, they fell fast and hard. Unforeseen risks always lurk: market crashes, regulatory whiplash, disruptive competitors, management scandals. You can know your company inside and out and still miss the storm.

Single-stock risk is brutal. Owning a lot of one stock — even if it's your own creation — equals outsized exposure to single-point failure. Individual stocks are much more volatile than diversified portfolios. While broad markets might exhibit 15% annual volatility, single tech stocks often swing 40% to 60% annually. Big swings. Big emotional pain. And big risks to your future.

Then there's the opportunity cost. Holding too much of one stock means missing out on gains elsewhere: other sectors, geographies, asset classes. True diversification — spreading wealth across a broad set of investments — doesn't just protect against downside. It enhances your ability to capture more consistent returns over time. It's not a surrender of faith in your company. It's a broadening of your financial future.

You don't have to dump your shares all at once. But you do need a plan. Gradual sales are the most straightforward method — selling a percentage of your holdings over a planned schedule. It spreads your tax liability and reduces the market impact of your sales. A well-designed 10b5-1 plan, a pre-arranged, SEC-sanctioned trading plan, can help sell shares at regular intervals without raising insider trading flags. It's clean. It's compliant. It's intelligent.

For more sophisticated moves, there's the exchange fund strategy. You pool your stock with other concentrated shareholders. In return, you receive a diversified portfolio without triggering an immediate tax bill. No fire sale. No tax hit. Just gradual, smart diversification.

Or consider collars and other hedging strategies. These use options to cap your upside while protecting your downside. It may feel like giving away the dream of endless upside, but the ability to sleep at night — knowing you've protected a significant floor of your wealth — is priceless. For those with philanthropic goals, gifting appreciated shares to a donor-advised fund (DAF) or a private foundation can unlock tax advantages while aligning wealth with values. Structured sales and direct indexing offer other paths to tailor the exit from concentration to your unique needs and tax circumstances.

But it's not just about strategy. It's about behavior. And that's where it gets tricky.

Your brain is hardwired against smart diversification. Overconfidence bias tells you, "I know this company better than anyone. I have an edge." Maybe you do. But risk doesn't care about insider knowledge when the world changes suddenly. Familiarity bias whispers, "I'm comfortable with this stock. It's been good to me." Comfort, however, doesn't equal safety.

Loss aversion kicks in — the fear of selling too soon, of missing the next big run-up. We don't fear missing gains; we fear locking in the feeling that we left money on the table. Status quo bias keeps you stuck. Doing nothing feels easier. But no action is a decision — and often a disastrous one. Anchoring — the fixation on a stock's high-water mark — is deadly. "It was $200. I'll wait until it gets back there to sell." Past prices have zero relevance to future outcomes.

The smartest founders — the ones who stay wealthy — understand these biases and build systems to counteract them. Plans. Advisors. Accountability. Discipline.

Let's walk through real-life scenarios. Scenario 1: The Smart Seller. A founder sells 10% of holdings each quarter over two years. They gradually reduce concentration, smooth the tax impact, and build a diversified portfolio alongside a philanthropic strategy. They still participate in their company's upside, but they've locked in financial independence along the way.

Scenario 2: The Overconfident Holder. Another founder refuses to sell. They watched the stock climb and can't bear to let it go. Then a market downturn cuts the stock by 60%. Their $20M becomes $8M. A hard, painful lesson.

Scenario 3: Exchange Fund Win. An early employee pools their shares into an exchange fund. No tax hit. In return, they get a diversified basket of assets. No more sleepless nights.

Scenario 4: Hedging Helps. A founder uses a collar to protect downside. They cap the upside at +20% but prevent a drop beyond -20%. They miss the absolute peak — but they preserve wealth and peace of mind.

Let's make it plain. Concentration risk means too much wealth in one stock. A 10b5-1 plan is a pre-set trading plan that sells shares gradually. An exchange fund lets you pool with others for diversification without selling. A collar is an option strategy that limits losses and gains. Diversification means spreading wealth across multiple investments to reduce risk.

So, what should you do next? First, inventory your concentrated positions. Know your numbers. Second, assess your risk tolerance honestly. Third, model scenarios: what happens to your life if the stock drops 50%? Fourth, explore 10b5-1 plans. Fifth, consider exchange funds or structured sales. Sixth, evaluate hedging options carefully. Seventh, develop a timeline for diversification. Eighth, work with a wealth advisor who understands founders and concentrated wealth. Ninth, check yourself for behavioral biases. And finally, commit to action. Without action, all of this is just words on a page.

Building a Post-Exit Portfolio: From Concentration to Curated Wealth

Now that you've understood the "why" of diversification, it's time to dive into the "how." Once you've reduced your concentration risk, what do you do with the cash? The post-exit portfolio is not about being average. It's about being strategic. It's about designing a wealth architecture that aligns with your ambitions, your values, and your vision of legacy.

The biggest mistake newly liquid founders make? Swinging from extreme concentration to passive, mindless allocation. You didn't build your company by copying everyone else — don't manage your wealth that way either.

Your portfolio isn't just a collection of stocks and bonds. It's the engine for the next chapter of your life: freedom, impact, and legacy.

Here's how the ultra-affluent founder approaches diversification.

8. Core-Satellite Portfolio Design: The Founder Edition

Think of your portfolio as a planet: the core is your gravity — stable, resilient, reliable. The satellites are your exploration — growth, innovation, impact.

8.1 Core Portfolio (50%-70% of Assets)

This is the foundation of your wealth. It's built for resilience, not adrenaline.

- **Global Equities**: Low-cost exposure to world markets — U.S., developed international, emerging markets.
- **Fixed Income**: High-grade bonds, municipal bonds (for tax efficiency), and global bonds for ballast.
- **Cash and Equivalents**: 1–2 years of living expenses in ultra-safe assets — cash, money markets, short-duration bonds.
- **Real Assets**: Inflation-protected assets like Treasury Inflation-Protected Securities (TIPS) and commodities exposure via ETFs.

This core portfolio is designed to survive market cycles, policy shocks, and the unknown. It's your fortress.

8.2 Satellite Portfolio (30%-50% of Assets)

This is where you flex the founder DNA — thoughtfully, strategically.

- **Private Equity and Venture Capital**: Direct investments or fund exposure to early-stage innovation.
- **Real Estate**: Income-producing real estate — multifamily, industrial, and niche sectors like logistics and medical offices.
- **Hedge Funds and Alternatives**: Low-correlation strategies that seek returns independent of market movements.
- **Direct Investments**: Co-investing in startups, emerging managers, or private deals — but with diligence, not emotion.
- **Impact Investments**: Align part of your portfolio with causes or innovations you care about — clean tech, education, financial inclusion.

The satellite portfolio is your opportunity to stay close to innovation — but without betting the farm.

9. Diversification Across Time Horizons: Today, Tomorrow, and Beyond

Wealth isn't static — your needs and goals will evolve. Smart portfolios are built across multiple time frames.

9.1 Short-Term (0–3 Years)

- Liquidity for lifestyle and known obligations (homes, taxes, philanthropy).
- High liquidity, low volatility assets.

9.2 Medium-Term (3–10 Years)

- Growth investments.
- Balanced exposure between public and private markets.
- Real estate for income generation.

9.3 Long-Term (10+ Years)

- Illiquid assets like private equity, venture capital, and impact funds.
- Dynasty planning vehicles (trusts, foundations).
- Endowment-style investing — patient capital.

Why this matters: By matching assets to time horizons, you avoid becoming a forced seller. You create resilience and optionality.

10. Advanced Ultra-Affluent Strategies

Once the foundation is set, the ultra-wealthy founder can add layers of sophistication:

- **Opportunity Zones**: Defer and reduce capital gains taxes while investing in underdeveloped communities.
- **Private Credit**: Lending to private companies — attractive yields, diversification away from traditional bonds.
- **Structured Notes**: Tailored risk-return profiles using customized products from investment banks.
- **Art and Collectibles**: Passion assets — part investment, part lifestyle.
- **Second Citizenship and Global Residency**: Diversifying not just assets, but residency options and tax exposure (think Portugal, UAE, New Zealand).

The goal isn't to dabble everywhere. It's to design a portfolio that's global, resilient, and aligned with your mission.

11. Philanthropy and Purpose: The Ultimate Diversification

As wealth grows, so does the desire to make an impact. Philanthropy isn't just charity — it's another form of diversification: emotional, reputational, and legacy.

Options for the ultra-affluent:

- **Donor-Advised Funds (DAFs)**: Immediate tax deduction, long-term charitable giving.
- **Private Foundations**: More control, more complexity — but powerful if you want to direct large-scale giving.
- **Charitable Remainder Trusts (CRTs)**: Receive income for life, then leave assets to charity — tax-efficient and impactful.
- **Mission-Aligned Investments**: Integrate environmental, social, and

governance (ESG) criteria into the broader portfolio.

Impact can — and should — be built into your wealth structure, not bolted on afterward.

12. The Behavioral Playbook for Ultra-Affluent Founders

Even with the best diversification strategy, behavior will determine success or failure.

12.1 Stay Disciplined

When markets swing, the instinct is to act. The best investors? They pause. They stick to their plan.

12.2 Rebalance Regularly

Markets move. Winners grow faster. Rebalancing enforces discipline — selling high, buying low.

12.3 Resist the Private Investment Siren Song

You'll see every deal post-exit. Friends, former colleagues, club deals. Don't confuse access with quality.

12.4 Remember the Goal

Freedom. Security. Legacy. Not excitement. Not headlines. Not empire-building 2.0 (unless you truly want it).

12.5 Use a Trusted Advisory Team

A personal CIO (Chief Investment Officer). Tax specialists. Estate planners. Behavioral coaches if needed. A good team protects you — not just from the markets, but from yourself.

13. Real-World Post-Exit Playbooks

Scenario 1: The Overloaded Angel Investor

A founder cashes out, invests in 50+ startups directly. Five years later: headaches, no liquidity, no diversification. Lesson: Concentration risk doesn't end with private markets.

Scenario 2: The Balanced Builder

Another founder allocates 60% to a diversified core portfolio, 30% to selective VC funds and co-investments, 10% to philanthropy. Ten years later: steady growth, impact, and the option to work — or not — on whatever she wants.

Scenario 3: The Quiet Philanthropist

A founder uses $50M to create a family foundation. He funds scholarships, endows research, and supports climate initiatives. The investments in the foundation are professionally managed for perpetuity. His wealth lives on — quietly but profoundly.

14. Ultra-Affluent Founder Diversification Checklist

- Build a Global Core Portfolio
- Design a Satellite Portfolio for Innovation and Impact
- Match Assets to Time Horizons
- Layer Advanced Strategies Where Appropriate
- Integrate Philanthropy Thoughtfully
- Rebalance Regularly
- Resist Behavioral Traps
- Use a Personal CIO-Level Advisory Team
- Think Multi-Generational
- Keep Freedom, Not Just Fortune, at the Center

You took bold risks to create wealth. But staying wealthy requires a different skill: discipline.

Concentrated wealth made you rich. Diversified, intentional wealth management keeps you free.

The exit was the beginning, not the end.

Make one money move before you go to bed tonight. Just one. Sketch out your diversified vision. Build a first draft. Interview advisors. Write down your goals beyond just numbers.

You've got this.

Your future self will thank you. So will your family. So will the generations that will live better because you built not just a company — but a legacy.

Welcome to the art of staying wealthy — and staying free.

Chapter 14: Hedging Strategies 101

You've spent years building wealth. Real wealth. Not paper dreams. Not startup promises. Tangible, extraordinary value created by sweat, sacrifice, and risk. But now, most of it is still tied up in one place — your company stock. You're not ready to sell. You're not ready to walk away. And you shouldn't have to. But here's the reality: the more concentrated your wealth, the more vulnerable you are.

That's where hedging comes in. Not magic. Not gambling. Not surrender. Pure risk management — the mark of founders who stay wealthy long after the exit confetti has settled.

This chapter is your no-nonsense guide to hedging strategies — what they are, how they work, why they matter, and how you can use them to protect what you've built without sacrificing what could still be. No jargon. No intimidation. Just clarity, control, and confidence.

Let's dive in.

1. Basics of Collars and Prepaid Forwards

When we talk hedging for founders, two strategies rise to the top: Collars and Prepaid Forwards. Let's demystify both.

1.1 Collars

A collar is an options-based strategy. If you own a stock, a collar involves two moves:

- **Buy a Put Option**: This gives you the right (but not the obligation) to sell your stock at a specified price — your floor.

- **Sell a Call Option**: This creates an obligation to sell your stock at a higher, specified price — your ceiling.

Why do this? The put protects you if the stock price collapses. The call, while capping your upside, subsidizes the cost of the put. It's protection on the downside, with an agreement to limit how much upside you'll participate in.

Example:

- Your stock: $100/share.
- Buy a put at $90: protect against anything lower.
- Sell a call at $120: cap your gains at $120.
- Outcome: If the stock drops to $70, you still get $90. If it soars to $150, you have to sell at $120.

It's a tradeoff — protection against loss in exchange for giving up some potential gain. But when you're sitting on millions, preservation beats lottery-ticket thinking.

1.2 Prepaid Forwards

A prepaid forward is different — it's a contract, not an options play. You agree to sell a certain number of shares in the future at a set price. In return, you get a large portion of the cash today, but you don't actually transfer the shares until delivery day. Here's the magic: no immediate sale means no immediate taxable event.

Example:

- You agree today to deliver 100,000 shares in three years.
- You receive $7 million today.
- You continue to hold voting rights and dividends (often negotiable).
- When delivery happens, taxes are due — not before.

It's liquidity without liquidation. And it's powerful for founders who need cash now but want to defer taxes and maintain optionality.

2. When Hedging Makes Sense

Not everyone needs to hedge. But if you're a founder, here are the scenarios when hedging deserves your full attention.

2.1 You Have Concentrated Risk

If 80% or more of your wealth is tied to one company's stock, you are exposed. No matter how great the company, markets, regulations, competitors, or black swans can derail it.

2.2 You Have Liquidity Needs

Maybe you want to buy a house. Maybe fund a foundation. Maybe pay taxes. Selling stock triggers tax. Hedging can provide liquidity without triggering that taxable event immediately.

2.3 You Want to Reduce Volatility

The more your wealth swings with a single stock, the harder it is to plan, sleep, or think clearly. Hedging can smooth the ride.

2.4 You Want to Delay Taxes

Prepaid forwards — and even some collar strategies — allow you to defer taxes until the sale is triggered later.

2.5 You're Restricted From Selling

If you're under lock-up post-IPO or limited by insider trading windows, traditional sales aren't an option. Hedging provides a workaround — carefully, and within regulatory bounds.

3. Cost and Complexity Considerations

Hedging is not free. It is not simple. And it demands a team that knows the territory.

3.1 Costs

- **Option Premiums**: Buying puts costs money. Selling calls offsets some of this, but not always fully.

- **Structuring Fees**: Banks love prepaid forwards — but they'll charge hefty fees for the privilege.
- **Opportunity Cost**: You cap your upside — meaning you might miss out on meteoric stock growth.

3.2 Complexity

- Legal review for all contracts.
- Regulatory compliance — Rule 144 if your shares are restricted.
- Margin and collateral considerations — banks may require you to post additional collateral if your stock plummets.
- Tax nuance — especially around constructive sales rules (Section 1259 of the Internal Revenue Code).

DIY hedging is a recipe for disaster. You need:

- A wealth advisor who's seen it before.
- A tax attorney fluent in equity compensation structures.
- A CPA who can model the tax implications.

4. Real-Life Scenarios

Scenario 1: The Smart Collar

A founder owns $20 million in stock, but she doesn't want to sell. She buys puts at 90% of market price and sells calls at 110%. The stock market stumbles. Her wealth is protected — she's locked in her financial independence regardless of market chaos.

Scenario 2: The Liquidity Bridge

An exec wants to buy a $5 million dream home but doesn't want a fire-sale on shares. He structures a prepaid forward, receives $5 million upfront, and defers taxes until future delivery. Home secured, tax deferred, portfolio intact.

Scenario 3: The No-Protection Catastrophe

A startup C-suite leader rides the stock from $200 to $500 and back down to $30 — in a year. No hedge. No liquidity. Paper wealth evaporates. When she finally sells, there's hardly anything left.

Scenario 4: Hedging + 10b5-1 Perfection

A founder structures a 10b5-1 plan to sell gradually but overlays it with a collar. He sells at intervals but protects against sudden market dives in the interim. He achieves liquidity, diversification, and downside protection — the holy trinity.

5. Plain-Language Breakdowns

Let's make sure we strip away the complexity:

- **Collar**: Protects your downside (put option) but limits your upside (call option).
- **Prepaid Forward**: Get cash now, deliver shares later, pay taxes later.
- **Put Option**: Insurance policy — right to sell at a set price.
- **Call Option**: Promise — obligation to sell if the stock hits a certain price.
- **10b5-1 Plan**: A safe, pre-set selling plan to gradually unwind holdings without insider trading risks.
- **Opportunity Cost**: The upside you give up to protect your downside.

Hedging is financial judo — using existing force to neutralize risk without fighting the market.

6. Action Steps

Hedging isn't a decision you make on gut feel. It's a process. Here's your founder's checklist:

- Inventory your concentrated positions
- Define your real liquidity needs

- Explore collar and prepaid forward structures
- Model outcomes — including tax implications
- Consult wealth, tax, and legal advisors
- Understand Rule 144 and insider constraints
- Compare costs versus benefits explicitly
- Structure hedges aligned with your future plans
- Monitor and adjust as market conditions shift
- Commit to a disciplined, documented strategy

7. Advanced Ultra-Affluent Hedging Techniques

If basic hedging isn't enough, or if you have substantial wealth to protect, consider:

- **Variable Prepaid Forwards**: Introduce flexibility on the number of shares delivered based on stock performance.
- **Equity Swaps**: Exchange your stock's return for a diversified index's return without selling the underlying.
- **Protective Puts Only**: For founders who hate capping upside — simply buy puts and eat the cost of protection.
- **Hedge Fund Overlay**: Hedge against market or sector-wide crashes rather than just individual stock risk.
- **Custom Derivatives**: Big banks will tailor products — at a cost — to meet exact liquidity, tax, and hedging objectives.

Hedging isn't about fear. It's about strategy. It's about treating your wealth the way you treated your company — with foresight, protection, and disciplined ambition.

You didn't work decades, endure sleepless nights, risk everything, and beat the odds just to leave your financial future hanging on the swings of a single stock.

This isn't about being pessimistic. It's about being intelligent.

Make one money move before you go to bed tonight. Just one. Call your advisor. Schedule a consultation. Map out your risk exposure.

Then do another next week. Understand your liquidity needs. Model the cost of a catastrophic loss versus the cost of insurance against it.

Your future self will thank you. So will your heirs. So will your peace of mind.

Welcome to founder-level wealth defense — the art of keeping what you've built, on your terms, for the long run.

Chapter 15: 10b5-1 Trading Plans

It's a paradox: the more successful you are, the harder it is to sell your own shares safely.

As a private company grows, or once you go public, the information asymmetry widens. Your board meetings are filled with nonpublic information. Your executive decisions — capital raises, acquisitions, layoffs, partnerships — move markets. Even if you're not directly acting on this information, regulators assume you know more than the average investor. That's the burden of success.

This is why 10b5-1 plans are not just advisable — they are critical. They institutionalize discipline. They protect your reputation. They future-proof your wealth strategy.

Imagine spending 10 years building a world-class company, and a poorly timed stock sale tarnishes your brand. Even if you're vindicated legally, public perception moves faster than courts. Smart founders think about both legal protection and reputational protection.

A well-designed 10b5-1 plan lets you:

- Sell shares legally and predictably.
- Protect against accusations even if unforeseen news breaks.
- Free your mind to focus on growth — not second-guessing every liquidity move.

9. Mistakes Founders Make Without a 10b5-1 Plan

You've probably heard the horror stories, but it's worth studying them.

9.1 Poor Timing

Selling shares right before a financing round, M&A transaction, or regulatory clearance — even if accidental — creates optics problems.

9.2 Overconcentration

Founders wait too long, remain overexposed to their own stock, and when markets turn, are unable to exit safely.

9.3 Panic Selling

Without a pre-set plan, founders sometimes sell emotionally during market volatility — locking in losses.

9.4 Tax Surprises

Without gradual sales, large single-year sales can trigger top federal and state capital gains taxes, plus Net Investment Income Tax (NIIT).

9.5 Insider Trading Allegations

Even if innocent, defending against an SEC or DOJ inquiry costs millions in legal fees — and drains your time, energy, and reputation.

A 10b5-1 plan won't prevent market volatility. But it will prevent poor timing, panic, overconcentration, and regulatory risk. In short, it protects both your money and your legacy.

10. Structuring a Founder-Friendly 10b5-1 Plan

A generic 10b5-1 plan is good. But for the ultra-affluent founder, customization makes it great.

10.1 Key Elements to Customize

- **Price Limits**: Set floors (sell if price is above $X) to avoid fire sales.
- **Discretionary Ranges**: Allow brokers to use discretion within a price band.
- **Escalating Volumes**: Sell a small amount early, more as price rises or as you near long-term capital gains thresholds.

- **Strategic Gaps**: Avoid trading around quarterly earnings or major corporate events.

10.2 Duration Strategy

Longer plans are safer. A 24-month plan signals you're not gaming the system. It spreads sales evenly. It minimizes market impact.

10.3 Broker Selection

Not all brokers are equal. Choose a desk experienced in executive sales and corporate insider rules — not a generalist.

Work with a wealth manager who can coordinate between your legal, tax, and broker teams.

11. Tax Optimization With 10b5-1 Plans

It's not just about *if* you sell — it's about *how* you sell.

Smart founders use 10b5-1 plans to:

- Harvest long-term capital gains.
- Spread sales across multiple tax years.
- Time sales to coincide with lower personal income years.
- Optimize state tax exposure (especially if you're considering moving to a no-income-tax state like Texas or Florida before liquidity events).
- Maximize charitable planning (selling low-cost basis shares to fund Donor-Advised Funds or foundations).

Example:

If you execute $5 million in sales under a 10b5-1 plan, and you're living in California (13.3% tax rate), you might consider moving before plan initiation to save over $600,000 in state taxes.

Layering tax strategy into your 10b5-1 plan is where ultra-affluent founders move from *rich* to *smartly rich*.

12. Advanced Moves for Ultra-Affluent Founders

You're not just any insider. You're the founder, the face, the legacy builder. You need tools sophisticated enough to match.

12.1 Multiple Parallel 10b5-1 Plans

- One plan for RSUs vesting quarterly.
- One plan for stock options.
- One plan for vested founder shares.

Each plan calibrated to different liquidity, tax, and diversification goals.

12.2 Integrating Hedging Strategies

Overlay a collar (buying puts, selling calls) alongside your 10b5-1 plan to protect the shares you're holding while gradually selling.

12.3 Staged Philanthropic Sales

Design sales under the plan to direct shares to your private foundation or DAF — locking in deductions, avoiding capital gains.

12.4 Customized Cooling-Off Periods

Some founders build a 90-120 day cooling-off period between plan signing and first trade — a more conservative stance in today's regulatory environment.

These advanced moves require coordination between your tax attorney, estate attorney, wealth manager, and corporate counsel. The payoff is freedom, security, and legacy preservation.

13. Real-World Founder Case Studies

Scenario 1: The Steady Architect

A SaaS founder designs a 24-month 10b5-1 plan, selling $1 million quarterly. He avoids insider trading risks, diversifies out of 80% company stock concentration, funds a family office, and seeds a DAF — all under the radar, no drama.

Scenario 2: The Overconfident Seller

An exec waits until post-IPO lockup ends. Sells $10 million in stock in a lump sum. Media speculates "insider knows bad news." Stock dips on perception alone. SEC opens inquiry. Even if cleared, the damage to reputation and company morale is real.

Scenario 3: The Strategic Giver

A founder uses a 10b5-1 plan to gradually donate appreciated shares to her foundation. She gains tax deductions at fair market value, avoids capital gains taxes, and funds her philanthropic vision — all built into the plan from day one.

14. Plain-Language Breakdowns

- **Insider Trading**: Buying or selling based on secret company news.
- **10b5-1 Plan**: Pre-set, automated sell schedule = no insider trading risk.
- **Cooling-Off Period**: Delay between signing a plan and executing the first trade to demonstrate good faith.
- **Safe Harbor**: Legal protection from regulatory penalties if the plan is properly constructed and executed.
- **Parallel Plans**: Multiple 10b5-1 plans for different types of equity (RSUs, options, founder shares).
- **Charitable Giving via 10b5-1**: Selling shares under plan, donating to DAFs, securing deductions.

15. Action Steps for the Ultra-Affluent Founder

- Take Inventory: How many shares, what types (RSUs, ISOs, NSOs, common)?
- Assess Information Risk: Are you routinely exposed to material nonpublic information?
- Map Your Goals: Liquidity needs, tax strategies, philanthropic ambitions.
- Engage Your Team: Legal, tax, wealth management, corporate counsel.

- Draft Plan: Clear, simple, defensible.
- Include Cooling-Off Period: Show regulators you're serious.
- Schedule Sales Gradually: Avoid lump-sum dumps.
- Layer Tax Planning: Coordinate sales with low-income years or relocation plans.
- Communicate Thoughtfully: Consider public disclosure or media strategy if you're high-profile.
- Monitor But Don't Tinker: Set it, forget it, stay disciplined.

You didn't build your company on luck. You built it on smart risks, disciplined execution, and long-term vision.

Managing your wealth post-exit requires the same mindset.

A well-crafted 10b5-1 plan is not just a defensive play — it's a strategic play. It's how the ultra-affluent founder exits elegantly. Protecting your wealth. Defending your reputation. Staying clear of legal landmines.

Make one move before you go to bed tonight. Sketch a draft plan. Call your advisor. Schedule a strategy meeting.

And next week, set the foundation for diversification on your terms — not the market's. Not the SEC's.

Your future self will thank you. Your family will thank you. Your legacy will stand taller for it.

Welcome to the art of selling wisely — and living freely.

Section 4: Life After Liquidity — Investing, Legacy, and Philanthropy

Liquidity is not the end of the journey.

It's the beginning of an entirely new chapter — one that requires a different mindset, a different playbook, and an entirely different set of financial skills.

When the deal closes, the wire hits, and the stock vests, you move into a new phase: wealth management, wealth growth, and — eventually — wealth stewardship.

And what you do in the months and years after liquidity will define whether your wealth simply supports you for a few years — or empowers you, your family, and your causes for generations.

Section 4 shows you how to transition from a builder to a steward of wealth.

We begin with post-exit wealth strategies — how to structure and manage your new portfolio. Cashing out is just the first move; now you must build a system for growing, protecting, and diversifying that wealth. You'll learn about the roles of public markets, private equity, venture capital, real estate, and alternative investments in a founder's new financial ecosystem.

Next, we move into family governance and the often unspoken reality of wealth: without education, planning, and communication, even large fortunes can vanish in a generation or two. You'll learn how to prepare your family for wealth — and how to prepare wealth for your family.

Then, we explore legacy and philanthropy: not just how to give, but how to give strategically, meaningfully, and tax-efficiently. Whether you want to launch a private foundation, establish a donor-advised fund, or weave philanthropy into your family's DNA, this section provides a roadmap to doing it right.

We end with the concept of the "Work Optional" life — designing a post-liquidity existence where work becomes a choice, not an obligation. Whether you launch new ventures, mentor others, travel, invest, or focus on personal passions, financial freedom is about having the ability to say "yes" or "no" on your own terms.

Life after liquidity isn't about coasting.

It's about redefining what success looks like, creating a legacy you're proud of, and using wealth as a tool for purpose, impact, and freedom.

Chapter 16: Building a Diversified Portfolio

You've done what very few ever manage: taken an idea, endured the chaos, survived the storms, and cashed out. You are liquid. Maybe for the first time in your adult life, you are staring at the wiring instructions of *real* wealth. Tens of millions. Hundreds of millions. Maybe more.

Now what?

This is where many founders make the first serious error of post-exit wealth. They get paralyzed. They let the money sit in cash, eroding under inflation. Or worse, they repeat old patterns — betting on the next hot startup, throwing capital into the sector they already know too well, or chasing returns without a system.

The truth is, the skill set that builds a company is not the same skill set that preserves wealth. And wealth preservation is the key to real freedom. Freedom to invest in passion projects. Freedom to fund your family's future. Freedom to give generously. Freedom to live without fear.

This chapter is your blueprint for transforming liquidity into lasting capital — not by guessing, not by gambling, but by building a carefully structured, purpose-driven, diversified portfolio.

Let's dive in.

1. Asset Allocation Fundamentals: The Bedrock of Wealth Preservation

1.1 What Is Asset Allocation?

Asset allocation is how you split your investments across different asset classes. It is the single biggest determinant of long-term returns and risk in your portfolio.

The basic building blocks:

- **Public Equities** (U.S. and International Stocks): High growth, high volatility.
- **Fixed Income** (Bonds): Stability and income.
- **Real Assets** (Real Estate, Infrastructure, Commodities): Inflation hedges, diversification.
- **Private Investments** (Private Equity, Venture Capital, Private Debt): Illiquid, potentially outsized returns.
- **Alternative Assets** (Hedge Funds, Structured Products, Art, Collectibles, Crypto): Specialized risk-return profiles.
- **Cash and Cash Equivalents** (Money Market Funds, Treasury Bills): Liquidity, dry powder.

Think of asset allocation as the architecture of a skyscraper. It's not glamorous — but without it, nothing else stands.

1.2 Why Asset Allocation Matters More for the Ultra-Affluent

You've graduated from the normal rules. When you're ultra-affluent, investment returns are just part of the equation. Your real risk is concentration, tax drag, and behavioral mistakes.

With $50M+ in assets:

- A 20% loss is not theoretical; it's eight figures.
- Tax efficiency matters more than chasing an extra 1% return.
- Illiquidity is not a bug; it's a feature — if managed right.

Diversification for you is not about maximizing return — it's about ensuring optionality, controlling volatility, and preserving purchasing power across decades, generations, and economic regimes.

1.3 Core Asset Allocation Models

Think of these as templates — but your final portfolio will be more customized.

- **Conservative Growth**: 40% equities, 40% bonds, 20% alternatives.
- **Balanced Growth**: 60% equities, 20% bonds, 20% alternatives.
- **Growth-Oriented**: 75% equities, 15% bonds, 10% alternatives.
- **Aggressive (Venture Focused)**: 60% equities, 30% private investments, 10% bonds.

For ultra-affluent portfolios, alternatives can swell to 30-40%, especially with the right liquidity planning.

Remember: it's not about fitting a mold — it's about crafting a portfolio that aligns with *your* life and goals.

2. Aligning Capital to Purpose: Your Financial Mission Statement

2.1 Know What the Money Is For

You're not investing for the sake of investing. You're investing to fund a life.

Typical ultra-affluent founder goals include:

- **Lifestyle Maintenance**: Your personal "spend rate."
- **Second Act Ventures**: Angel investing, new startups.
- **Philanthropy**: Donor-Advised Funds, Foundations.
- **Family Wealth**: Trusts, generational transfers.
- **Personal Passions**: Art, real estate, adventure.

You must map your money to your mission. Otherwise, you end up wealthier on paper but poorer in meaning.

2.2 Matching Investments to Goals

Here's how it usually maps:

Goal Investment Focus

Liquidity for Expenses

Cash, Short-Term Bonds

Legacy and Endowment

Growth Assets: Stocks, Private Equity

Philanthropy

Impact Investing, Donor-Advised Funds

Income to Live On

Dividend Stocks, Municipal Bonds, Real Estate Income Funds

Opportunistic Capital

VC, Private Equity, Hedge Funds

Each dollar has a job. Don't confuse them.

3. Advanced Diversification Techniques

You already know "don't put all your eggs in one basket." Let's go beyond the basics.

3.1 Geographic Diversification

U.S. stocks are 60% of global equity markets. But 96% of the world's consumers live outside the U.S.

A truly global portfolio might have:

- 50-60% U.S. Equities.
- 20% International Developed Equities.
- 10% Emerging Markets Equities.
- 10-20% Global Fixed Income.

Emerging markets and developed ex-U.S. exposures aren't just for return — they're insurance against U.S.-centric risk.

3.2 Private Market Diversification

In today's world:

- Private equity consistently outperforms public markets.
- Private credit fills the void left by banks post-2008.
- Venture capital offers asymmetric upside — with illiquidity risk.

Allocate intentionally:

- 10-20% Private Equity (Buyout, Growth Equity)
- 5-10% Private Credit (Direct Lending, Special Situations)
- 5-10% Venture Capital (Seed, Series A, B)
- 5% Opportunistic (Real Assets, Infrastructure)

But beware: access matters. If you're not accessing top-decile funds, you're taking illiquidity risk without commensurate return.

3.3 Inflation Protection

Ultra-affluent portfolios cannot ignore real assets:

- Real estate.
- Infrastructure.
- Inflation-protected bonds (TIPS).
- Commodities (in moderation).

These hedges protect real purchasing power across economic cycles.

4. Behavioral Risk Management

Your greatest risk isn't the market — it's you.

4.1 Behavioral Biases to Recognize

- **Recency Bias**: Overweighting what's worked lately.
- **Overconfidence**: Thinking your past success predicts market success.
- **Loss Aversion**: Fear of short-term losses derailing long-term strategy.

- **Confirmation Bias**: Seeking info that supports your current view.

4.2 The Founder Psychology

As a founder, you are wired for action, control, and risk. Great for startups. Toxic for wealth preservation.

You must shift from *builder* to *steward.*

Good investors:

- Are patient.
- Are diversified.
- Are humble.
- Stick to process, not feelings.

Wealthy founders who succeed post-exit cultivate a different kind of discipline — the discipline of *staying invested.*

5. Real-Life Scenarios: Founders Post-Liquidity

Scenario 1: The Serial Over-Concentrator

Exited at $50M. Reinvested 80% into three tech startups. Two failed. Portfolio down to $15M.

Lesson: Concentration can build wealth, but diversification preserves it.

Scenario 2: The Disciplined Diversifier

Exited at $100M. Allocated:

- 50% Global Equities.
- 20% Fixed Income.
- 20% Private Markets.
- 10% Real Assets.

Portfolio compounded at 7% annually. Avoided major losses during COVID crash.

Lesson: Stay diversified. Stay disciplined.

Scenario 3: The Philanthropic Strategist

Exited at $30M. Donated $5M to a Donor-Advised Fund. Allocated DAF portfolio for growth. Created a legacy that will last beyond his lifetime.

Lesson: Purpose drives good portfolio design.

6. Plain-Language Breakdowns

- **Asset Allocation**: How you split your money among asset classes.
- **Diversification**: Spreading investments to reduce risk.
- **Private Markets**: Investments not traded on public exchanges.
- **Behavioral Risk**: Emotional mistakes that cost money.
- **Rebalancing**: Adjusting back to your target allocation.
- **Impact Investing**: Investments that aim for financial and social returns.

7. Action Steps

- Inventory All Assets: Public, Private, Real Estate, Cash.
- Clarify Goals: Income, Growth, Legacy, Philanthropy.
- Risk Tolerance Assessment: What drawdown can you stomach?
- Time Horizon Mapping: Liquidity in 0-5 years vs. legacy assets 20+ years out.
- Build an Initial Allocation: Tailored to you, not off-the-shelf.
- Layer in Private Markets: Opportunistically, with access to top-tier managers.
- Automate Rebalancing: Annual or semi-annual schedule.
- Engage a Multi-Disciplinary Team: Wealth advisor, tax advisor, estate attorney.
- Regular Portfolio Reviews: Annual, or after major life events.
- Stay the Course: Ignore noise. Trust process.

This isn't just about money.

It's about freedom. About choice. About creating a life you don't need a vacation from. It's about protecting what you've built — and multiplying its impact over decades, not just market cycles.

Diversification isn't a hedge against growth. It's a *system for lasting wealth.*

Make one move before you go to bed tonight. Map out your goals. Schedule a meeting with your team. Sketch out your asset allocation.

And then build — not the next startup — but the future you truly want.

Your future self will thank you. So will your family. So will your legacy.

Chapter 17: Real Estate as a Diversifier

You've spent years scaling companies, enduring the sleepless nights, raising capital, shipping products, leading teams, and navigating uncertainty. Now, finally, you have liquidity — and choices. Most founders instinctively glance toward another startup, or a venture fund, or perhaps public equities to grow their wealth. But there's one asset class you may have overlooked, or dismissed as "for old money types," yet it deserves a front-row seat in your portfolio: real estate.

Not speculative flips. Not get-rich-quick schemes. Serious, structured, tax-advantaged real estate ownership. If built correctly, it can deliver income, stability, tax efficiency, and a generational wealth anchor that other asset classes struggle to match.

This chapter is your founder's guide to deploying your liquidity in real estate intelligently, strategically, and profitably.

Let's dive in.

1. Why Founders Should Think Differently About Real Estate

1.1 The Wealth Preservation Problem

Tech founders are wired for asymmetric bets. Small risk, massive upside. Startups. Angel deals. Crypto. Public tech stocks. And for years, that mindset worked. You weren't looking for a 6% yield; you were looking for 100x.

But now? You're in a different phase. Post-liquidity, wealth preservation and slow, steady compounding matter more than another lottery ticket.

Real estate plays a different game:

- **Income**: Recurring, predictable cash flow.
- **Tangible asset**: Unlike stocks, real estate is real. It exists.
- **Tax efficiency**: Depreciation, 1031 exchanges, Opportunity Zones — huge advantages for the ultra-affluent.
- **Inflation hedge**: As money becomes worth less, rents and property values tend to rise.
- **Wealth anchoring**: Real estate tends to stay, persist, endure.

1.2 What Real Estate Is — and Is Not

It's not passive without setup. It's not risk-free. It's not guaranteed to beat equities. But real estate offers one thing few asset classes can: **durability**. Done right, it won't 10x your wealth overnight — but it can preserve and grow it predictably over decades.

2. Pros and Cons — The Clear-Eyed View

2.1 Pros of Real Estate

- **Diversification**: Low correlation with the stock market. When tech stocks crash, apartments still collect rent.
- **Cash Flow**: Quality properties in good markets generate stable, tax-efficient income streams.
- **Appreciation**: Long-term price appreciation driven by population growth, economic development, and inflation.
- **Tax Benefits**: Depreciation, mortgage interest deductions, 1031 exchanges — more on this soon.
- **Leverage**: Real estate allows you to borrow cheaply to control more assets, amplifying returns if managed well.
- **Control**: You can directly influence returns — upgrade units, reposition assets, raise rents.
- **Impact**: Invest in local communities, create housing, develop real

assets with lasting utility.

2.2 Cons of Real Estate

- **Illiquidity**: You can't just hit "sell" like a stock. It takes time and often cost to liquidate.
- **Operational Complexity**: Property management, leasing, repairs, tenant issues — headaches unless outsourced.
- **Concentration Risk**: A single building in a single city ties you to local market cycles.
- **Leverage Risk**: Debt cuts both ways. It amplifies gains — and losses.
- **Market Cycles**: Real estate is cyclical. Buying at the wrong time (top of the market) can set you back years.

No investment is perfect. But real estate, managed well, can be a powerful counterbalance to the volatility of tech-heavy portfolios.

3. Real Estate for the Ultra-Affluent: How to Play at Scale

3.1 Direct Ownership vs. Indirect Ownership

Direct Ownership: You buy the building, you control the asset, you collect the rent.

- Pros: Maximum control, potential for operational alpha (forced appreciation).
- Cons: Time, complexity, management burden.

Indirect Ownership:

- **REITs (Real Estate Investment Trusts)**: Publicly traded, highly liquid. Low yield compared to direct ownership but ultra-convenient.
- **Private Real Estate Funds**: Higher returns, less liquidity, often reserved for accredited or qualified purchasers.

- **Syndications**: Pool money with other investors in single or multiple deals. Moderate liquidity, limited control.

Which you choose depends on:

- Your desired control.
- Your time commitment.
- Your liquidity preferences.
- Your need for yield vs. appreciation.

Many ultra-affluent individuals blend — holding both direct and fund investments.

3.2 Key Strategies and Structures

Buy and Hold Rentals: Residential or commercial properties that generate steady income.

Value-Add Properties: Buy, renovate, reposition, re-lease at higher rates.

Development: Riskier but higher potential reward — ground-up projects.

Triple-Net Lease Commercial Properties: Tenant pays taxes, insurance, and maintenance — pure cash flow.

Industrial: Warehousing, logistics — a growing asset class in the age of Amazon.

Vacation Rentals: High yields in tourist markets, but with higher management intensity and seasonality.

Opportunity Zones: Special tax incentives for investing in designated areas.

4. Real Estate Tax Advantages: Quietly Transformative

4.1 Depreciation Magic

The IRS lets you depreciate (i.e., deduct) a portion of your property's value each year — even if the asset appreciates. For residential property, it's 27.5 years; for commercial, it's 39 years. This paper loss can often wipe out taxable rental income.

4.2 1031 Exchanges

Sell a property. Reinvest proceeds in a "like-kind" property. Defer capital gains tax indefinitely. You can 1031 repeatedly — until your death, at which point your heirs get a stepped-up basis, erasing the tax liability.

Tax deferred = wealth compounded.

4.3 Opportunity Zones

If you have a massive capital gain from your liquidity event, you can defer and reduce taxes by reinvesting gains into a Qualified Opportunity Fund that targets Opportunity Zones.

Properly executed, this can:

- Defer your gain.
- Reduce your taxable gain (up to 15%).
- Potentially eliminate gains on the new investment if held 10+ years.

4.4 Leverage: Non-Recourse Loans

Banks lend against real estate with favorable terms:

- Non-recourse (they can take the property but not personal assets if you default).
- Low interest rates.
- Long durations.

Used wisely, leverage can amplify returns while preserving personal wealth.

5. Managing Real Estate at Scale

5.1 Professional Property Management

Once you have more than one property, managing directly becomes a burden.

Property managers:

- Collect rent.
- Handle repairs.
- Manage tenants.
- Enforce leases.
- Deal with regulatory compliance.

Good managers charge 6-10% of gross rents — worth every penny.

5.2 Risk Management Must-Haves

- Insurance: Comprehensive property and liability insurance.
- Legal Structure: Hold properties in LLCs or limited partnerships for liability protection.
- Reserves: Maintain 6-12 months of expenses in cash.
- Conservative Leverage: Target 50-65% LTV.

6. Real-Life Founder Playbooks

Scenario 1: The Focused Multifamily Investor

$20M liquidity.

Allocates $5M into Class B multifamily apartments across Sunbelt cities.

- Cash flow: 6%+.
- Target IRR: 12-15%.
- Tax efficiency via depreciation.
- Outcome: Stable income, long-term appreciation, tax shelter.

Scenario 2: The Diversified Real Estate Fund Investor

$50M liquidity.

Allocates $10M into a mix of real estate private equity funds:

- Core-plus real estate.
- Opportunistic funds.
- Industrial real estate funds.

- Outcome: 10-12% targeted net returns, minimal operational headaches.

Scenario 3: The Vacation Rental Strategist
$5M allocated to:

- High-end short-term rentals in Aspen, Scottsdale, and Maui.
- Managed by premium property management firms.
- Lifestyle + Income.

Outcome: 8-12% annual returns plus personal use benefits.
Scenario 4: The Opportunity Zone Visionary
Post-exit, $10M gain.
Invests $5M into an Opportunity Zone Fund.

- Defers capital gains tax for up to 10 years.
- Eliminates tax on new gains after 10 years.
- Outcome: Powerful tax shield + impact investing.

7. Plain-Language Breakdowns

- **Cap Rate**: Annual net operating income / property purchase price.
- **Depreciation**: IRS tax benefit to offset rental income.
- **1031 Exchange**: Tax-deferred swapping of properties.
- **Opportunity Zone**: Special tax-favored investment zones.
- **Loan-to-Value (LTV)**: Ratio of loan to property value — lower = less risk.
- **Triple-Net Lease**: Tenant pays taxes, insurance, and maintenance — pure income.
- **REIT**: Fund that owns real estate — like stocks for property investing.

8. Action Steps

- Define Your Goals: Income, Appreciation, Lifestyle, Tax Benefits?
- Decide Direct vs. Indirect Ownership
- Research Target Markets
- Engage a Top-Tier Property Manager or Fund Manager
- Build Your Real Estate Team: CPA, Attorney, Broker, Manager
- Plan Financing Strategy: Conservative Leverage
- Analyze Tax Strategy: Depreciation, 1031, Opportunity Zones
- Structure Properly: LLCs, Trusts, LPs
- Diversify Across Geographies and Property Types
- Commit to Long-Term Discipline

Real estate isn't about chasing fast returns. It's about anchoring wealth. It's about converting liquidity into longevity. It's about tangible, durable assets that produce income, protect against inflation, and offer a fortress against volatility.

If you've cashed out, don't leave your wealth naked to the storms of public markets. Build pillars. Build permanence. Build the legacy that outlives you.

Make one move before you go to bed tonight. Start scanning target markets. Sketch a real estate plan. Call a trusted advisor. Plant the seeds of serious, sustainable wealth.

Your future self will thank you. So will your balance sheet. So will the generations after you.

Chapter 18: Private Equity and Venture Investments

You've built. You've exited. You've created liquidity. You're standing at the crossroads, staring at what's next. Yes, you can allocate to the public markets — ETFs, blue-chip stocks, some municipal bonds for ballast. Yes, you can load up on real estate, anchor your wealth in hard assets. But in your gut, you know that neither is where your edge lies. You didn't create wealth playing it safe. You created it understanding growth before others saw it, betting on teams and technology others didn't yet believe in.

Now, there's a way to keep playing — smarter, more diversified, more structured: private markets.

Private equity, venture capital, private credit, infrastructure, and real assets. These are the vehicles where the next layer of generational wealth is compounded. But there's a right way and a wrong way to participate. This chapter is your guide to the sophisticated, founder-informed path through private market investing — how to access it, how to evaluate it, and how to use it to build real, lasting wealth.

Let's dive in.

1. Accessing Private Market Investments

1.1 What Are Private Markets?

Private markets are simply investments made into companies, assets, or structures not traded on public exchanges. The primary categories:

- **Private Equity**: Buying stakes in private companies, often later-stage, with the goal of improving and exiting profitably.
- **Venture Capital**: Funding early-stage, high-growth startups that may not yet be profitable but are scaling quickly.
- **Private Credit**: Lending directly to private companies, filling the gap where banks are too risk-averse.
- **Real Assets**: Infrastructure, timberland, farmland — physical assets that produce yield.

Private markets are less liquid, less transparent, less regulated — and that's precisely where the opportunity lies for the right kind of investor.

1.2 Why Founders Are Well-Positioned

Founders are uniquely suited for private market investing. You understand the dynamics others don't: the messy middle, the product-market fit journey, the scaling pain points. You know what good leadership looks like. More importantly, you've lived the complexity that can't be captured in a deck or a financial model.

You also bring to the table:

- **Deal Access**: Your network will offer early glimpses of the best opportunities.
- **Pattern Recognition**: You can see the difference between a gimmick and a real business model.
- **Risk Tolerance**: You've already bet on yourself; you understand asymmetric payoff profiles.

You're not just capital. You're informed capital. That's a huge edge.

1.3 Ways to Access Private Markets

1.3.1 Direct Investments

Angel investing, seed rounds, co-investments alongside bigger firms — direct investments allow you to handpick your opportunities.

- **Pros**: Potential for massive upside. Personal influence. Deep engagement.
- **Cons**: High failure rates. Complete illiquidity. Time-intensive diligence.

1.3.2 Funds

Venture capital funds, private equity funds, and even private credit funds allow for professional management and diversification.

- **Pros**: Professional vetting. Spread risk across multiple deals. Less time commitment.
- **Cons**: Fees — usually a 2% management fee and 20% performance carry. Less direct control.

1.3.3 Secondary Markets

Platforms like Forge, EquityZen, and private deals can give you access to late-stage companies at a pre-IPO valuation.

- **Pros**: Reduced risk. Shorter time to liquidity.
- **Cons**: Higher pricing. Crowded trades in hot companies.

1.3.4 Funds of Funds

Instead of picking individual funds, you invest in a vehicle that spreads your allocation across dozens of top-tier managers.

- **Pros**: Diversification across managers and strategies.
- **Cons**: Additional layer of fees. Potential dilution of standout returns.

The point isn't that one is better than the other — it's that access is not the challenge for you. **Selection** and **construction** are.

2. Evaluating Opportunities and Risks

2.1 Key Evaluation Metrics

Every private investment opportunity can (and must) be filtered through a disciplined lens:

2.1.1 Team

Even more than product, the founding or leadership team is the highest leverage variable. Look for:

- **Resilience**: Have they survived real adversity?
- **Adaptability**: Can they pivot, learn, grow?
- **Coachability**: Will they take feedback?
- **Network**: Can they attract capital, talent, customers?

2.1.2 Market

- **TAM (Total Addressable Market)**: Big enough to create a category leader?
- **Market Growth Rate**: Are secular tailwinds in your favor?
- **Competition**: Is the field crowded or wide open?

2.1.3 Product

- **Differentiation**: Clear, defensible advantage.
- **Traction**: Are there paying customers, growing metrics?
- **Scalability**: Can they grow without linear cost increases?

2.1.4 Financials

- **Burn Rate and Runway**: How long can they survive at current cash flow?

- **Unit Economics**: Is there a clear path to profitability?

Early-stage investing focuses on team and market. Growth-stage investing focuses on traction and margins.

2.2 Risks

2.2.1 Illiquidity

You could be locked into your investment for 7–10 years with no exit window.

2.2.2 High Failure Rate

In venture, the standard is 70–90% of investments return nothing or lose money. Success is the exception, not the rule.

2.2.3 Capital Calls

If you invest in a fund, they don't take your full commitment upfront. They "call" capital over 3–5 years. Your cash flow needs to match.

2.2.4 Valuation Risk

Private company valuations are often more art than science. There's less frequent, less transparent market pricing.

2.2.5 Concentration Risk

Overweighting any single sector, geography, or stage can expose you to systemic failure.

2.3 The Power Law

Especially in venture, **one** investment can return the entire fund or portfolio and then some. It's not about hitting 7/10 wins — it's about finding the one company that delivers 100x. That's why diversification is critical.

2.4 Due Diligence Process

Founders who want to excel in private markets need a rigorous diligence process:

- Background checks on founders.
- Cap table review.
- Customer interviews.

- Revenue and churn analysis.
- Manager track record for fund investments.

Due diligence protects your downside, even if it can't eliminate it.

3. Building a Diversified Alternative Portfolio

3.1 Asset Allocation

General guidance:

- 10%–25% of your total investable wealth in alternatives.
- Higher if you have deep expertise, high net worth, and long time horizons.

3.2 Staging and Vintage Year Diversification

Commit capital over multiple years. Catch different parts of the economic cycle. It's the alternative asset equivalent of dollar-cost averaging.

3.3 Stage Diversification

- **Seed/Early**: Highest risk, highest reward.
- **Series A/B**: Traction evident, still early upside.
- **Growth**: More de-risked, lower upside, but higher certainty.

A smart portfolio has exposure to all stages.

3.4 Sector Diversification

Don't just do tech. Add:

- Fintech.
- Healthcare.
- Biotech.
- Consumer.
- Climate tech.
- Diversifying sectors protects against bubble risk.

3.5 Geography Diversification

The next Shopify could be in Canada. The next MercadoLibre could be in Latin America. Global diversification matters.

3.6 Portfolio Construction

Direct deals:

- 15–30 startups across sectors, stages, geographies.

Fund commitments:

- 5–10 funds across vintages, strategies, managers.

This gives you enough shots on goal while still being manageable.

3.7 Monitoring and Reporting

Alternatives are paperwork-heavy. Expect:

- Quarterly updates.
- K-1 tax forms (delivered late).
- Limited liquidity reporting.

Consider private wealth reporting software or an advisor to organize.

3.8 Exit Planning

Realize:

- Private exits are unpredictable.
- Liquidity comes through M&A, IPO, or secondary markets.
- Be prepared to hold for 7–10 years.

Patience isn't optional — it's the asset.

4. Real-Life Scenarios

Scenario 1: Angel Portfolio

Founder invests $1M into 20 early-stage startups. 15 fail. 3 deliver modest returns. 2 become unicorns — and return 20x and 50x, driving a 5x portfolio return.

Scenario 2: Fund Investor

Founder commits $500K to a top-quartile VC fund. 10-year hold. 20% net IRR. Consistent, diversified exposure. Minimal time involvement.

Scenario 3: Secondary Market Win

Founder buys shares in a late-stage SaaS company pre-IPO through a secondary platform. The company IPOs two years later. 2x return. Quick liquidity compared to early-stage investing.

Scenario 4: Over-Concentration Pain

Founder invests $5M directly into one biotech company based on a friend's tip. FDA trial fails. Company folds. $5M loss.

Lesson: No matter how good it looks, **diversify**.

5. Plain-Language Breakdowns

- **Private Equity**: Buying, improving, and selling private companies.
- **Venture Capital**: Investing early in startups, hoping to find the next unicorn.
- **Secondary Markets**: Buying shares from other private investors before IPO.
- **Power Law**: A small number of investments drive most returns.
- **Capital Calls**: Periodic fund requests for committed capital.

6. Action Steps

- Define how much of your wealth you want in private markets.
- Decide on mix: direct investments, funds, or secondaries.
- Clarify sectors and stages where you have edge or interest.

- Build a vintage year strategy: stagger commitments across years.
- Vet funds and co-investment opportunities rigorously.
- Commit to diversification across sector, stage, geography.
- Organize reporting early — it compounds in complexity fast.
- Expect illiquidity — don't invest dollars you might need soon.
- Work with a trusted private wealth advisor if needed.
- Be patient. Alternatives reward time, not speed.

Private markets are the playground where serious wealth gets compounded — not overnight, but over time. You already have the instincts: you've lived the startup journey. Now, you have the capital to put those instincts to work again — carefully, diversified, wisely.

Alternatives aren't a shortcut. They're a commitment. But done right, they deliver something no public market ETF can match: asymmetric upside, exposure to innovation, access to the next generation of value creators.

Make one move before you go to bed tonight. Sketch your alternative investment strategy. Review a fund's deck. Map a vintage plan. Start building.

You've got this.

Your future self will thank you. So will your net worth. So will the generations that come after you.

7. Model Private Market Allocations for Founders

Different liquidity levels require different strategies. But the principles remain the same: diversification, patience, discipline.

Here's how a founder might approach building a private market allocation at $10M, $50M, and $100M liquidity levels.

Model 1: $10 Million Liquidity — The Focused Starter Portfolio

At $10M liquidity, you have room to be ambitious but still must protect your core wealth. You want exposure to alternatives but in a measured way.

Target Allocation

- 60% Public Markets (Stocks, Bonds, Cash)
- 20% Real Estate (Direct or REITs)
- 20% Private Markets (Venture, Private Equity, Private Credit)

Private Market Breakdown

- 10% Venture Capital Funds (early and growth stage blend)
- 5% Direct Angel Investments (network deals, personal diligence)
- 5% Private Credit Funds (senior secured debt for stability)

Portfolio Design

- 2–3 Venture Capital Funds ($200K–$500K commitments each).
- 5–10 direct startup investments ($50K–$100K per check).
- 1–2 Private Credit Funds for cash yield.

Rationale

You're building exposure while limiting illiquidity. Private credit adds income and reduces reliance on venture exits. Real estate brings stable diversification. Public markets are your liquidity buffer.

Caution

At this level, **don't overcommit**. Illiquid capital locks can bite if you need access for life changes — another startup, real estate purchase, unexpected family needs.

Model 2: $50 Million Liquidity — The Strategic Growth Portfolio

With $50M, you're no longer building — you're optimizing. You have the ability to lean further into alternatives without risking core financial security.

Target Allocation

- 40% Public Markets

- 25% Real Estate (Commercial, Multi-Family, REITs)
- 35% Private Markets (Venture, Private Equity, Private Credit, Real Assets)

Private Market Breakdown

- 15% Venture Capital (funds + direct deals)
- 10% Private Equity Funds (growth buyout strategies)
- 5% Private Credit (senior debt and distressed credit)
- 5% Real Assets (timber, farmland, infrastructure)

Portfolio Design

- 5–7 Venture Capital Funds ($500K–$1M commitments).
- 10–20 direct investments ($100K–$250K per check).
- 3–5 Private Equity Funds (late-stage/growth-stage bias).
- 2 Private Credit Funds (for yield).
- Real Asset exposure through funds or direct partnerships.

Rationale

You can afford true diversification. You can balance venture's risk with private equity's steadier cash flows and credit's yield. Real assets hedge inflation and add decorrelation.

Tactical Edge

You can also consider building a **personal syndicate** — investing alongside a trusted group of founders or executives to access deal flow that solo angels can't.

Caution

At this level, **manager selection** is critical. Being invited into top-decile venture or private equity funds is key — access matters more than theory.

Model 3: $100 Million Liquidity — The Institutional-Style Portfolio

At $100M+ liquidity, you move into an institutional mindset. You're managing legacy capital. Preservation becomes as important as growth.

Access to the best funds becomes non-negotiable.

Target Allocation

- 30% Public Markets
- 20% Real Estate (operating properties, development, REITs)
- 50% Private Markets (Venture, Private Equity, Private Credit, Real Assets, Secondaries)

Private Market Breakdown

- 20% Venture Capital (Tier 1 + emerging managers).
- 15% Private Equity (growth buyout, mid-market, special situations).
- 5% Secondaries (VC and PE — to balance illiquidity).
- 5% Private Credit (senior loans, asset-backed lending).
- 5% Real Assets (infrastructure, ag, timber).

Portfolio Design

- 10–15 Venture Capital Funds (access matters more than check size).
- 30–50 direct startup investments (network co-investments, late-stage secondaries).
- 5–10 Private Equity Funds (diversified across strategies).
- Secondary fund exposure (liquidity and vintage diversification).
- Private credit and real assets to manage cash flows and inflation risks.

Tactical Layer

- **Custom SMA (Separately Managed Account)**: For opportunistic co-investments.
- **Private Market Secondaries**: For faster liquidity and potential discount buys.
- **Impact or ESG Funds**: If mission-aligned capital deployment matters.

Rationale

At this size, you can think in terms of *perpetual capital.* You want assets that are self-sustaining: distributions feed your lifestyle, philanthropy, future investing.

You can also afford to build a **family office infrastructure** — staff or outsource tax, legal, investment operations to manage complexity at scale.

Caution

With size comes complexity. **Oversight** becomes your biggest risk. Poor monitoring of dozens of illiquid positions can destroy returns. You need quarterly review structures, not annual ones.

8. Additional Tactical Considerations for All Portfolios

8.1 Commitment Planning

Funds call capital over years — not all at once. Build a pacing model: commit a set amount each year to build diversification across **vintage years**.

8.2 Cash Flow Management

Private investments don't provide liquidity on demand. Make sure your **cash reserve planning** accounts for lifestyle needs + unexpected events.

8.3 Fee Awareness

Two-and-twenty (2% management fee + 20% carried interest) structures are common. Carefully model net returns, not just gross IRR.

8.4 Co-Investments

Once you're in good funds, you'll get offered co-investments — larger, direct exposures with no carry. **Selective co-investing** can enhance returns if done judiciously.

8.5 Reporting

Your public assets update daily. Your private investments? Annually — at best. Build or buy reporting systems that:

- Aggregate NAVs (Net Asset Values).
- Track capital calls and distributions.

- Monitor vintage year diversification.
- This allows clear performance visibility.

8.6 Tax Optimization

Consider:

- QSBS (Qualified Small Business Stock) eligibility.
- 1202 gains exclusions.
- 1045 rollovers.
- Donor-Advised Funds or private foundations for charitable giving of private shares pre-exit.

Tax-optimized structures make a 20%+ difference in net outcomes.

You didn't build a startup to take ordinary risks. You didn't walk away from a liquidity event to accept average returns. Private markets — approached strategically — allow you to **own innovation** in a way the public markets can't. They allow you to continue leveraging the skills, pattern recognition, and instinct that got you here.

But the private markets demand respect.

They reward **disciplined risk-takers**, not gamblers. They reward **patient capital**, not tourists chasing the next shiny thing. They reward those who **diversify intelligently**, not those who concentrate blindly.

Make one move before you go to bed tonight. Pull your liquidity plan. Map your alternatives allocation. Call a manager you trust.

Chapter 19: Crafting Your Investment Policy Statement

You built your company on a framework. On discipline. On systems. You scaled it with a vision that most people couldn't see — and you made it real. So now that you're building your personal wealth, why would you do it without the same rigor?

That's where the Investment Policy Statement — the IPS — comes in.

If you think IPSs are just for endowments, pension funds, or bureaucratic committees, think again. The IPS is for founders like you — with capital to protect, complexity to navigate, and too much to lose by flying blind.

Let's get into the why, the how, and the what-next of creating your personal wealth blueprint.

1. Why an IPS Is Critical

1.1 What Is an Investment Policy Statement?

At its core, an IPS is a written document that defines how your wealth will be invested. It outlines your objectives, your risk parameters, your liquidity needs, and the rules of the road for your financial life.

Think of it not as paperwork, but as a **pre-commitment device** — a way to hardwire discipline into a system where emotion will try to sabotage you.

It's your blueprint. Your constitution. Your operating manual. It ensures you and your advisors make decisions aligned with your long-term goals, not short-term noise.

1.2 Why Founders Need One

Founders have a unique relationship with risk. You're no stranger to volatility. You've survived markets, investors, competitors, downturns. But post-liquidity wealth has a different texture of risk — and the stakes are higher because the downside is not just lost capital — it's lost security, lost optionality, lost legacy.

Why else does a founder need an IPS?

1.2.1 Complexity

Your wealth post-exit is likely not just a brokerage account and a 401(k). It's a hybrid of cash, public equities, venture stakes, private equity, real estate, maybe art, maybe philanthropy vehicles. Complexity doesn't scare you — but managing it without a plan is reckless.

1.2.2 Volatility

The markets will not care about your exit story. They will do what they do — fluctuate. There will be downturns. There will be headlines. Your company's volatility was operational; the market's volatility is emotional. An IPS helps you manage it with logic instead of gut.

1.2.3 Behavioral Biases

Even the smartest founders fall prey to behavioral finance traps:

- Overconfidence after a big win.
- Loss aversion that paralyzes action.
- Recency bias after a market rally or crash.
- An IPS is the antidote.

1.2.4 Accountability

When you were a founder, you had a Board. Milestones. Accountability. Your wealth deserves the same. An IPS holds you — and your advisors — to account.

1.3 What Happens Without One?

Drift. Indecision. Reactivity. Chasing hot sectors. Panicking during downturns. Without a plan, even elite founders can turn wealth into a mess of missed opportunities and avoidable mistakes.

An IPS is not about restricting you. It's about freeing you — to invest intentionally, live freely, and protect the empire you worked so hard to build.

2. Components of a Solid IPS

2.1 Statement of Purpose

Start with *Why* — just like you did when you started your company. Why are you investing? What is the money for?

- Early retirement?
- Generational wealth?
- Funding your next venture?
- Philanthropy?
- A family office?

Define it clearly. Your purpose informs your risk profile, your time horizon, and your asset allocation.

2.2 Investment Objectives

Quantify your goals. Not just "grow wealth." How much? By when? With how much volatility are you willing to ride it out?

Example:

- Target 7% annualized return, net of fees and taxes.
- Willing to tolerate 15%-20% drawdowns without deviating from plan.
- Desire $500,000 annual cash flow to fund lifestyle needs.

Numbers anchor your ambitions to reality.

2.3 Time Horizon

When will you need the money?

- 0-5 years? You're playing defense — cash, bonds.

- 5-15 years? Balanced growth.
- 15+ years? Growth mode — equities, venture, private equity.

Wealth compounds with time — but only if you match the right assets to the right time horizon.

2.4 Risk Tolerance

Be honest. It's not just how much risk you *think* you can handle when markets are calm — it's how much you can handle when they're crashing.

Ask:

- How would you feel if your portfolio dropped 25%?
- Could you stay invested?
- Would you be tempted to sell at the worst possible time?

Define it, in writing.

2.5 Asset Allocation Targets

Set strategic targets — your investment recipe:

Example:

- 50% Global Equities
- 20% Fixed Income
- 15% Alternatives (Private Equity, Venture)
- 10% Real Assets (Real Estate, Infrastructure)
- 5% Cash

Set bands around these targets (+/- 5%) to allow flexibility without drift.

Asset allocation isn't a detail. It's 90% of your long-term outcomes.

2.6 Rebalancing Policy

How will you rebalance?

- Annually on a set date?
- When an asset class drifts more than 5% from target?

Rebalancing is systematic risk control — selling high, buying low, on a schedule — not based on your gut or CNBC headlines.

2.7 Liquidity Needs

Define:

- Emergency reserves.
- Known large expenses (home purchase, philanthropy).
- Capital for future investments (next venture, real estate play).

Liquidity protects you from forced selling when markets are down — and allows you to seize opportunities when others can't.

2.8 Constraints

List your guardrails:

- ESG constraints?
- No private crypto funds?
- No more than 10% in a single private deal?
- Minimum credit quality for bonds?

Set them now. Prevent regret later.

2.9 Roles and Responsibilities

Who does what?

- You: Define goals, approve strategies.
- Advisor: Implement, monitor, adjust.
- CPA: Tax optimization, reporting.
- Attorney: Estate planning, legal risk mitigation.

Clear lines prevent confusion — and mistakes.

2.10 Review Schedule

Markets change. You change.

Set a cadence for review:

- Annual formal review minimum.
- After major life events — exit, divorce, illness, family expansion.
- Quarterly investment performance snapshots.

Plan for change — but resist changing the plan impulsively.

3. Reviewing and Updating Your IPS

3.1 Why Review Matters

Your wealth journey isn't static. Neither is life. You'll launch new ventures. Move cities. Have children. Face new opportunities and risks.

A stale IPS is a dead IPS. Review it. Keep it alive.

3.2 How to Review

Your annual meeting should answer:

- Are investment objectives being met?
- Is asset allocation still appropriate?
- Has risk tolerance shifted?
- Any life events requiring change?
- Are advisors delivering on their mandates?

If yes, tweak. If no, update. If massively no, overhaul.

3.3 When to Update

Update only for *life* changes, not *market* changes.

- IPOed your next startup? Update.
- Got married/divorced? Update.
- Markets down 20%? Ignore.

Stay stoic. Stay strategic.

3.4 Real-Life Example: The IPS Advantage

Founder A exits with $80M. No IPS. Leverages up, concentrates in tech. 2022 hits — markets down 30%. Panics. Sells low. Losses lock in.

Founder B exits with $80M. IPS in place. 60/30/10 portfolio. Rebalances during downturn. Deploys fresh capital at market lows. Five years later — Founder B's wealth is up 40% net of fees and taxes.

Same exit. Same opportunity. Different outcomes — because of a plan.

4. Plain-Language Breakdowns

- **IPS**: Your financial constitution.
- **Asset Allocation**: Your portfolio's recipe.
- **Risk Tolerance**: Your pain threshold.
- **Rebalancing**: Discipline over drama.
- **Liquidity**: Sleep-well-at-night money.

5. Action Steps

- Draft your Statement of Purpose.
- Quantify your investment objectives.
- Define your time horizon.
- Get brutally honest about risk tolerance.
- Set your initial target allocations.
- Write your rebalancing rules.
- Note liquidity needs and constraints.
- Define advisor roles clearly.
- Set your first review date.
- Commit. Stick to it.

Your company had a business plan. Your wealth demands an investment plan.

The IPS isn't just for today's decisions — it's for tomorrow's crises. It's not just about money — it's about discipline. Legacy. Freedom.

It's your wealth's *operating system* — invisible when things are good, indispensable when things get rough.

Make one money move before you go to bed tonight. Just one. And then another next week.

Draft the purpose.

Define the structure.

Schedule the review.

Build your wealth the same way you built your company — with clarity, conviction, and a plan.

Welcome to serious wealth stewardship.

Chapter 20: Investment Vehicles for Tech Founders

You've crossed the chasm.

You've built, scaled, and exited—or you're somewhere mid-flight but already created liquidity most people only dream about. Either way, you're standing at a profound inflection point. The world of capital isn't just open to you — it's calling your name. But in that cacophony of opportunities, how do you decide where to place your chips?

You know how to build a company. You know how to operate at scale. But wealth — serious, enduring wealth — demands a different skill set. It's not about hustle anymore. It's about design. Precision. Patience.

This chapter breaks down the core investment vehicles every founder must master: public equities, bonds, real estate, alternatives, and cash. More importantly, it shows you how to assemble them into a blueprint — a portfolio that works as hard as you once did.

Let's dive in.

1. Public Equities — The Engine of Growth

Public equities are the bread and butter of serious wealth-building. Stocks — ownership in public companies — are what drive growth over long periods. They're transparent, liquid, global, and historically, one of the most powerful engines of wealth creation.

You may have built your fortune in private markets, but public markets are the rebalancing point. They're what gives your wealth legs when you're no longer willing to sprint.

Why Founders Should Care

Liquidity. Flexibility. Access. Public equities allow you to step out of the opaque, illiquid world of startups and into an arena where prices update every second and buyers are always available.

Stocks complement the illiquidity of your venture capital or private equity positions. They are the counterweight to your operating company.

Pros and Cons

Pros:

- Liquidity: You can exit anytime.
- Transparency: Daily valuations, regulatory disclosures.
- Global Access: Invest anywhere, instantly.

Cons:

- Volatility: Markets swing, and swings can be brutal.
- Behavioral Risk: It's easy to make emotional mistakes — panic selling during downturns is the death knell of compounding.

Key Strategies

You don't need to guess the next Tesla or Amazon. Focus on:

- Broad-market index funds (U.S. and international).
- Factor investing (tilts toward value, size, or profitability).
- A global equity allocation — don't anchor too heavily to one market, even the U.S.

The best strategy? Automate. Set it. Forget it. Rebalance once a year.

You didn't get rich by being reactive. Don't lose it that way.

2. Bonds — The Shock Absorber

Bonds don't get founders excited — but they should. Bonds are loans to governments or corporations. They pay interest and return your capital at maturity. In a founder's portfolio, bonds are the adult in the room. They temper risk. They smooth volatility.

Why Founders Should Care

Bonds provide stability, which offsets the growth volatility of equities and the uncertainty of private markets.

Pros and Cons

Pros:

- Lower volatility than stocks.
- Predictable income stream.
- Portfolio ballast during market downturns.

Cons:

- Lower returns compared to equities.
- Vulnerable to inflation eroding real returns.

Key Strategies

Focus on:

- High-quality government and corporate bonds.

- Laddering maturities (spreading bonds across different expiration dates).
- Keeping duration moderate — long-duration bonds can be crushed when rates rise.

Bonds aren't sexy, but they're necessary. You don't buy bonds to get rich. You buy bonds to stay rich.

3. Real Estate — The Tangible Diversifier

Real estate isn't just about rental income or capital appreciation. It's about diversification, cash flow, inflation protection, and, in some cases, tax optimization.

You know this intuitively — real estate, properly chosen and managed, performs differently than stocks or bonds.

Why Founders Should Care

- Real estate is a tangible asset — you can see it, feel it, touch it.
- It's often less volatile than public markets.
- It can generate passive income — and founders value cash flow once they step away from operating businesses.

Pros and Cons

Pros:

- Inflation hedge — rents and property values tend to rise with inflation.
- Potential tax benefits — depreciation, 1031 exchanges.
- Passive income stream.

Cons:

- Illiquidity — selling a property can take months.
- Management headaches — tenants, repairs, taxes.

Key Strategies

Options include:

- Direct ownership of rental properties.
- REITs (Real Estate Investment Trusts) — public or private.
- Private real estate funds — for access to institutional-grade properties.

Mix and match based on your appetite for involvement and liquidity needs. Own a few properties for cash flow and equity appreciation. Add REITs for diversification and liquidity.

Real estate should be part of your financial ecosystem — just like it's part of the economy's ecosystem.

4. Alternatives — The Alpha Generator

Founders are no strangers to alternatives. Venture capital. Private equity. Hedge funds. Commodities. Private credit. Alternatives are where outsized returns live — but also where risks multiply.

Why Founders Should Care

Private markets are where you first built your fortune. You understand risk. You understand uncertainty. Alternatives allow you to stay in the arena — but on your terms, with diversification.

Pros and Cons

Pros:

- Access to innovation and hypergrowth companies.
- Potential for higher returns compared to public markets.
- Diversification — alternatives often move differently than stocks and bonds.

Cons:

- Illiquidity — your money is locked up for years.
- High fees — 2% management + 20% performance is still common.
- Opaque valuations.

Key Strategies

- Allocate 10%-25% of your portfolio to alternatives.
- Diversify by vintage year — don't commit everything at once.
- Use a mix of direct investments and funds.
- Stay disciplined — don't let excitement override liquidity planning.

Alternatives are a weapon. Use them carefully — but use them.

5. Cash — The Quiet Power

Cash doesn't make headlines. But in a founder's portfolio, cash is the foundation.

Why Founders Should Care

Cash is optionality. Cash is peace of mind. Cash is the ability to seize opportunity when others are frozen in fear.

Pros and Cons

Pros:

- Absolute liquidity.
- Safety.

Cons:

- Negligible returns.
- Purchasing power erosion from inflation.

Key Strategies

- Keep 6-12 months of living expenses.
- Maintain additional reserves for taxes, business investments, and emergencies.
- Park excess cash in high-yield savings accounts or Treasury bills.

Cash is boring. But when markets tank, boring is beautiful.

6. Building the Blueprint — How to Allocate

6.1 The Foundation: Asset Allocation

Asset allocation is the single biggest driver of your investment outcomes.
Example allocation for a UHNW founder:

- 50% Global Public Equities.
- 20% Bonds.
- 15% Real Estate.
- 10% Alternatives (Private Equity, VC, Private Credit).
- 5% Cash.

Tailor it to your risk tolerance, liquidity needs, and time horizon. This is your *personal capital stack.*

6.2 Factors to Consider

Risk Tolerance: How much volatility can you handle emotionally — not just on paper?

Time Horizon: Longer time horizons favor equities and alternatives.

Liquidity Needs: Money you'll need in the next 1-3 years should be in cash or short-term bonds.

Tax Considerations: Tax location matters. Place tax-inefficient assets (bonds, REITs) in tax-deferred accounts if possible.

6.3 Rebalancing Discipline

Markets move. Your portfolio will drift. Annual rebalancing forces you to:

- Sell winners (sell high).
- Buy laggards (buy low).

Simple. Powerful. Necessary.

7. Matching Assets to Goals

7.1 Liquidity Spectrum

Asset ClassLiquidity

Cash

Daily

Public Equities

Daily

Bonds

Daily

REITs

Daily

Direct Real Estate

Months

Private Equity / Venture

7-10 years

Match the liquidity of the asset to the timeline of the goal.

7.2 Bucketing Strategy

BucketTimeframeAssets

Bucket 1

0-2 Years

Cash, Short-term Bonds

Bucket 2

2-7 Years

Public Equities, Intermediate Bonds, REITs

Bucket 3

7+ Years

Private Equity, Venture Capital, Direct Real Estate

Align your investments to when you'll actually need the money.

8. Real-Life Scenarios

Scenario 1: The Overconcentrated Founder

Founder holds 90% of net worth in one company stock. Company falters. Wealth evaporates.

Solution: Diversify early and often. Sell gradually through 10b5-1 plans. Build a portfolio across public, private, real assets.

Scenario 2: The Ultra-Conservative Founder

Founder sells company, parks 80% in cash and bonds. Inflation erodes purchasing power. Portfolio underperforms.

Solution: Increase equity exposure. Layer in growth-oriented alternatives. Be cautious, but don't be paralyzed.

Scenario 3: The Balanced Founder

Founder builds:

- 60% public equities.
- 20% bonds.
- 10% real estate.
- 10% venture funds.

Outcome: Growth. Stability. Opportunity. Weathered downturns without panic. Stayed invested. Compounded wealth.

Wealth isn't about home runs. It's about avoiding wipeouts.

9. Plain-Language Breakdowns

- **Public Equities**: Ownership in companies. Liquid. Growth engine.
- **Bonds**: Loans to governments or companies. Income. Stability.
- **Real Estate**: Physical or securitized property. Inflation hedge.
- **Alternatives**: Private markets. Venture, PE, hedge funds.
- **Cash**: Safety and optionality.
- **Asset Allocation**: How you spread your wealth across asset classes.
- **Rebalancing**: Resetting to original allocations.
- **Liquidity**: Ease of converting to cash without loss.
- **Bucketing**: Aligning assets to time-specific goals.

10. Action Steps

- Inventory current holdings.
- Define your investment objectives.
- Quantify liquidity needs.
- Sketch your asset allocation.
- Segment investments by time horizon.
- Commit to annual rebalancing.
- Start diversifying — immediately.
- Avoid concentration traps.
- Prioritize tax efficiency.
- Review goals and adjust annually.

Founders are wired to concentrate. To bet everything on one big idea. But wealth management? It's a different game.

It demands balance. Patience. Process.

You can't control the markets. But you can control your discipline.

Make one money move before you go to bed tonight. Just one. And then another next week.

Sketch your asset allocation. Revisit your cash needs. Commit to rebalancing.

Section 5: The Founder's Playbook — Tools, Tactics, and Action Steps

Knowledge without action is just noise.

And in the high-stakes world of tech founders, *action* is what separates those who build lasting wealth from those who let opportunity slip away.

Section 5 is your blueprint for moving from theory to practice — your real-world guide to turning the strategies and insights of this book into tangible results.

We open with a structured set of **financial action steps** tailored to every stage of the founder journey — before, during, and after liquidity. Whether you're pre-exit and grappling with your cap table, in the heat of negotiations for a sale, or post-exit managing new wealth, you'll find clear, founder-specific checklists and frameworks to guide your next move.

Next, we dive into **real-world case studies** — stories of founders who navigated their financial lives successfully (and those who made painful mistakes). You'll see the common pitfalls and the powerful strategies that made the difference between fleeting wealth and lasting legacy.

Then, we focus on **red flags** — the mistakes founders most often make when managing money: procrastinating on tax planning, misunderstanding liquidity, underestimating risk, and neglecting estate planning. Knowing these red flags equips you to avoid them in your own journey.

You'll also find **checklists and frameworks** — simplified, actionable tools that help you audit your personal financial life the way you audit your company's operations. From a liquidity event checklist to a legacy-building starter guide, this section gives you what every founder needs: clarity and execution steps.

Finally, we share how working with experienced, founder-focused professionals — like those at **Tech Business Founders** led by Pat Brown — can streamline your process. Having a strategic partner who knows the terrain ensures you make smart moves, not costly mistakes.

This isn't just another "money book."

This is a playbook designed to help you — the founder — protect, grow, and multiply what you've built.

When you close this section, you won't just know what to do — you'll have a concrete path forward, clear next steps, and the confidence to own your financial future like you own your business destiny.

Chapter 21: Advanced Investment Strategies

You're here. You're not playing defense anymore — you're playing to win.

You spent years grinding, risking, betting on yourself when few would. You built something from nothing. You crossed the chasm. You created real liquidity.

Now the game changes. Protecting wealth is a different art than creating it. The blunt instruments of basic investing — index funds, real estate, public markets — got you stability. But from here on out? The best founders, the serious wealth stewards, use sharper tools. They think differently. They plan differently.

Welcome to advanced investment strategies — a toolkit not designed for everyone, but specifically engineered for founders like you. Founders who have liquidity. Founders who have ambition. Founders who are thinking about decades, not quarters. These strategies, properly deployed, can be the difference between rich and wealthy, between having money and creating a legacy.

Let's get strategic. Let's get surgical.

1. Direct Indexing — Tax Alpha on Autopilot

1.1 What Is Direct Indexing?

Imagine buying the S&P 500 — but instead of holding one ETF or mutual fund, you own each of the 500 companies individually. That's direct indexing.

Why bother? Because it gives you control — control over what you own, how you own it, and more critically, how you manage taxes. Instead of waiting for the fund manager to make moves, you harvest tax losses yourself at the individual stock level, systematically, surgically.

Customization is the real secret. Hate fossil fuels? Remove them. Overexposed to tech through your career? Underweight the sector. Want to tilt toward companies that match your personal values? Done.

1.2 Why Founders Should Care

Founders are often overexposed — to their own industry, sector, or even their former company's stock post-exit. Direct indexing lets you customize away from those risks while aggressively optimizing taxes.

You didn't get where you are by using off-the-shelf solutions. Why start now?

1.3 Pros and Cons

Pros:

- Hyper-personalization.
- Enhanced tax-loss harvesting (true "tax alpha").
- Lower tracking error to the benchmark, if done right.

Cons:

- More complex than buying an ETF.
- Can come with management fees — though technology is driving those

down fast.

1.4 Key Strategies

- Set up systematic tax-loss harvesting. Capture losses throughout the year, not just in December.
- Tilt away from your old industry or sectors you're already heavily invested in.
- Apply ESG, social impact, or other personal screens.

Tax alpha is real. Direct indexing captures it — efficiently, consistently, quietly.

2. Structured Notes — Engineering Outcomes

2.1 What Are They?

Structured notes are custom-designed debt instruments. Think of them like a bet with training wheels. You loan money to a bank, but your return is tied to the performance of an index, stock, or basket of assets — with downside protection, or enhanced yields, built in.

It's finance meeting engineering: you define your risk/return profile, and the note is tailored to fit.

2.2 Why Founders Should Care

Public markets are volatile. Structured notes let you design outcomes: partial downside protection if markets fall, enhanced yield if markets stay flat, or higher participation in upside with defined risk.

It's the ability to play offense while still protecting the foundation.

2.3 Pros and Cons

Pros:

- Custom outcomes based on risk appetite.
- Potential for better risk-adjusted returns.
- Yield enhancement in low-rate environments.

Cons:

- Complexity — you must understand the fine print.
- Counterparty risk — if the issuing bank fails, you could lose money.
- Limited liquidity — typically you must hold to maturity.

2.4 Key Strategies

- Use for income enhancement when rates are low and bonds are unattractive.
- Deploy during uncertain markets when downside protection is more valuable.
- Only work with advisors or banks who can fully model and explain your structured notes — these are tools, not toys.

Well-designed structured notes give founders surgical precision when broad markets feel blunt and unpredictable.

3. Private Credit — Yield in a Starved World

3.1 What Is It?

Private credit is exactly what it sounds like: loans made directly to businesses, but not through traditional banks. Think middle-market companies that are too small for public debt markets but too big to go to a local bank. Private debt funds lend to them — and you, the investor, can participate.

3.2 Why Founders Should Care

Public bond yields are pitiful. If you're looking for stable income without tying yourself to public market volatility, private credit offers a compelling solution.

More importantly, private credit's performance is often uncorrelated with equities, offering real diversification.

3.3 Pros and Cons

Pros:

- Higher yields than public bonds.
- Predictable cash flows.
- Portfolio diversification.

Cons:

- Illiquidity — you're locked up for several years.
- Credit risk — you must trust the underwriting.

3.4 Key Strategies

- Focus on senior secured loans first — they get paid first in bankruptcy.
- Blend with some mezzanine debt for higher returns, but limit exposure.
- Work with managers who have survived multiple credit cycles, not just the easy years.

Private credit brings institutional-grade yield opportunities to UHNW portfolios. Founders, with their appetite for complexity and risk-awareness, belong in this space.

4. Opportunity Zone Investments — Taxes Meet Impact

4.1 What Are They?

Born from the 2017 Tax Cuts and Jobs Act, Opportunity Zones are designated distressed areas where the government incentivizes private investment — with massive tax breaks.

Roll over eligible capital gains into a Qualified Opportunity Fund (QOF), and you can defer taxes on your gains, reduce them, and — if you hold the new investment long enough — eliminate future taxes on any new gains.

4.2 Why Founders Should Care

Exiting a startup often triggers massive capital gains. Opportunity Zones offer a way to:

- Defer immediate taxation.
- Reduce taxes on gains if held long enough.
- Erase taxes on appreciation inside the QOF.

All while investing in communities that need revitalization. It's legacy and leverage in one.

4.3 Pros and Cons

Pros:

- Deferral and reduction of capital gains.
- Potential tax-free growth.
- Impact-driven investing — real change.

Cons:

- Long holding periods — typically 10+ years.
- Regulatory complexity.
- Quality of projects varies — due diligence is critical.

4.4 Key Strategies

- Roll gains from your exit within the 180-day window.
- Partner with reputable Opportunity Zone funds or operators.
- Focus on zones with real potential — not just tax gimmicks.

Impact. Tax optimization. Legacy. Opportunity Zones check every box a modern founder should care about.

5. Tailored Investment Strategies — Post-Exit, No Playbooks

5.1 The Problem: Standard Playbooks Don't Fit

You're not a W-2 employee with a 401(k) and a house in the suburbs. You have:

- Concentrated stock positions.
- Huge one-time tax liabilities.
- Family trusts.
- Dynamic liquidity needs.
- Maybe multiple businesses still running.

You need a bespoke playbook. One designed around *your* variables.

5.2 Building Your Custom Strategy

5.2.1 Liquidity Timeline

- Immediate (0-2 years): Cash, Treasuries.
- Short-term (2-5 years): Bonds, public equities.
- Long-term (5+ years): Venture, private equity, real estate.

5.2.2 Risk Budget

- Define how much portfolio volatility you can tolerate.
- Allocate accordingly: more equities and alternatives if you can accept the swings.

5.2.3 Tax Management

- Use direct indexing for efficient harvesting.
- Locate tax-inefficient assets in tax-deferred accounts.
- Plan charitable giving (DAFs, private foundations).

5.2.4 Values Alignment

- ESG investing.
- Impact funds.
- Philanthropic capital — start aligning dollars with what you want to change in the world.

5.2.5 Legacy Planning

- Dynasty trusts to protect assets across generations.
- Private foundations to institutionalize family giving.
- Structures that minimize estate taxes while maximizing impact.

A real wealth strategy isn't just spreadsheets. It's values, vision, velocity.

5.3 Real-Life Founder Blueprint

Founder X sold his company for $50M. His allocation:

- $20M into a direct indexing portfolio — efficient, diversified, tax-managed.
- $10M into private credit and real estate — stable income, inflation hedge.
- $5M into venture and private equity funds — upside, familiarity.
- $10M seeded into a family trust — legacy protection.
- $5M allocated to Opportunity Zones — impact and tax optimization.

Outcome: Diversified. Tax-optimized. Legacy in motion.
That's the difference between rich and ultra-affluent.

6. Plain-Language Breakdowns

- **Direct Indexing**: Customized stock portfolios that mirror an index but allow tax and value-based optimization.
- **Structured Notes**: Financial instruments that offer tailored return profiles linked to market performance.
- **Private Credit**: Private lending to mid-sized companies for higher yields and diversification.
- **Opportunity Zones**: Government-incentivized investments offering capital gains tax breaks.
- **Tailored Strategy**: A personalized, dynamic investment plan crafted around your liquidity, risk, and legacy goals.

7. Action Steps

- Assess your current portfolio's complexity and risks.
- Review tax management strategies — engage a strategist.
- Evaluate if direct indexing can replace your current index exposure.
- Consider structured notes for yield enhancement.
- Explore private credit funds for stable returns.
- Research high-quality Opportunity Zone investments.
- Draft a post-exit wealth blueprint with clear buckets and allocations.
- Align your portfolio to your personal values and mission.
- Set quarterly or annual wealth review dates.
- Engage a wealth team that understands founder-level complexity.

Advanced wealth requires advanced planning.

These strategies aren't about being flashy. They're about being smart, surgical, intentional.

You didn't build your company on shortcuts. You don't build lasting wealth on shortcuts either.

Intentional. Strategic. Focused.

Make one money move before you go to bed tonight. Just one. And then do another next week.

Book that call with a tax strategist. Draft a liquidity bucket plan. Review an Opportunity Zone fund.

Chapter 22: Mitigating Taxes Through Smart Investments

You built. You sold. You scaled. You made it through the fire of startup life, crossed the chasm, and created liquidity. Now? It's time to think bigger — and smarter.

You've already realized the hard truth: You can't control markets. You can't control valuations. You can't control the next macroeconomic shock. But there's one arena where you still hold considerable power: taxes.

And here's the part no one tells you early enough — your investment strategy and your tax strategy are inseparable. Smart investment planning *is* smart tax planning. The more intentional you get here, the more wealth you preserve — and the more freedom you create for your future self.

Let's dive deep into how truly wealthy founders approach tax optimization — not by accident, not reactively — but surgically, strategically, with precision.

1. Tax-Loss Harvesting — Your Tactical Ally

1.1 What Is It?

Tax-loss harvesting sounds complicated, but it's remarkably simple. It's the act of selling investments that have declined in value to realize a capital loss. You can then use that loss to offset realized capital gains elsewhere in your portfolio. Net result? Lower taxable income. Lower taxes.

And the beauty? You can reinvest the proceeds into similar (but not identical) investments to stay in the market.

1.2 Why Founders Should Care

When you have liquidity from a major event — a company sale, a secondary transaction, a liquidity window — you're often staring down massive capital gains. Tax-loss harvesting helps you systematically trim your tax bill and boost your after-tax returns year after year.

More importantly? Over time, the compounding benefits of "tax alpha" — the incremental return generated through tax savings — can add millions to your bottom line.

1.3 Pros and Cons

Pros:

- Immediate tax savings.
- Reinvest proceeds to maintain market exposure.
- Systematic source of "tax alpha."

Cons:

- Wash-sale rules: you can't repurchase the same (or "substantially identical") investment within 30 days.
- Timing risk: markets could rebound after you sell.

1.4 Key Strategies

- Use *direct indexing* platforms that allow systematic tax-loss harvesting across individual stocks.
- Harvest not just once a year, but monthly or quarterly — more frequent harvesting = more opportunities.

- Replace sold securities with highly correlated ETFs or funds to maintain your exposure without tripping wash-sale rules.

The best time to start tax-loss harvesting? Yesterday. The second-best time? Now.

2. Tax Deferral Strategies — Buy Time, Buy Optionality

2.1 What Are They?

Tax deferral is exactly what it sounds like: strategies that push your tax obligations into the future. Why defer? Because every year you delay paying taxes, you retain more capital in your portfolio to compound and grow.

More capital compounding, longer runway — simple math, profound impact.

2.2 Why Founders Should Care

Liquidity events trigger enormous gains — and immediate tax obligations. Deferring that tax gives you time to grow your money further, potentially at a lower future tax rate, or position it for even more sophisticated estate planning strategies.

Deferral = control. Control buys freedom.

2.3 Key Strategies

- **Qualified Opportunity Zones (QOZs):** Invest gains within 180 days into a QOZ fund, defer your original gain, and potentially eliminate taxes on new gains if held 10+ years.
- **1031 Exchanges (for real estate):** Swap one investment property for another, deferring capital gains taxes.
- **Charitable Remainder Trusts (CRTs):** Donate appreciated assets,

get a charitable deduction now, and receive income over time.

- **Deferred Sales Trusts (DSTs):** Sell business or real estate assets, defer capital gains by rolling proceeds into a trust.

2.4 Real-Life Example

A founder sells their company for $25M. Rather than pay taxes on the entire gain, they roll $5M into a Qualified Opportunity Zone fund. Result? Immediate deferral on $5M, tax-free growth if held 10 years.

Leverage the law. Maximize the benefit. That's the game at this level.

3. Roth Conversions During Low-Income Years — Play the Brackets

3.1 What Are Roth Conversions?

A Roth conversion is the process of moving money from a traditional IRA or 401(k) (tax-deferred) into a Roth IRA (tax-free growth and withdrawals). Yes, you pay taxes now. But you never pay taxes again on those funds — ever.

3.2 Why Founders Should Care

Most founders have volatile income years. If you've exited and you're taking a breather — a sabbatical, a pivot, a "retirement" — your income may temporarily drop. Those low-income years are the golden window for Roth conversions.

Convert while your tax bracket is low. Enjoy a lifetime of tax-free growth.

3.3 Pros and Cons

Pros:

- Tax-free future withdrawals.
- No Required Minimum Distributions (RMDs).
- Potential estate planning benefits (Roth IRAs can stretch tax-free growth across heirs).

Cons:

- Immediate tax hit.
- Complexity in tax planning.

3.4 Key Strategies

- **Partial conversions:** Spread large conversions over multiple years to stay in lower tax brackets.
- **Offset conversion income:** Pair conversions with charitable giving to blunt the tax impact.
- **Roth 401(k) rollovers:** If you had a Roth 401(k), roll it into a Roth IRA post-exit to avoid future RMDs.

Front-load the tax pain. Back-load the tax-free freedom. Your future self will thank you.

4. Asset Location Strategies — Placement Matters

4.1 What Is Asset Location?

Asset location is about putting the right investments in the right accounts to minimize taxes. It's not *what* you invest in — it's *where* you hold those investments.

Think of it like asset allocation's smarter, tax-savvier cousin.

4.2 Why Founders Should Care

After a liquidity event, you're likely juggling multiple accounts:

- Taxable brokerage accounts.
- IRAs and 401(k)s (tax-deferred).
- Roth IRAs (tax-free).

Each type of investment generates different types of tax consequences. Optimizing where you hold what can meaningfully improve your after-tax returns.

4.3 Pros and Cons

Pros:

- Boost long-term returns by reducing tax drag.
- More efficient compounding.

Cons:

- Requires planning.
- Potential liquidity trade-offs.

4.4 Key Strategies

- **Put tax-inefficient assets** (like bonds, REITs, actively managed funds) into tax-deferred accounts.
- **Hold tax-efficient assets** (like index funds, ETFs, municipal bonds) in taxable accounts.
- **Park high-growth assets** in Roth IRAs to maximize tax-free growth.

4.5 Example

Own municipal bonds? Keep them in taxable accounts (they're already tax-advantaged). Actively managed small-cap funds throwing off short-term gains? Shelter them in your IRA. Growth stocks you plan to hold forever? Put them in your Roth IRA for tax-free appreciation.

Location matters. In real estate — and in investing.

5. Real-Life Scenarios — Lessons from the Front Lines

Scenario 1: The Harvesting Hustler

A founder exits and builds a $50M portfolio. In a volatile year, she harvests $500K in tax losses across her direct indexing portfolio. That $500K offsets gains from other sales — saving over $100K in taxes. She stays fully invested, rebalances, and pockets the tax savings.

Outcome: Immediate savings. Improved portfolio efficiency.

Scenario 2: The Deferral Dynamo

Another founder, facing $2M in gains from a liquidity event, rolls $2M into a top-tier Opportunity Zone fund. Ten years later, the investment doubles — and he pays *zero* tax on the new gains.

Outcome: Deferred pain. Maximized gain. Legacy wealth built.

Scenario 3: The Conversion Strategist

A founder exits at 40, takes a two-year sabbatical. During those low-income years, she converts $2M from her traditional IRA to a Roth IRA across two years — staying in a reasonable tax bracket. Future withdrawals? Tax-free.

Outcome: Lifetime tax-free income. Estate planning win.

Scenario 4: The Location Legend

A founder strategically allocates:

- Bonds and REITs in IRAs.
- Index funds in taxable accounts.
- Growth stocks in Roth IRAs.

Result? 1%-2% annual improvement in after-tax returns — compounded over decades.

Outcome: Meaningful wealth multiplication.

6. Plain-Language Breakdowns

- **Tax-Loss Harvesting:** Selling underperformers to offset winners and cut your tax bill.
- **Tax Deferral:** Pushing taxes into the future to retain and grow more capital now.
- **Roth Conversions:** Pay tax once. Grow and withdraw tax-free forever.
- **Asset Location:** Putting each investment in the right account to boost after-tax returns.

7. Action Steps — Your Tactical Checklist

- Review your capital gains exposure.
- Implement a tax-loss harvesting program.
- Assess deferral opportunities (QOZs, CRTs, DSTs).
- Identify windows for Roth conversions.
- Optimize asset location across all your accounts.
- Build a tax strategy calendar — annual and quarterly checks.
- Hire a tax-savvy wealth advisor.
- Integrate charitable giving for tax leverage.

- Stay informed on tax law changes — they evolve.
- Review and refresh your plan annually.

Final Thought — Smart Founders Keep What They Earn

Smart founders don't just make money. They keep it.

Mitigating taxes isn't about gimmicks. It's about intention. Precision. Strategy. It's about building wealth efficiently, intentionally, methodically.

You didn't spend a decade sacrificing nights, weekends, and normalcy to hand 40% of your hard-won gains to the IRS.

Be proactive. Be tactical. Be strategic.

Make one money move before you go to bed tonight. Just one. And then another next week.

Chapter 23: Establishing Foundations and Charitable Entities

You built the dream. You scaled the company. You achieved the exit. You reached a level most only dream of — and you know deep down that your work isn't finished. You've conquered the wealth game, but the real question now becomes: what will you do with it?

Because true wealth isn't just measured by what you accumulate. It's measured by what you leave behind — the ideas you plant, the communities you uplift, the legacy you etch into the lives of those you'll never even meet.

And strategic philanthropy, done right, can be one of the most powerful tools for building that legacy. Beyond the tax deductions, beyond the grants, it's about living intentionally — aligning your capital with your deepest convictions.

Let's have the real conversation about giving. Let's not treat it as a footnote. Let's treat it as what it is — a pillar of a life well-lived.

1. Private Foundations — Legacy With Control

1.1 What Is a Private Foundation?

A private foundation is a charitable organization that you, as the founder, create and control. It's a separate legal entity — typically structured as a 501(c)(3) — that can make grants to nonprofits, run its own programs, and invest its endowment. But unlike public charities, private foundations are funded by a single source — you.

There are rules, of course: the foundation must distribute at least 5% of its assets annually for charitable purposes. It's also subject to reporting requirements, excise taxes, and public transparency.

But what you gain is unparalleled control over how your charitable dollars are deployed — today and for generations to come.

1.2 Why Founders Should Care

Founders are builders by nature. A private foundation allows you to build a platform for impact. It's a way to formalize your values, to teach stewardship to your children, and to create a lasting philanthropic engine long after you're gone.

And yes, the tax benefits are significant:

- Deduct up to 30% of your Adjusted Gross Income (AGI) for cash contributions.
- Deduct up to 20% of AGI for contributions of appreciated assets.
- Avoid capital gains taxes by donating highly appreciated stock directly.

But the real win? It's about purpose. About influence. About legacy.

1.3 Pros and Cons

Pros:

- Total control over grants, investments, and strategy.
- Family involvement for generations.
- Credibility and platform to attract other donors.

Cons:

- Administrative burden — governance, recordkeeping, IRS compliance.

- 5% mandatory distribution requirement annually.
- 1.39% excise tax on net investment income.

1.4 Key Steps to Set Up

- Engage legal counsel to draft governing documents (Articles of Incorporation, Bylaws).
- File IRS Form 1023 to secure tax-exempt status.
- Build your initial board — typically yourself, family members, or trusted advisors.
- Develop an investment policy statement (IPS) for the endowment.
- Design a mission and grant-making strategy that reflects your deepest values.

Legacy doesn't happen by accident. You architect it — brick by brick.

2. Donor-Advised Funds (DAFs) — Simplicity Meets Impact

2.1 What Is a Donor-Advised Fund?

Think of a Donor-Advised Fund (DAF) as a "charitable investment account." You make a contribution — cash, stock, or other assets — receive an immediate tax deduction, and then recommend grants over time to your favorite charities.

It's one of the fastest-growing vehicles in philanthropy because it democratizes legacy planning. You don't need $50M to make an impact. You can start with $50,000 — or less.

2.2 Why Founders Should Care

DAFs solve a huge problem for founders: the timing mismatch between liquidity events and philanthropic planning.

Just sold your company and facing a massive tax bill? Contribute appreciated stock to a DAF:

- Immediate deduction.
- No capital gains taxes.
- Time to decide where the money ultimately goes.

Plus, your contributions can be invested inside the DAF, allowing your philanthropic dollars to grow tax-free while you're deciding.

2.3 Pros and Cons

Pros:

- No administrative burden.
- Immediate tax deduction — up to 60% of AGI for cash donations, 30% for appreciated assets.
- Tax-free growth inside the DAF.
- Family-friendly — involve children in recommending grants.

Cons:

- Less control compared to private foundations.
- Grants must be recommended through a sponsoring organization.

2.4 Key Strategies

- *Bunching Strategy:* Consolidate several years' worth of giving into one high-income year to maximize deductions.
- *Appreciated Stock Contributions:* Donate highly appreciated shares — avoid capital gains, deduct full fair market value.
- *Family Engagement:* Use the DAF as a platform to involve your family in strategic philanthropy.

DAFs are proof: Legacy doesn't have to be complicated to be powerful.

3. Charitable Trusts — Giving and Receiving

3.1 Charitable Remainder Trust (CRT)

A CRT is an irrevocable trust that provides you (or another beneficiary) with an income stream, either for life or a fixed term. Afterward, the remaining assets go to charity.

Benefits:

- Current-year partial charitable deduction.
- Capital gains tax deferral if funded with appreciated assets.
- Income for life or a term of years.

3.2 Charitable Lead Trust (CLT)

With a CLT, the charity gets the income stream first for a period of time, and then the remainder returns to you or your heirs.

Benefits:

- Immediate charitable impact.
- Potential to transfer wealth to heirs at a reduced gift and estate tax cost.

3.3 Why Founders Should Care

Trusts are strategic tools — especially when dealing with highly appreciated assets like company stock or real estate. They let you:

- Defer or minimize taxes.
- Support charities you care about.
- Maintain an income stream.

- Reduce your taxable estate.

Philanthropy can be more than generosity — it can be a finely tuned financial strategy.

3.4 Example

Imagine a founder with $10M in low-basis stock. By contributing to a CRT, they avoid an immediate $2M capital gains tax hit, receive a $1.5M deduction upfront, and establish an income stream of $500K annually for life. Upon death, the remaining assets support causes they believe in.

Smart giving. Smart tax strategy. Enduring impact.

4. Aligning Giving Strategies With Wealth Preservation

4.1 Tax Benefits

- Immediate income tax deductions.
- Capital gains tax avoidance on donated appreciated assets.
- Estate tax minimization via strategic gifting.

4.2 Multi-Generational Legacy

Philanthropy isn't just about writing checks. It's about building values. It's about training your children and grandchildren to think about impact, stewardship, and responsibility.

Family foundations and DAFs create platforms where financial literacy meets empathy. Where next-gen leaders are forged.

4.3 Strategic Planning

- Time major gifts in years when income (and tax exposure) are highest — like the year of a major liquidity event.
- Use charitable giving to offset Roth conversion tax bills or sale of appreciated assets.
- Incorporate philanthropy into your estate plan — reduce estate taxes while leaving a legacy.

Your giving should be as intentional and strategic as your investing.

5. Real-Life Scenarios and Relatable Stories

Scenario 1: The Foundation Builder

After selling her company for $50M, a founder creates a private foundation with $5M. Her adult children serve on the board, learning governance and grant-making firsthand.

Outcome:

- Deep family engagement.
- Hands-on legacy.
- Annual grants to causes aligned with family values.

Scenario 2: The DAF Dynamo

Another founder donates $1M of appreciated startup stock into a DAF the same year they exit. They avoid a large capital gains tax bill and take a deduction against their high income year. The family meets quarterly to recommend grants.

Outcome:

- Immediate tax benefit.

- Meaningful, ongoing giving.
- Low administration.

Scenario 3: The Trust Strategist

A founder contributes $10M of low-basis stock into a CRT. They receive an income stream for life, enjoy a major tax deduction, and support education-focused charities upon death.

Outcome:

- No immediate capital gains.
- Higher after-tax income.
- Legacy impact locked in.

Legacy and liquidity can coexist. You just have to be strategic about it.

6. Plain-Language Breakdowns

- **Private Foundation:** Your personal charitable organization. High control, high responsibility.
- **Donor-Advised Fund (DAF):** Simplified charitable account. Immediate deduction, long-term giving flexibility.
- **Charitable Trust:** Split-interest tool — income now, charity later (or vice versa).

7. Action Steps — Building Your Legacy Plan

- Assess your charitable goals: What impact do you want to have?
- Evaluate your net worth and liquidity: How much can you allocate?
- Meet with a philanthropic advisor: Strategy first.
- Decide between a Foundation, DAF, or Trust: What structure fits your goals?
- Engage attorneys and CPAs for setup: Get it right from the start.

- Draft a charitable mission statement: Clarify your "why."
- Educate your family: Bring them along early.
- Create an annual giving plan: Stay proactive, not reactive.
- Integrate giving into your estate plan: Legacy is intentional, not accidental.
- Review annually and adjust: Life changes. So should your strategy.

Philanthropy Isn't a Footnote. It's a Pillar.

Great founders build great companies. Legendary founders build great legacies.

Philanthropy isn't just a charitable act. It's a strategic financial decision. It's a platform for impact. It's a way to align your capital with your convictions, to build a story that extends beyond yourself.

Private foundations. Donor-Advised Funds. Charitable trusts.

Different tools. Same goal: to matter. To last. To give back at scale.

Make one money move before you go to bed tonight. Just one. And then another next week.

Sketch out your legacy goals. Call a philanthropic advisor. Explore setting up a DAF.

Chapter 24: Can You Do This On Your Own?

You've done it all before.

You built a company from scratch.

You raised capital, hired a team, scaled it, maybe even exited.

Surely you can manage your own wealth, right?

Maybe.

Maybe not.

Let's have the honest conversation about DIY wealth management as a tech founder.

Because when it comes to managing significant, complex, and volatile wealth—the kind that comes from startups and exits—the stakes are higher.

This isn't your college checking account.

This isn't a $10,000 investment account you set up on Robinhood.

This is your life's work.

Your legacy.

And it deserves the same level of attention, intention, and expertise that you brought to your company.

1. The Case for DIY Financial Planning

1.1 Why Some Founders Prefer DIY

- Control.
- Cost savings.
- Confidence.
- Access to information.

You're a builder. A problem solver. It's only natural to think you can manage this yourself.

1.2 Pros of DIY

1. Control:
You're in charge. You call the shots.
2. Cost Savings:
No advisory fees.
3. Learning Opportunity:
Financial literacy is empowering.
4. Flexibility:
Move quickly without committee approvals.

1.3 Cons of DIY

1. Time:
Managing complex wealth is a job.
You already have one.
2. Complexity:
Taxes, estate planning, investment management, risk management—they're separate fields for a reason.
3. Behavioral Biases:
DIY investors often fall prey to emotional decisions.
4. Opportunity Cost:
What's the value of your time?

5. Missed Optimization:

Tax strategies alone could save you millions.

If you know how to implement them.

2. Complexity and Risk Factors

2.1 Unique Challenges for Founders

1. Illiquidity:

Most of your wealth is tied up in private company stock.

2. Concentration Risk:

Too much tied to one company—yours.

3. Tax Landmines:

ISOs. AMT. QSBS. 83(b) elections.

4. Exit Planning:

M&A vs IPO? Secondary sales?

5. Estate Planning:

You have more to protect.

And more at risk.

6. Charitable Planning:

Philanthropy can unlock tax benefits—if structured correctly.

Founders have a uniquely complex financial landscape.

One that demands nuanced, proactive planning.

2.2 The Risk of "I'll Figure It Out Later"

You didn't scale your company by winging it.

Don't wing your wealth either.

Wealth planning mistakes are expensive.

Sometimes irreversible.

Think:

- Missing a critical 83(b) election window.

- Triggering AMT without a strategy.
- Paying unnecessary capital gains.
- Exposing your estate to avoidable taxes.

2.3 Real-Life Founder Pitfalls

- Founder exercised stock options without AMT planning—owed a $3M tax bill.
- Sold company without estate freeze techniques—lost 40% to taxes.
- Ignored concentrated risk—watched net worth evaporate when stock price fell.

We don't tell you these stories to scare you.

We tell you these stories to save you.

3. When It's Time to Seek Professional Help

3.1 Signs You Need Help

- You're losing sleep over tax or investment decisions.
- Your net worth exceeds $5M.
- You're planning for an IPO or acquisition.
- You have significant equity comp.
- You're considering charitable giving but don't know where to start.
- You're trying to balance business reinvestment with personal financial security.

3.2 What a Great Advisor Should Bring

- **Experience:**
- Working with founders.
- **Tax Expertise:**
- ISOs, AMT, QSBS, liquidity events.

- **Investment Management:**
- Post-exit allocation strategies.
- **Estate Planning Coordination:**
- Integrating legacy goals.
- **Charitable Giving Strategies:**
- Foundations, DAFs, CRTs.
- **Risk Management:**
- Insurance. Concentration hedging.
- **Team Coordination:**
- CPAs, attorneys, investment bankers.

Founders need quarterback-level advice.
Someone who sees the full field.

3.3 How to Vet an Advisor

1. **Ask About Experience:**
"How many founders have you worked with?"
2. **Demand Transparency:**
Fee-only? Fiduciary?
3. **Assess Chemistry:**
Do they get you?
Do they speak your language?
4. **Verify Credentials:**
CFP®? CPA? JD?
5. **Review Services Offered:**
Investment management alone isn't enough.
You need comprehensive planning.
Your advisor should feel like a partner, not a product pusher.

4. Pros and Cons of Hiring a Wealth Manager

4.1 Pros

- Expertise.
- Time savings.
- Risk reduction.
- Tax efficiency.
- Behavioral guardrails.

4.2 Cons

- Cost (typically 0.25% – 1% of AUM).
- Finding the right fit can take time.
- Loss of total control.

4.3 Is the Cost Worth It?

Run the numbers.

- If tax savings alone exceed fees?
- If reduced mistakes preserve millions?
- If peace of mind increases?

Then yes.

Smart founders know when to DIY.

And when to delegate.

5. Real-Life Scenarios and Relatable Stories

Scenario 1: The DIY Diehard

Founder manages wealth solo.

- Misses QSBS eligibility on $10M gain.

- Owes $2M+ more in taxes than necessary.

Scenario 2: The Balanced Delegator

Founder builds wealth team.

- CPA handles taxes.
- Estate attorney manages trusts.
- Wealth advisor oversees investments.

Outcome?

- Integrated, proactive planning.
- Reduced taxes.
- Preserved legacy.

Scenario 3: The Late-Stage Learner

Founder waits too long.

- Over-concentrated.
- Market correction.
- 40% wealth decline.

Learning:
Don't wait until the market teaches you a lesson.

6. Plain-Language Breakdowns

DIY Financial Planning

Good for:

- Simple wealth structures.
- Founders with time and appetite for learning.

Risky for:

- Complex tax situations.
- Significant equity holdings.

Professional Financial Planning

Good for:

- High-net-worth individuals.
- Founders facing liquidity events.

Brings:

- Expertise.
- Strategy.
- Structure.

You're the CEO of your life.

But even CEOs need a great CFO.

7. Action Steps

1. **Evaluate Your Net Worth Complexity**
2. **List Your Financial Priorities**
3. **Assess Time and Expertise Available**

4. **Interview at Least Three Advisors**
5. **Verify Fiduciary Status**
6. **Check Credentials**
7. **Ask About Founder-Specific Experience**
8. **Understand the Fee Structure**
9. **Get References**
10. **Decide: DIY, Hire, or Hybrid**

You didn't bootstrap a company on luck alone.

You built it on vision, strategy, and execution.

Your wealth deserves the same.

DIY can work.

Until it doesn't.

Professionals can't guarantee success.

But they dramatically increase your odds.

Whether you choose DIY or professional guidance, choose intentionally.

Choose wisely.

Because this isn't just money.

It's your legacy.

Make one money move before you go to bed tonight. Just one. And then do another next week.

Sketch out your financial blueprint.

Interview an advisor.

Audit your DIY processes.

Chapter 25: Hiring a Wealth Manager

When to Seek Professional Financial Help

As a tech founder, there comes a point when the financial complexity of your life outgrows DIY spreadsheets and gut decisions. Your wealth isn't a paycheck-to-paycheck situation anymore; it's an intricate web of equity grants, private investments, tax traps, and legacy questions.

Knowing when to seek professional financial help is crucial. There's no flashing neon sign telling you it's time. Instead, there are subtle, but important, signals:

- Your company's valuation is climbing, but so are your tax worries.
- You've got significant stock options, RSUs, or illiquid equity, and you're unsure when and how to unlock their value.
- You're experiencing liquidity events or tender offers and wondering about the long-term impact.
- Your personal financial goals (buying a home, funding children's education, creating a charitable foundation) feel distant and disconnected from your current financial activity.
- You're ready to stop managing your wealth reactively and start planning proactively.

If any of these resonate, it's time to consider working with a wealth manager.

What a Wealth Manager Does

A wealth manager is more than someone who picks stocks or rebalances a portfolio. Think of a wealth manager as your personal CFO.

Their role is comprehensive:

1. **Holistic Financial Planning**: They consider every aspect of your financial life — investments, taxes, estate planning, insurance, philanthropy, cash flow, and business interests.
2. **Investment Management**: They design and execute an investment strategy tailored to your goals, risk tolerance, time horizon, and liquidity needs.
3. **Tax Strategy**: They work to minimize your lifetime tax liability through proactive planning around stock sales, charitable contributions, and strategic relocations.
4. **Estate and Legacy Planning**: They help structure your assets to not only serve you during your lifetime but support your family and causes you care about for generations.
5. **Business Succession Planning**: If you're transitioning out of a startup, they help strategize what's next, whether it's retirement, launching another venture, or moving into angel investing.
6. **Risk Management**: They ensure you have the right protections in place, including liability coverage, umbrella policies, and personal cybersecurity measures.
7. **Philanthropic Planning**: They guide you in establishing donor-advised funds, private foundations, or charitable trusts if giving back is part of your vision.

Benefits of Working with an Advisor

Partnering with a wealth manager offers profound benefits that go beyond financial returns.

1. Expertise and Experience

Wealth managers specialize in the exact challenges you face. They understand the nuances of tech founder equity, pre-IPO planning, secondary market liquidity, and the psychology of sudden wealth.

2. Time Freedom

Managing significant wealth is a full-time job. Delegating to a professional frees up your time and mental energy for what you do best — building, innovating, and leading.

3. Customization

Your financial situation is unique. A great wealth manager tailors strategies to you — not a one-size-fits-all solution, but a bespoke plan designed for your goals and values.

4. Tax Efficiency

With significant equity positions and business exits come significant tax bills. Wealth managers design strategies to minimize taxes legally and efficiently.

5. Emotional Detachment

Money can evoke fear, greed, and indecision. A wealth manager provides a rational, disciplined approach to managing investments and financial decisions.

6. Coordination of Advisors

Your wealth manager becomes the quarterback of your financial team, coordinating with CPAs, estate attorneys, insurance specialists, and business advisors.

7. Legacy and Impact Planning

A wealth manager helps ensure that your financial success extends beyond you — supporting your family, your community, and the causes you care about.

Real-World Scenario

Imagine you're a founder with $50 million in illiquid private company shares. You're pre-IPO, facing an AMT bomb from ISO exercises, and wondering if you should move to Texas or Florida to reduce state income taxes before the liquidity event.

On top of that, you want to set up a donor-advised fund to support education initiatives.

Without professional help, you're trying to:

- Navigate complex tax law.
- Analyze liquidity strategies.
- Evaluate estate planning tools.
- Optimize charitable giving.

All while running your company.

A seasoned wealth manager can design a plan that addresses all of these, helping you unlock liquidity, mitigate taxes, protect your wealth, and achieve your personal and philanthropic goals.

A Call to Action

Start by interviewing wealth managers. Ask about their experience with founders, their investment philosophy, their planning process, and their fee structure.

And remember, this isn't just about managing money.

It's about:

- Managing complexity.
- Maximizing opportunities.
- Minimizing risks.
- Creating a life and legacy that reflect your values.

You built your business with vision and strategy.

Your financial life deserves the same care.

Make one move today: Schedule an introductory call with a wealth manager. Your future self will thank you.

(If you're ready to start that conversation, I'm here to help. Reach out to me, Pat Brown, at info@techbusinessfounders.com or visit www.techbusinessfounders.com. Let's build the next phase of your legacy.)

Final Note

This isn't about abdicating responsibility for your financial future.

It's about bringing in the right partners to help you:

- Navigate the complexity.

- Seize the opportunities.
- Protect what you've built.

It's about ensuring that your wealth — hard-earned, hard-won — becomes a tool for freedom, impact, and peace of mind.

Hiring a wealth manager isn't a sign of weakness.

It's a sign of wisdom.

You didn't build a groundbreaking company just to live with financial anxiety.

You built it to create freedom.

Let's make sure your financial life reflects that.

[Pat Brown LinkedIn: https://www.linkedin.com/in/patrick-brown-mba-5a75b08/]

Chapter 26: What to Look for in a Wealth Manager

Your wealth as a tech founder is complex. It's volatile, concentrated, and highly illiquid—until it isn't. You've spent years pouring everything you have—time, energy, relationships—into your company. Now, whether you're still in growth mode or eyeing a major liquidity event, you need someone in your corner who understands not just wealth, but *founder wealth*.

And here's the truth: Not all wealth managers are created equal.

The wrong advisor can cost you millions in opportunity. The right one can help you not only protect what you've built but amplify it—turning a successful exit into generational wealth.

This chapter is about helping you know what to look for when hiring a wealth manager—and what to avoid. Whether you're interviewing firms or thinking about it for the first time, consider this your founder's checklist.

Let's dive in.

1. Credentials and Experience Matter — More Than You Think

When it comes to finding a wealth manager, the first thing you want to examine is professional credibility.

Are they qualified to advise someone with your specific financial profile?

Founders need more than a generalist. They need someone who understands the intersection of entrepreneurship, equity compensation, tax strategy, liquidity planning, and legacy building.

Here's what to look for:

Look for the Right Letters After Their Name

- **CFP® (Certified Financial Planner):** This is the gold standard. A CFP® has undergone rigorous training in financial planning, tax planning, retirement, insurance, and estate planning.
- **CFA® (Chartered Financial Analyst):** If you're looking for heavy expertise in investments, this designation signals serious chops in portfolio management and analysis.
- **CPA (Certified Public Accountant):** Useful for those wealth managers who integrate deep tax planning into their services.
- **MBA (Master of Business Administration):** An MBA is particularly valuable for founders. It suggests a manager who not only understands personal finance but also business finance—meaning they can think about your wealth from the perspective of an operator and strategist, not just a number cruncher.

Founder-Focused Experience

Having the right credentials is important. But you also want someone who has worked with tech founders before—especially if they've guided others through major exits, stock option planning, and liquidity events.

Ask:

- "How many founders have you worked with?"
- "Can you share examples of clients with similar profiles to mine?"
- "What's your experience navigating pre-IPO liquidity strategies or QSBS planning?"

You're looking for real-world experience, not just a pretty resume.

2. Understanding Fee Structures

Let's talk money—specifically how your wealth manager gets paid.

Fee-Only vs. Commission-Based

- **Fee-Only:** These advisors charge a flat fee, hourly fee, or percentage of assets under management (AUM). They don't earn commissions on products they sell. This is the gold standard for transparency.
- **Commission-Based:** These advisors earn money when they sell insurance policies, annuities, or mutual funds. This can create conflicts of interest—you don't want your wealth manager recommending products because they get paid more.
- **Fee-Based:** This is a hybrid. They may charge fees but also earn commissions. If you go this route, make sure you understand exactly how they're compensated.

What's Normal?

For assets under management, 1% of your portfolio annually is standard for the first $1 million. Larger portfolios often have a sliding scale. Ultra-high-net-worth clients can negotiate lower fees.

But fees aren't the whole story. The real question is *value.*

If your wealth manager saves you millions in taxes, helps structure your portfolio for long-term growth, and guides you through a successful exit—you'll find their fee is worth every penny.

3. Evaluating Fit and Communication Style

Choosing a wealth manager isn't just about credentials and cost. It's about *fit.*

You're trusting this person with the financial legacy you've worked so hard to build. You'll be sharing details about your goals, fears, dreams, and failures. This is a high-trust relationship.

So ask yourself:

- **Do they listen more than they talk?**
- **Do they educate without being condescending?**
- **Do they seem to genuinely care about your goals—not just your assets?**
- **Can they explain complex concepts (like AMT, QSBS, or 10b5-1 plans) in plain language?**

Great wealth managers don't make you feel stupid. They make you feel smart, empowered, and confident.

Communication Frequency

You also want to be clear about how often you'll meet and what support looks like between meetings.

- Quarterly reviews?
- Ad hoc strategy sessions before a funding round or liquidity event?
- Annual deep dives on tax and estate planning?
- Are they accessible when life throws you a curveball?

The relationship should feel proactive, not reactive.

4. Look for a True Team, Not a Lone Ranger

Wealth management for tech founders isn't a one-person show.

You want a wealth manager who works as part of a coordinated team—bringing in tax experts, estate attorneys, insurance specialists, investment strategists, and even business succession planners.

Think of it like this: You're the CEO of your life and wealth. Your wealth manager should act like a personal CFO—coordinating the entire team so you don't have to.

Ask:

- "Do you work with CPAs and estate planning attorneys?"
- "Will you coordinate with my business attorney if needed?"
- "How do you approach liquidity events from a team perspective?"

5. Specialized Planning for Founders

Many wealth managers are fantastic with typical high-net-worth clients—executives, doctors, retirees. But founders? Founders are different.

Your wealth is likely tied up in illiquid assets—stock options, private shares, ownership interests. You might have AMT risk, QSBS planning opportunities, tender offers to evaluate, and the need to diversify post-IPO without tanking your company's stock price.

You need someone who speaks that language fluently.

Look for a manager who offers:

- **Equity compensation planning:** ISOs, NSOs, RSUs, and 83(b) elections.
- **Liquidity event planning:** Secondary sales, tender offers, pre-IPO loans.
- **Tax optimization:** AMT mitigation, QSBS strategies, domicile planning.
- **Legacy planning:** GRATs, IDGTs, DAFs, charitable trusts.

- **Risk management:** Hedging strategies, cybersecurity protections, D&O coverage reviews.
- **Lifestyle planning:** Cash flow projections post-exit, investment policy statements tailored to founder wealth.

6. Red Flags to Avoid

Sometimes it's not just about what a wealth manager *has*—it's about what they *lack*.

Be cautious of:

- **Product pushers:** If they spend more time pitching insurance or annuities than understanding your equity structure—walk.
- **One-size-fits-all portfolios:** You're not a mass-market investor. You're a founder with unique risk exposure.
- **Overpromising returns:** If it sounds too good to be true, it is.
- **Poor communication:** If it's hard to get a meeting or they don't return calls—keep looking.
- **Limited founder experience:** This can't be their first rodeo. You need expertise born of experience.

7. Questions to Ask During the Interview

When you sit down with a potential wealth manager, come prepared. Here are key questions to ask:

- "What's your experience working with founders?"
- "How do you charge for your services?"
- "What's your approach to equity compensation planning?"
- "Can you walk me through how you'd help me prepare for a liquidity event?"
- "How do you coordinate tax, estate, and investment planning?"
- "Who else will be on my advisory team?"

- "How often will we meet, and what do those meetings cover?"

Their answers will tell you everything you need to know.

8. Building a Long-Term Relationship

Hiring a wealth manager isn't a one-and-done decision. It's the start of a long-term relationship.

As your life evolves—marriage, kids, liquidity events, new ventures, philanthropy, retirement—your financial needs will evolve too.

You want someone who can grow with you. Someone who sees not just the founder you are today, but the multi-dimensional legacy-builder you're becoming.

Look for a manager who's in it for the long haul—not just the IPO.

9. How Pat Brown, MBA, Helps Tech Founders

When you're ready to build a financial future as ambitious as your startup vision, you don't want just any advisor. You want a strategic partner who *gets it.*

That's where I come in.

With an MBA background, 20+ years of experience, and a founder-first approach, I help tech entrepreneurs:

- Navigate complex equity compensation plans.
- Structure smart pre- and post-liquidity strategies.
- Mitigate taxes creatively and legally.
- Build diversified investment portfolios.
- Create legacy plans that honor their families and their futures.
- Coordinate with top-tier CPAs, attorneys, and private bankers to quarterback the entire financial plan.

This isn't cookie-cutter wealth management. This is bespoke, founder-specific planning designed to turn today's success into tomorrow's freedom and impact.

Let's build your financial legacy—intentionally, intelligently, and ambitiously.

Want to start a conversation?

Reach out:

📧 **info@techbusinessfounders.com**

🌐 **www.techbusinessfounders.com**

🔗 LinkedIn – Patrick Brown, MBA

A Call to Act:

Make one move before you go to bed tonight. Schedule an initial conversation with a wealth manager—or review your current one. And next week? Start building your personal financial dream team. Because you deserve it.

Chapter 27: How Pat Brown Can Facilitate the Journey

The life of a tech founder is one defined by volatility, vision, and velocity. The path you take to build a company from scratch—the highs, the lows, the late nights, the hard decisions—demands an exceptional level of commitment and skill. Managing your personal finances requires that same level of discipline and expertise.

Yet, the financial complexities you face as a tech founder go well beyond the reach of traditional wealth management. Your situation is distinct: concentrated equity positions, stock options, pre-IPO shares, liquidity event tax traps, and the ever-looming task of turning paper wealth into real, lasting security.

You don't need a generalist.

You need a founder-centric, customized financial strategy.

That's where I, Pat Brown, MBA, come in.

Founder-Centric, Customized Financial Planning

Unlike traditional financial planning firms that might treat you like any other high-net-worth client, my approach starts with one fundamental belief:

Your wealth isn't just numbers. It's personal. It's strategic. It's dynamic.

I focus solely on working with entrepreneurs, founders, and innovators like you. Because building wealth through a tech company is different.

What makes my approach founder-centric?

- **Understanding Your Lifecycle:** From seed to Series A, from Series C to pre-IPO to exit—I've seen the founder's arc and understand how your financial needs evolve.
- **Stock Option Strategy:** ISOs, NSOs, RSUs, 83(b) elections, and QSBS tax treatments aren't buzzwords—they're tools we deploy strategically.
- **Liquidity Event Planning:** Secondary sales, tender offers, structured loans, and pre-IPO planning are part of the custom roadmaps I design.
- **Risk Mitigation:** I help you hedge concentrated positions, manage AMT, and diversify without derailing your potential upside.
- **Legacy and Lifestyle Planning:** Beyond the exit, it's about freedom, family, philanthropy, and future ventures. We create a plan that honors it all.

Every plan is tailored, founder-specific, and future-focused.

Coordination with Tax, Legal, and Investment Teams

Financial independence is a team sport.

That's why my work extends beyond creating spreadsheets and asset allocations. I quarterback an integrated team—or collaborate with yours—to ensure your tax, legal, and investment strategies are working in concert.

- **Tax Coordination:** AMT exposure, QSBS qualification, tax-loss harvesting, Roth conversions during low-income years, and maximizing the benefits of domicile strategies—all timed and tailored to your liquidity and income trajectory.
- **Legal Coordination:** We engage with attorneys to set up trusts, private foundations, donor-advised funds, and customized estate plans that not only secure your legacy but optimize your tax position.
- **Investment Strategy:** Public equities, bonds, private equity, venture

funds, real estate, structured notes, and direct indexing—we construct a personalized, diversified portfolio aligned with your liquidity needs, risk tolerance, and long-term goals.

Your world doesn't operate in silos. Neither should your wealth plan.

My role is to simplify, synchronize, and elevate every aspect of your financial journey.

Long-Term Partnership to Guide Every Financial Stage

Founders are different.

You're not building wealth for the next quarter—you're building for the next generation.

That's why I view our relationship not as a transactional engagement but as a long-term partnership. One that evolves alongside you:

- **Early-Stage:** Helping you manage personal cash flow, strategize around early equity grants, and build a defensive foundation while you grow your company.
- **Growth Stage:** Planning liquidity timelines, managing risk exposure, and maximizing tax advantages through key company milestones.
- **Exit Stage:** Structuring liquidity events, harvesting tax opportunities, and transitioning from founder to investor without losing momentum.
- **Post-Exit Stage:** Crafting a sustainable investment strategy, scaling philanthropy, teaching the next generation, and building enduring wealth.

Founders deserve founder-specific financial advice—not a recycled retirement plan built for a W-2 employee.

Why Work With Me, Pat Brown, MBA?

My foundation isn't just built on finance—it's built on *founders.*

I've spent decades working with entrepreneurs who, like you, have poured everything into their companies. I understand the personal risks, the emotional ups and downs, and the nuanced decisions you face.

And as an MBA, I bring a rigorous, business-savvy perspective to personal finance. I don't just see your wealth—I see your entrepreneurial DNA embedded in it.

When you work with me, you get:

- Deep expertise in founder-specific financial planning.
- A fiduciary partner whose only agenda is your success.
- Clear, plain-language advice—no jargon, no BS.
- Proactive strategies to protect, grow, and transition your wealth.
- A personal CFO for your life—who knows that wealth is about more than just money. It's about freedom.

Let's Build Your Financial Legacy

If you've made it to this chapter, chances are you're not just a founder.

You're a visionary. A builder. A person who understands that while exits create opportunity, *planning* creates freedom.

I'm here to help you:

- Claim your financial freedom.
- Build a legacy that extends beyond your business.
- Sleep better at night knowing your wealth is working as hard as you do.

Let's get started.

Contact Pat Brown, MBA

✉ **Email:** info@techbusinessfounders.com

🌐 **Website:** www.techbusinessfounders.com

🔗 **LinkedIn:** Patrick Brown, MBA

A Call to Act:

Make one move tonight—book a call, send an email, or simply make the decision to stop "winging it" with your financial future. Just one move. And next week? Let's map the next 20 years.

Because you didn't come this far just to come this far.

Your future self will thank you.

So will your family.

So will your legacy.

And yes—so will your peace of mind.

Chapter 28: My Wealth Management Process

Discovery, Design, and Execution

Let's begin at the beginning. Before a plan is made, before numbers are crunched, before any investments are considered, the most important part of the process is discovery.

Discovery is about understanding you.

And not just your balance sheet or your cap table. It's about understanding who you are, what you care about, how you think, and what you dream about—especially once the hectic pace of building your company starts to slow down. Discovery isn't a quick questionnaire or a one-and-done meeting. It's a series of honest, thoughtful conversations.

The Discovery Process

We dive deep into:

- Your story: How did you get here? What's your origin story?
- Your goals: What does success look like for you beyond your company?
- Your values: What matters more to you—impact or accumulation? Freedom or influence?
- Your current financial picture: Assets, liabilities, cash flow, equity positions, investment accounts, real estate, and more.
- Your blind spots: What haven't you thought about yet? Where are the risks you might not see coming?

Discovery is about depth over speed. If this process takes three meetings, great. If it takes six, even better. We're not in a rush.

The better we understand you, the better we can design a plan that works for you—not just a plan that looks good on paper.

The Design Process

Once we've done the hard work of discovery, we move to design.

Design is where we build the financial blueprint. It's where strategy meets reality.

Here's what it involves:

- **Cash flow and liquidity planning:** How much cash do you need on hand today, and how much should you plan to access in the next 3, 5, or 10 years?
- **Equity strategy:** How to handle your concentrated stock positions—whether that's through gradual liquidation, hedging, gifting strategies, or diversification.
- **Tax strategy:** How to minimize taxes legally and smartly, from AMT management to QSBS qualification to Roth conversions.
- **Investment portfolio design:** Building an allocation strategy that reflects your goals, time horizon, and tolerance for risk—across public markets, private investments, real estate, and more.
- **Estate and legacy planning:** How do you want your wealth to impact your family, your causes, your community?
- **Insurance and risk management:** Protecting what you're building from the unexpected—disability, liability, life insurance.
- **Philanthropy and impact:** Whether through donor-advised funds, private foundations, or direct charitable giving.

Everything is customized. No cookie-cutter portfolios. No templated advice.

The Execution Process

Design without execution is a nice idea.

Execution is where your financial plan becomes real.

We help:

- Coordinate the professionals you already work with—your CPA, your attorney, your family office, your board.
- Select and manage investment vehicles aligned with your strategy.
- Review and adjust liquidity strategies based on your company's growth and exits.
- Implement estate strategies to protect and preserve wealth.
- Integrate philanthropic strategies without disrupting your personal financial goals.

Execution is ongoing. It's proactive. It's not a one-time set-it-and-forget-it.

Ongoing Review and Strategy Adjustment

Life changes. Markets shift. New laws get passed. Opportunities emerge. Risks evolve.

That's why ongoing review is a non-negotiable part of our wealth management process.

Here's how we stay on top of it:

- **Quarterly review meetings:** Where are we? What's changed? What needs to be updated?
- **Annual strategic refresh:** Is the overall strategy still aligned with your life and goals?
- **Tactical adjustments as needed:** Maybe the IPO window opens, and it's time to revisit a liquidity strategy. Maybe new tax laws create opportunities to save. Maybe your personal life changes—marriage, divorce, kids, relocation.

We're not reactive. We're anticipatory.

We don't just build the plan—we walk with you as the plan evolves.

Helping Founders Build Sustainable Wealth

If you're reading this book, you probably already know that building a company is one of the hardest things you can do.

Building sustainable wealth afterward can be just as tricky.

The challenges are real:

- Concentrated risk in your company's equity.
- Volatile cash flows.
- Massive tax exposures.
- Lifestyle creep.
- Pressure to invest in friends' startups or do "smart" deals.
- Legacy and estate complexities.

That's why a wealth management process designed specifically for tech founders matters.

Because what got you here—vision, hustle, resilience—isn't the same skill set that will help you manage, protect, and grow wealth for the next 40 years.

You deserve a process that's as sophisticated as the business you've built.

You deserve a partner who gets it—someone who understands how tech wealth is created, how it grows, and how it can be lost.

That's the point of everything we've designed.

A founder-centric, custom-built, real-world process that turns business success into financial peace of mind.

Contact Pat Brown

Email: info@techbusinessfounders.com

Website: www.techbusinessfounders.com

LinkedIn: Patrick Brown, MBA

Call to Act:

Make one money move before you go to bed tonight. Just one. And then do another next week.

You've got this.

And if you want a guide to help you get there—you know where to find me.

Chapter 29: Estate Planning Basics

Building a groundbreaking company demands vision, sacrifice, and relentless energy. But if all that work ends without a plan for what happens next, your achievements risk slipping away. Estate planning is not just a "rich person" exercise. It's about protecting your legacy, your family, and your life's work—whether you're worth $5 million or $500 million.

Most founders think estate planning is something for later. After the IPO. After the acquisition. After "someday." But life has its own timeline, and the best time to plan is now.

Let's break it down, piece by piece—no legal jargon, no scare tactics. Just real talk about how to protect what you've built.

Why Estate Planning Matters

You didn't hustle to create wealth only to leave it vulnerable. Estate planning matters because:

- **You Want to Decide**: Without a will or trust, the state decides who gets what.
- **You Want to Protect**: Without careful planning, taxes can wipe out a chunk of your wealth.
- **You Want to Provide**: For your spouse, your children, your causes—in a way that's intentional, not accidental.
- **You Want to Preserve**: Your company's future, your investments,

your philanthropic legacy.

Failing to plan isn't just an oversight. It's a risk you can't afford.

Key Documents Every Founder Needs

1. **Will**
A will is the cornerstone of any estate plan. It spells out:

- Who gets what.
- Who manages the process (your executor).
- Who becomes the guardian of your minor children, if needed.

Without a will, state laws (called "intestacy laws") determine all of that—and it might not align with what you want.

2. **Living Trust**
A living trust isn't just for the ultra-wealthy. It lets you:

- Bypass the public, time-consuming probate process.
- Retain control over how and when your assets are distributed.
- Protect beneficiaries who may not be ready for a lump sum inheritance.

For founders with complex assets—private company stock, real estate, investments—trusts provide flexibility and protection.

3. **Durable Power of Attorney**
Who handles your finances if you're incapacitated? Who pays the bills, manages the investments, makes legal decisions? Without a durable power of attorney, courts may appoint someone for you.

A durable POA ensures it's someone you trust.

4. **Healthcare Power of Attorney & Living Will**

- **Healthcare POA**: Designates who makes medical decisions if you can't.
- **Living Will**: Specifies what kind of life-sustaining treatments you

want (or don't want).

These documents ensure your wishes are honored—and relieve your family of painful guesswork.

5. **Beneficiary Designations**

Your 401(k), IRA, and life insurance policies pass according to the beneficiary designations—not your will. Review them regularly.

A common pitfall? Founders forgetting to update beneficiaries after a divorce, marriage, or birth of a child.

Updating Your Plan After Major Life Events

Estate planning isn't "one and done." Major life events mean it's time for a refresh:

- Marriage
- Divorce
- Birth or adoption of a child
- Significant wealth events (IPO, acquisition)
- Starting or selling a business
- Major real estate purchases
- Death of a spouse or heir

Think of your estate plan like a business plan—it evolves.

Special Considerations for Tech Founders

1. **Private Company Stock**

Your biggest asset may be illiquid. Planning for:

- How it will be valued.
- Who will manage it.
- How heirs can convert it to cash if needed.

2. **Concentrated Positions**

   Too much wealth tied to one company? Explore:

   - Charitable Remainder Trusts (CRTs)
   - Grantor Retained Annuity Trusts (GRATs)
   - Family Limited Partnerships (FLPs)

These structures can reduce taxes and transfer wealth efficiently.

3. **Philanthropy and Legacy**

   You've changed the world with your company. Why stop there? Consider:

   - **Donor-Advised Funds (DAFs)**
   - **Private Foundations**
   - **Charitable Trusts**

Giving back isn't just good for the soul—it's smart tax strategy.

Common Mistakes Founders Make

- **Procrastination**: Waiting until "someday"—which never comes.
- **DIY Estate Planning**: You're a founder, not an estate attorney. Complex wealth needs expert guidance.
- **Not Coordinating with Other Advisors**: Your estate plan must align with your tax strategy, investment portfolio, and business succession plan.
- **Ignoring State Laws**: Estate laws vary by state. Domicile planning matters.

Action Steps

1. **Take Inventory**: List all your assets—company equity, investments, real estate, insurance policies.
2. **Meet with an Estate Planning Attorney**: Preferably one who understands founders and complex assets.
3. **Draft Core Documents**: Will, trust, POA, healthcare directives.
4. **Update Beneficiaries**: Make sure designations reflect your current wishes.
5. **Communicate**: Talk with your family about your wishes. Clarity now avoids conflict later.
6. **Review Regularly**: Life changes, laws change—so should your plan.

Estate Planning is Wealth Planning

Think of estate planning not as an end-of-life task, but as part of your overall wealth strategy.

It's about:

- Maximizing what you leave behind.
- Minimizing taxes.
- Protecting your family.
- Preserving your legacy.

It's the final stage of entrepreneurship—building not just a company, but a life well-lived and a legacy well-protected.

You've built something extraordinary.

Now—make sure it outlives you.

A Call to Act:

Before you go to bed tonight, take one action toward protecting your legacy:

- Schedule a consultation with an estate planning attorney.

- Review your beneficiary designations.
- Make a list of who you'd want to handle your affairs if something happened.

Just one move tonight.

Another next week.

Keep going.

Your future—and your family's future—will thank you.

This isn't just about wealth.

This is about dignity.

This is about freedom.

This is about legacy.

You didn't build your company to leave its future to chance.

You didn't work this hard to watch others decide your family's future.

Estate planning is your final act of leadership.

Your future self will thank you.

So will your family.

So will every generation that follows.

Stay the course. Build your legacy with the same precision and passion you built your business.

Chapter 30: GRATs and IDGTs for Founders

If you've made it to the point where you're considering wealth transfer strategies, congratulations. You've reached a level few ever do. You're not just building a company. You're building a legacy. And legacy requires its own skill set — its own strategies — just like building a company did.

The truth is, at this level of success, you face a new kind of risk. It's not operational. It's not product-market fit. It's not your competitors.

It's the IRS.

Without planning, the IRS could claim 40% or more of your hard-earned wealth at your death through estate taxes. But with the right strategy? You can minimize — even eliminate — that exposure.

Enter two of the most powerful tools in the ultra-affluent founder's playbook: GRATs (Grantor Retained Annuity Trusts) and IDGTs (Intentionally Defective Grantor Trusts).

These aren't exotic. They aren't black magic. They are tested, vetted, and proven. They are how the ultra-wealthy preserve wealth across generations.

Let's walk through it — clearly, calmly, and practically.

1. What Is a GRAT?

A GRAT, or Grantor Retained Annuity Trust, is an irrevocable trust structure. You, as the grantor, contribute assets into the trust — often pre-IPO shares or other appreciating assets. In exchange, the trust agrees to pay you an annuity — a fixed payment — over a set number of years.

At the end of that term, anything left over in the trust — above and beyond the IRS-assumed rate of return (the Section 7520 rate) — passes to your beneficiaries (typically your children) free of gift or estate tax.

The genius of the GRAT is in the difference between reality and assumption. If your assets outperform the IRS's low assumed rate, that extra growth bypasses taxes and lands directly in your heirs' hands.

1.1 Why Is This Powerful for a Founder?

Because pre-IPO stock is often undervalued relative to its true long-term potential. You are sitting on the very type of asset that GRATs were born to amplify — high-growth, high-potential, early-stage wealth. The IRS locks in today's value; your company's trajectory does the heavy lifting.

If you set it up right — if your company's shares appreciate significantly while in the trust — most of that upside passes to your heirs with no additional tax burden.

2. Real-World GRAT Example

Imagine you transfer $5 million worth of your pre-IPO shares into a GRAT today. The IRS assumes that those shares will grow at the Section 7520 rate — say, 3%.

But your company, your vision, your execution — grows those shares tenfold.

By the end of the GRAT's term — maybe five or seven years — your $5 million has become $50 million.

You've been paid back your annuity along the way, slowly "zeroing out" the value you transferred. And that $45 million in excess appreciation?

It passes to your children or heirs, estate-tax free.

No additional gift tax.

No estate tax.

Just generational wealth — created by your ingenuity, protected by your planning.

3. Why GRATs Work Best Pre-IPO

The timing here is critical. Pre-IPO, your shares are valued by appraisal, typically with discounts for lack of marketability and minority interest. Translation: a lower valuation.

Once your company goes public, the valuation shifts to market value — and it's much higher.

The pre-IPO window is when the IRS is most lenient about valuation — and when your company's potential for explosive growth is greatest.

If you're on the cusp of a liquidity event, or if you're still a few years out but scaling fast, the time to set up a GRAT is now.

Catch the low valuation.

Capture the upside.

Preserve the wealth.

4. What Is an IDGT?

The Intentionally Defective Grantor Trust, or IDGT, sounds complicated. And in a way, it is — but the basic concept is simple.

You sell assets — say, your private company stock — to the trust in exchange for a promissory note. The trust now owns the appreciating asset. You receive the note — and the promise of repayment with modest interest, typically pegged to the IRS's applicable federal rate (AFR).

The "defect" comes into play for tax purposes. For income tax purposes, you still own the trust — meaning you're personally responsible for paying any taxes due on the trust's income. But for estate tax purposes? The trust is separate — and outside your taxable estate.

Why is that powerful?

Because the trust's assets can grow tax-free. You're paying the tax bill out of your pocket — leaving the assets inside the trust to compound, untouched and untaxed.

And by freezing the value at the time of sale, you effectively lock in today's lower valuation for estate tax purposes.

5. Real-World IDGT Example

Let's say you transfer $10 million of your pre-IPO stock into an IDGT. In return, the trust issues you a promissory note promising to pay you $10 million plus 3% annual interest over a set period.

Now, your company goes public.

Your $10 million stake explodes to $100 million in value.

But the trust's obligation to you hasn't changed — it still only owes you the original $10 million plus the 3% interest.

All that extra $90 million in growth?

It stays inside the trust.

Outside your estate.

No estate tax.

No gift tax (assuming a properly structured sale).

Just leveraged legacy.

6. GRATs vs. IDGTs: Which Should You Use?

This isn't a binary choice. Many founders use both.

GRATs are best when:

- You want minimal or no gift tax exposure.
- You want a "no risk" transfer — if the asset underperforms, it just reverts to you.
- You prefer to receive annuity payments back to yourself.

IDGTs are best when:

- You want to freeze an asset's value for estate tax purposes.
- You're comfortable paying the trust's income taxes personally.
- You prefer a more flexible trust design — for example, allowing generation-skipping transfer tax (GST) planning.

Each tool has strengths. Each fits a different stage of your wealth journey.

Smart founders layer them strategically.

7. Timing Is Everything

If you take only one thing from this chapter, let it be this: timing is everything.

The single biggest driver of GRAT or IDGT success is catching a low valuation.

- Before the IPO.
- After a down round.
- During a market correction.

The lower the valuation when you transfer the assets, the greater the upside your heirs will capture tax-free.

Once your company is public, once the markets price in all the growth you've created, it's too late. The IRS sees that value — and so do estate tax calculators.

Move early.

Move thoughtfully.

Move now.

8. Action Steps to Take

- **Talk to your estate attorney.** Find one experienced in GRATs and IDGTs for founders. This isn't DIY territory.
- **Get a qualified appraisal.** You'll need defensible valuation numbers. The IRS scrutinizes low valuations closely.
- **Align your wealth manager and CPA.** These are not standalone strategies. Your investment, tax, and estate plans must be coordinated.
- **Model different scenarios.** What happens if your company triples? If it tanks? Model it out.
- **Move quickly.** If you're within two years of a liquidity event, the clock is ticking.

9. Pros and Cons of GRATs and IDGTs

GRAT Pros:

- Minimal to no gift tax if structured properly.
- Retain some income via annuity payments.
- IRS-accepted, straightforward structure.

GRAT Cons:

- Must survive the term of the GRAT.
- No benefit if assets underperform the Section 7520 rate.

IDGT Pros:

- Freezes asset value at today's lower levels.
- All future appreciation passes outside your estate.
- Highly flexible in trust terms.

IDGT Cons:

- You personally pay income taxes.
- Slightly more complex to set up and administer.

10. Real-Life Founder Stories

Founder A set up an IDGT two years before their IPO, selling $5 million of private shares to the trust. Post-IPO, those shares were worth $50 million. The excess appreciation stayed outside their estate — a $20 million+ estate tax savings.

Founder B transferred $10 million into a GRAT just after a down round. Over the next five years, the company grew 10x. Their heirs received the appreciation tax-free, with minimal gift tax exposure.

Two founders. Two strategies. One common theme: legacy preservation through thoughtful planning.

11. Why It Matters

You built something remarkable. Something rare.

But without careful planning, the IRS could be your biggest creditor at death.

40% — or more — of your wealth, gone.

But it doesn't have to be that way.

GRATs and IDGTs — properly timed, properly structured — are your playbook for keeping what you've built. For your family. For your foundation. For the world you want to impact.

Because real success isn't just about creating wealth. It's about preserving it. Protecting it. Directing it.

This is where founders become architects — not just of companies, but of legacies.

Leadership Beyond Liquidity

This isn't about loopholes. This isn't about beating the system.

This is about leadership.

Leadership of your family's future.

Leadership of your values.

Leadership that extends far beyond your IPO or liquidity event.

You didn't build your company by accident. You built it with foresight, strategy, and resilience.

Now — build your legacy the same way.

Start tonight. Write down the name of a trusted estate planning attorney. Or ask your wealth manager for a recommendation. Book a call. Take one small step.

Because in wealth — as in startups — the biggest moves often start with the smallest steps.

Chapter 31: Charitable Giving with Impact

When you think about the wealth you've built, the innovation you've driven, the risks you've taken—it's only natural to think about the legacy you want to leave behind. For many tech founders, philanthropy isn't just a feel-good afterthought. It's an integral part of a holistic financial life—one that fuses money with meaning, and legacy with leverage.

But just like your journey from founder to exit wasn't accidental, impactful charitable giving isn't either. It demands as much strategic thought as any product launch or funding round. And the best news? Done correctly, charitable giving can not only align with your values but also deliver tangible tax and estate planning benefits.

Let's walk through what that really looks like.

Why Charitable Giving Matters for Founders

The first and most important truth: you don't have to wait until you've "made it" to start giving with impact. In fact, some of the best opportunities to amplify your giving — and reduce your tax bill — come well before a big liquidity event.

When structured intentionally, charitable contributions can:

- Minimize current and future tax liabilities.

- Remove highly appreciated assets from your estate.
- Amplify the long-term impact of your dollars.
- Embed your personal values into your financial legacy.

More than that, thoughtful philanthropy allows you to define success on your terms. You've already disrupted an industry—why not disrupt the status quo of traditional giving?

Structuring Giving Through DAFs and CRTs

There are many vehicles for charitable giving, but two of the most powerful for tech founders are Donor-Advised Funds (DAFs) and Charitable Remainder Trusts (CRTs). Let's unpack these in plain language.

Donor-Advised Funds (DAFs)

Think of a DAF as your "charitable investment account." You contribute cash, stock, or other assets to the fund and get an immediate tax deduction. Those assets can grow tax-free within the DAF, and you (or your heirs) can recommend grants to your favorite nonprofits over time.

Why DAFs Work for Founders:

- **Tax Timing Flexibility:** Make a large contribution in a high-income year (e.g., the year of an IPO or acquisition) and dole out the actual grants over many years.
- **Asset Flexibility:** Donate highly appreciated stock directly, avoiding capital gains tax.
- **Low Maintenance:** No annual tax filings, administrative overhead, or required distributions.

Common Pitfalls:

- Once you contribute, it's irrevocable—you can't take it back.
- Funds can only be granted to IRS-recognized 501(c)(3) organizations.

Charitable Remainder Trusts (CRTs)

A CRT is more complex but powerful. It's a split-interest trust: you transfer assets into the trust, and the trust pays you (or another beneficiary) a stream of income for a set term or life. When the trust ends, the remainder goes to charity.

Why CRTs Work for Founders:

- **Income Stream:** Convert highly appreciated assets into a lifetime income without an immediate capital gains hit.
- **Estate Reduction:** Remove large assets from your taxable estate.
- **Charitable Legacy:** Ensure substantial gifts to causes you care about.

Key Considerations:

- Must follow strict IRS rules for payout rates and terms.
- Irrevocable—once assets are in, they're committed.
- Upfront legal and administrative costs.

Tax Benefits of Charitable Contributions

Beyond the feel-good factor, the tax benefits of strategic charitable giving are significant.

1. **Immediate Income Tax Deduction:** Depending on the asset type and your adjusted gross income (AGI), you can deduct a significant percentage of your AGI in charitable contributions.
2. **Capital Gains Tax Avoidance:** When you donate appreciated assets (e.g., stock, real estate), you avoid realizing capital gains.
3. **Estate Tax Reduction:** Assets given to charity are removed from your estate, reducing potential estate taxes.
4. **Tax-Free Growth:** Assets in DAFs and CRTs grow tax-free until distributed.

Example: Let's say you have $10 million in pre-IPO stock with a $1 million basis. Selling it outright could trigger massive capital gains. Donating it to a DAF or CRT sidesteps that immediate tax hit.

Aligning Philanthropy with Personal Values

Charitable giving is most impactful when it's personal. This isn't about writing a check to whatever big-name nonprofit knocks on your door. It's about:

- **Defining Your Mission:** What causes matter to you? Education? Climate? Healthcare? Racial equity?
- **Identifying Strategic Partners:** Seek organizations aligned with your mission, ones that use resources effectively.
- **Measuring Impact:** Ask for metrics and transparency.

Your philanthropic strategy should feel as clear and intentional as your business strategy.

Pros and Cons of Charitable Giving Vehicles

Strategy Pros Cons

DAF

Immediate deduction, tax-free growth, flexible giving timeline

Irrevocable, administrative fees

CRT

Lifetime income stream, capital gains deferral, estate tax reduction

Complex setup, irrevocable, must comply with IRS rules

Action Steps: How to Get Started

1. **Meet with Your Advisors:** Tax, legal, and financial advisors should work together to design your giving strategy.
2. **Inventory Your Assets:** Identify highly appreciated assets.
3. **Define Your Mission:** Write a personal giving statement.
4. **Choose Your Vehicles:** DAF, CRT, or a combination?
5. **Start Small:** Set up a DAF and make a contribution.
6. **Review Annually:** Adjust your giving strategy as your life and liquidity change.

Breaking Down the Complex Ideas

What's a Donor-Advised Fund (DAF) Really?

- Think of it as a personal charitable foundation, but simpler.
- You get the tax break immediately but can give grants slowly.
- Assets inside the DAF grow tax-free.

What's a Charitable Remainder Trust (CRT) in Simple Terms?

- You give the asset to a trust.
- The trust pays you or someone you love income.
- After a set time, what's left goes to charity.

Real-Life Scenarios and Relatable Stories

Scenario 1: The IPO Year

Sara, a 35-year-old founder, is expecting a major liquidity event. She sets up a DAF and contributes $2 million in pre-IPO shares, locking in a tax deduction and bypassing capital gains. Over the next 20 years, she directs grants to causes she loves.

Scenario 2: The Serial Entrepreneur

Jason, 45, has already exited two companies. He funds a CRT with $10 million in stock. The CRT pays him an annual income. When he passes, the remaining $8 million funds scholarships for underrepresented students in STEM.

Scenario 3: The Legacy Builder

Elena, 55, wants her giving to outlast her lifetime. She establishes a family DAF, naming her children as successor advisors. Her legacy of giving will live on through her family.

Education, Empowerment, and Engagement

Education:

You now understand the basics: DAFs, CRTs, tax deductions, capital gains avoidance.

Empowerment:

You don't need to be Bill Gates to be strategic. Smart giving multiplies your impact.

Engagement:

Talk with your family. Make it a tradition. Giving is a muscle that strengthens with use.

A Call to Act

Make one money move before you go to bed tonight:

- Read about donor-advised funds.
- Write down three causes you're passionate about.
- Book a call with your wealth advisor.

Then make another move next week. The best time to start building your legacy was yesterday. The second-best time is now.

This isn't just about donations. It's about dignity. It's about freedom. It's about building a legacy that's bigger than you, one that stretches beyond balance sheets and bank accounts.

You didn't build a groundbreaking company just to walk away with a bigger number in your checking account. You built it to leave a mark.

Chapter 32: Risk Management for Entrepreneurs

Risk is a constant companion for every entrepreneur. It lurks in every investment, every strategic decision, and every innovation you dare to bring into the world. Yet for many founders, the focus is so heavily skewed toward growth and opportunity that risk management becomes an afterthought — until it's too late.

Here's the truth: successful wealth-building isn't about eliminating risk. It's about identifying it, respecting it, and managing it smartly.

If you're reading this chapter, you're likely already further along than most. You're asking the right questions. How do I protect what I'm building? How do I safeguard my future wealth against the unknown?

Let's walk through it together.

Identifying Key Financial Risks

The first step to managing risk is knowing where it hides.

1. Concentrated Stock Risk

As a founder, you're heavily exposed to your company's fortunes. Your wealth is tied to the company's valuation, and while that can create extraordinary upside, it can also expose you to devastating downside.

2. Liquidity Risk

Your net worth might look impressive on paper, but if it's locked in illiquid assets like private company stock or real estate, you could find yourself asset-rich but cash-poor — unable to fund your life, cover taxes, or seize opportunities.

3. Tax Risk

A sudden liquidity event — a big exit, IPO, or secondary sale — can trigger a massive tax bill if you haven't planned properly. Timing is everything. Structure is everything.

4. Market Risk

Even if you diversify, no portfolio is immune to broad market downturns. Investing is not about avoiding volatility — it's about preparing for it.

5. Legal and Liability Risk

Founders are often targets for lawsuits — whether from employees, customers, investors, or competitors. Without proper asset protection, your personal wealth could be at risk.

6. Personal Risk

Illness, disability, death. Founders often neglect personal insurance coverage in their rush to build the business. But without it, a tragedy can cascade into financial ruin for your family.

7. Inflation Risk

Today's dollars won't be tomorrow's dollars. If your portfolio isn't structured to outpace inflation over time, you're losing purchasing power quietly but steadily.

8. Succession Risk

If you plan to exit your business eventually (and you should), what's the plan? Lack of a clear succession strategy can torpedo enterprise value — and your legacy.

Building a Comprehensive Risk Management Plan

Identifying the risks is only half the job. Now comes the strategy.

1. Diversify Your Wealth

Start by gradually shifting from concentrated company stock into a broad, diversified portfolio. Think public equities, bonds, real estate, private investments, and alternatives.

Diversification doesn't guarantee no losses. But it does reduce the probability of catastrophic losses.

2. Build Liquidity Buffers

Create layers of liquidity:

- **Emergency Fund**: 6-12 months of personal living expenses.
- **Opportunity Fund**: Capital set aside for new investments.
- **Tax Reserve Fund**: Set aside taxes before you spend.

Liquidity gives you the power to stay patient, ride out downturns, and move fast when opportunities arise.

3. Smart Tax Planning

Work with tax professionals early and often. Consider strategies like:

- **QSBS Exemption**
- **Charitable Giving Strategies**
- **Opportunity Zone Investments**
- **Deferred Sales Trusts**

The right moves could save you millions.

4. Asset Protection

Use legal structures to separate personal and business assets. Consider:

- LLCs for real estate holdings.
- Proper use of insurance (D&O, E&O, umbrella coverage).
- Irrevocable trusts.

Get a solid estate plan. It's not just for the ultra-wealthy. It's for anyone who cares about what happens to their family.

5. Personal Insurance Coverage

Founders need more than basic insurance. Review:

- **Life Insurance**: Protect your family. Potentially fund buy-sell agreements.

- **Disability Insurance**: Your greatest asset is your ability to generate income.
- **Long-Term Care Insurance**: A rising cost few plan for.
- **Umbrella Liability Insurance**: Because lawsuits happen.

6. Inflation Protection

Tilt part of your portfolio to inflation-sensitive assets:

- Real estate
- Treasury Inflation-Protected Securities (TIPS)
- Commodities
- Equities (long-term growth)

7. Succession Planning

Start early. Build systems, processes, and leadership teams that can function without you. When the time comes to sell or transition, the company is worth more.

8. Mental Resilience

Risk isn't just numbers on a page. It's how you react under pressure. Build your emotional and mental resilience. Surround yourself with a team that brings calm, clarity, and discipline.

Periodically Reviewing Insurance Coverage

Insurance isn't a set-it-and-forget-it tool. Your life changes. Your business grows. Your needs evolve.

Review your coverage at least annually:

- Has your net worth increased?
- Have you acquired new assets?
- Have you sold assets?
- Have you moved states?

- Have you had children?
- Has the business valuation changed?

Work with an independent insurance advisor — not someone tied to selling specific products — to audit your coverage.

Remember, the goal isn't to pay for every conceivable risk. It's to cover the risks that would be financially devastating.

Real-Life Scenarios and Relatable Stories

You just closed a $50M Series C.

You're still pulling a $150K salary and living modestly. But your paper wealth is now enormous. What's the risk?

- Your concentration is 90% company stock.
- No liquidity.
- No estate plan.
- No insurance.

It's time to:

- Build an emergency and opportunity fund.
- Set up umbrella insurance.
- Draft your estate documents.
- Start working a staged diversification plan.

You're selling your company for $300M.

Your personal take will be $20M after taxes and fees. A life-changing number.

But:

- You have no tax strategy. Uncle Sam will take a big bite.
- You have no estate plan. Your heirs could face a 40% estate tax.

- You have no liquidity plan.

It's time to:

- Engage tax, legal, and investment advisors immediately.
- Structure charitable donations to reduce taxable income.
- Consider GRATs or IDGTs.

You're 45, worth $10M on paper, with two kids.

You've always been "self-insured" — no life insurance, minimal health insurance, no disability insurance.

But:

- What happens if you're disabled and can't work?
- What happens if you die suddenly?
- What happens if you're sued personally?

It's time to:

- Get a thorough insurance review.
- Set up appropriate coverage.
- Shield personal assets.

Education, Empowerment, Engagement

Risk management isn't sexy.

It's not the exciting pitch deck. It's not the glitzy IPO party. It's not the profile in Forbes.

But it's what turns "one-time wealth" into "lifetime wealth."

Founders who thrive over decades understand this. They play offense, but they also play defense.

And defense wins championships.

You don't have to become a risk management expert overnight. You just have to care enough to build the right team around you. CPA, estate planning attorney, insurance advisor, wealth manager.

You just have to care enough about your family's future, your legacy, your peace of mind.

You've already beaten enormous odds by building something from nothing. Now make sure you keep what you've built.

Call to Act

Tonight, before you go to bed, do one thing:

Make a list of the financial risks you know you haven't addressed yet.

Tomorrow, set a date to meet with a professional to start plugging the holes.

Start. Protect. Preserve.

You didn't come this far to lose it all to risks you can see coming.

This is about dignity.

This is about freedom.

This is about the power to say no to burnout and yes to wealth, wellness, and peace of mind.

You didn't build a groundbreaking company just to feel trapped by uncertainty.

Tech Business Founders is your permission slip to build the financial life you actually want — and deserve.

Chapter 33: Insurance Essentials

You are a tech founder. You carry ideas, teams, and investors on your shoulders. You disrupt industries. You break things, you build better ones. But here's the secret most founders learn too late: you are also carrying risk. Heavy, invisible, underestimated risk.

Insurance is not the most glamorous topic. It's not going to dazzle at your next pitch meeting. It won't trend on LinkedIn. But if you want to keep what you've built—and protect the wealth you're working so hard to accumulate—you have to get this right.

Today's conversation is about getting real about risk. This isn't about fear. It's about freedom. It's about putting a safety net under everything you've worked for so you can swing bigger, live bolder, and stop worrying about the what-ifs.

Because there's one thing no founder can afford: catastrophic loss without a plan.

Let's walk through it together.

D&O Insurance: Protecting Yourself and Your Startup

What Is D&O Insurance?

Let's start with the basics. D&O stands for Directors and Officers liability insurance. It protects your personal assets—and the company's—if you're personally sued for something connected to your leadership role.

Translation: if a shareholder, employee, vendor, or competitor decides you made a bad call and sues you, D&O is what stands between your house, your bank account, and a pile of legal fees.

Think you're too small? Think again. Early-stage companies are often the most vulnerable because they don't have deep pockets to fight litigation. And lawsuits don't wait until you're a unicorn.

D&O insurance typically covers:

- Legal defense costs
- Settlements and judgments
- Allegations of mismanagement, breach of fiduciary duty, errors, omissions, misleading statements

In a lawsuit-happy world, D&O is not optional. It's foundational.

Why Founders Need D&O Insurance

Founders are targets. You're visible. You're making decisions under uncertainty. Even with the best intentions, mistakes happen—or at least the perception of mistakes.

You can be sued by:

- Disgruntled employees (wrongful termination, discrimination)
- Angry investors (misrepresentation, breach of fiduciary duty)
- Customers or clients (misleading claims)
- Competitors (unfair competition)

Here's the kicker: even if you did nothing wrong, you still have to defend yourself. Legal defense alone can sink a startup without D&O coverage.

And here's the second kicker: personal liability means your own savings, your house, your future earnings are at risk. Without D&O, you're naked.

When to Get D&O Insurance

Sooner than you think.

The minute you take outside capital, you should have D&O. Many VCs will require it before wiring funds. It signals maturity and prudence. Even if you're bootstrapping, consider it once you start scaling or hiring.

Rule of thumb: if you have a board, if you have investors, if you have employees, you need D&O.

How Much Coverage Do You Need?

Typical startup policies range from $1 million to $5 million in coverage. The right amount depends on:

- Company size and revenue
- Industry (some, like fintech and healthcare, are riskier)
- Investor requirements
- Number of employees
- Prior claims history

A seasoned insurance broker can guide you. Don't cheap out on this. A $5,000 premium now can save you $500,000 later.

Umbrella Policies: Personal Protection for Founders

What Is an Umbrella Policy?

An umbrella insurance policy provides extra liability coverage beyond the limits of your other policies (like auto and homeowners). Think of it as a backup plan for your backup plan.

For example, say you're involved in a serious car accident. Your auto policy covers up to $250,000 in damages, but the injured party wins a $1 million judgment. That $750,000 gap? Covered by your umbrella policy.

Without it? Your bank account, investments, future wages, and assets are on the hook.

Why Founders Need an Umbrella Policy

You're not just another citizen anymore. You're a founder. People perceive you as wealthy (even if you're still living on ramen). That perception makes you a target.

Common scenarios where an umbrella policy saves you:

- Major car accidents with high medical bills
- Slip-and-fall accidents on your property
- Dog bites or injuries caused by pets
- Slander, libel, and other personal lawsuits
- Boating accidents (yes, really)

An umbrella policy steps in when your underlying coverage limits are exhausted. It protects your lifestyle and your future.

How Much Umbrella Coverage Do You Need?

Start with at least $1 million. Many high-net-worth individuals carry $5 million to $10 million. If you're on the verge of an exit, about to come into serious wealth, or already have significant assets, lean higher.

Premiums are surprisingly affordable. A $1 million umbrella policy might cost $200 to $500 per year. It's one of the highest-value protections you can buy.

Personal Insurance Needs Post-Exit

Congratulations. You sold your company. The wire hit. The champagne popped.

Now what?

This is where founders make big mistakes: assuming that exiting a company means exiting risk. In many ways, the risks just shift.

You need to rethink your entire insurance structure post-exit. Here's how.

Life Insurance

Why It Matters: If you have dependents or estate tax exposure, life insurance can preserve your family's financial security.

If you sold your company for millions, congratulations—but also, be careful. Estate tax laws can claw away up to 40% of your estate above exemption limits. Life insurance can provide liquidity to pay estate taxes without forcing your heirs to sell assets.

Consider permanent life insurance (whole or universal life) if you're planning for estate liquidity. If you're simply protecting young kids and a spouse, term life may still be the best fit.

Pro Tip: Buy it before you're older or your health deteriorates. Life insurance costs rise dramatically with age and health issues.

Health Insurance After an Exit

Don't Go Naked

Here's a scenario I see too often: a founder sells their company and suddenly loses their employer-sponsored health insurance. They think, "I'm healthy. I'll just wait until I figure out my next move."

Dangerous thinking.

Medical bankruptcies aren't a myth, and they don't only happen to people without money. One serious illness, one unexpected accident, and suddenly you're writing seven-figure checks. Even if you can technically afford it, why would you want to?

Post-exit, you have a few options:

- **COBRA Continuation**: Keep your old employer-sponsored plan for up to 18 months. Expensive, but easy.
- **Individual Market Insurance**: Through ACA exchanges or private insurers.
- **Short-Term Health Insurance**: Cheaper but limited. Often doesn't cover pre-existing conditions.
- **Health Sharing Ministries**: Not technically insurance, and very risky for high-net-worth individuals.

For most founders, COBRA is the immediate solution, followed by shopping for a high-quality individual policy.

Pro Tip: If you plan to retire early (before Medicare eligibility at 65), build private health insurance costs into your financial plan. It's often the biggest blind spot.

Disability Insurance: Protect Your Earning Power

The Overlooked Risk

You're young. You're healthy. You've built a successful company. Disability feels irrelevant—until it isn't.

Founders are particularly vulnerable because so much of their financial life is tied to their ability to work, network, invest, create, lead. If an illness or injury takes that away, how do you replace it?

Disability insurance provides income if you can't work due to illness or injury. It's not cheap, but neither is being unable to provide for yourself and your family.

Key things to look for:

- **Own Occupation Coverage**: Pays if you can't do your specific job, even if you could theoretically work in another role.
- **High Coverage Limits**: Especially important for founders who expect income spikes post-exit.

- **Cost-of-Living Adjustments**: Benefits that increase over time to keep up with inflation.

Pro Tip: Buy it while you're healthy and before an exit. Once you have liquidity, underwriters may assume you "don't need income" and either deny coverage or make it very expensive.

Long-Term Care Insurance: Planning for the Inevitable

The Statistic No One Wants to Think About

70% of people over 65 will need some form of long-term care. Think nursing homes, assisted living, home health aides. It's not covered by Medicare. It's brutally expensive. And it can drain even large portfolios if unplanned.

Long-term care (LTC) insurance helps cover these costs. It's not right for everyone, but it should be part of a serious wealth preservation conversation, especially post-exit.

Modern LTC policies come in different flavors:

- **Standalone LTC Insurance**: Pure LTC coverage. Premiums not guaranteed and can rise.
- **Hybrid Policies**: Life insurance policies with LTC riders. More expensive, but if you never need care, your heirs get a death benefit.

Pro Tip: The best time to buy LTC coverage is in your 50s, before health issues arise and premiums spike.

Founders exiting in their 40s should plan for it even if they don't buy immediately.

Asset Protection Strategies

Lawsuits Happen. Be Ready.

Founders are lawsuit targets during and after their careers. Wealth is a beacon.

Beyond basic insurance, consider:

- **Homestead Exemptions**: Certain states protect your primary residence from creditors.
- **LLCs for Real Estate and Businesses**: Hold rental properties, vacation homes, and side businesses in LLCs to shield personal assets.
- **Irrevocable Trusts**: Advanced strategy for higher net-worth individuals to shield assets from creditors and predators.
- **Retirement Accounts**: 401(k)s and IRAs often have strong legal protections. Max them out.

Work with an experienced asset protection attorney early. These strategies are worthless if you try to implement them after a lawsuit is filed.

Pro Tip: Make asset protection boring and automatic. You want it to work in the background while you live your life.

Real-Life Scenarios: Insurance Lessons from Founders

Case Study 1: The Founder Who Skipped D&O Insurance

Alex launched a fast-scaling SaaS company. Everything looked great—until a minority investor sued the board for mismanagement after a pivot didn't pan out. Legal defense cost over $800,000. Without D&O insurance, the founders had to cover it out of pocket. It derailed their Series B raise and forced a fire-sale acquisition.

Lesson: D&O is not an optional extra. It's as essential as your product roadmap.

Case Study 2: The Car Accident That Cost Millions

Jessica exited her company and bought a dream house and two sports cars. She figured she was set. Then came the car accident. Her standard auto insurance covered $300,000—but the judgment was $2.2 million. She had to sell the house to cover the rest because she didn't have an umbrella policy.

Lesson: Wealth without protection is a house of cards.

Case Study 3: The Founder Who Planned Ahead

Marcus sold his e-commerce company for $25 million. Before closing, he set up D&O, bought umbrella insurance, and worked with a financial planner to review his personal insurance. When an unexpected health crisis hit a year later, his disability policy kicked in, preserving his standard of living and protecting his investment portfolio from forced liquidation.

Lesson: Smart insurance planning is wealth protection planning.

Building Your Insurance Strategy: Step-by-Step

Step 1: Audit Your Risks

Make a list:

- Professional liability (D&O)
- Personal liability (umbrella policy)
- Health risks (health insurance)
- Income risks (disability insurance)
- Longevity risks (long-term care insurance)
- Asset risks (property and casualty, cyber liability)

If you're unsure where you're exposed, bring in a professional to conduct a risk audit.

Step 2: Prioritize

You don't have to buy everything at once. Prioritize based on:

- Likelihood of occurrence
- Financial impact if it happens
- Affordability of coverage

Typically, D&O, umbrella, and health insurance are table stakes. Disability and long-term care come next as wealth accumulates.

Step 3: Find the Right Advisors

Insurance is complex and often sales-driven. Work with:

- Independent brokers (access to multiple carriers)
- Fee-only planners (no commission bias)
- Specialist attorneys for asset protection

Good advisors focus on strategy, not sales. They're partners, not hawkers.

Step 4: Review Annually

Life changes. So do risks.
Review your coverage:

- After funding rounds
- After exits
- After major purchases (houses, boats, art)
- After marriages, divorces, or births
- At milestone birthdays (40, 50, 60)

Adjust as needed. Insurance is not set-it-and-forget-it.

Common Mistakes Founders Make (And How to Avoid Them)

1. Underinsuring Early

Founders tend to skimp on D&O and umbrella policies when cash is tight. Understandable, but risky.

Solution: Budget for insurance from Day 1. It's a line item, not an afterthought.

2. Letting Coverage Lapse Post-Exit

Once the business sells, founders often drop D&O and personal coverage.

Solution: Keep coverage until all personal liabilities (like earn-outs or escrow periods) have cleared—and personal wealth protection is firmly in place.

3. DIY Insurance Shopping

Buying insurance isn't like shopping for a toaster. Online quotes can be misleading. Terms matter.

Solution: Work with pros. A good broker can tailor policies to your real risks, not just sell you something cookie-cutter.

4. Assuming Wealth Equals Safety

Some founders think, "I have $10 million. I can self-insure."

Sure. But why? A $500 umbrella premium can protect millions. Leverage insurance where it makes sense.

Solution: View insurance as a tool for protecting, not replacing, wealth.

Expanding the Risk Management Playbook

Cyber Insurance: Protecting Your Digital Assets

You're a founder. Even post-exit, your digital footprint is enormous.

- Personal financial accounts
- Business residuals
- Emails with sensitive information
- Intellectual property
- Cloud storage

Hackers know this. They're patient. They're ruthless. And they target individuals just as much as corporations.

Cyber liability insurance protects you against:

- Identity theft
- Financial fraud
- Data breaches
- Ransomware attacks
- Legal liabilities if your compromised information impacts others

This is not paranoia—it's reality. Post-exit founders are prime targets. Your wealth is bait.

Pro Tip: Pair insurance with cybersecurity best practices—password managers, two-factor authentication, regular software updates, encrypted devices, and a dedicated security consultant if your profile is particularly high.

Specialty Insurance: Covering the Unusual

As wealth grows, so do your interests—and your risks.

- **Fine Art and Collectibles**: Standard homeowners' insurance usually won't cover expensive art, wine, jewelry, or memorabilia at full value.
- **Yachts, Planes, and Exotic Cars**: These require specialized coverage, not standard auto or homeowner policies.
- **Vacation Homes**: Often in areas prone to floods, wildfires, hurricanes—requiring bespoke policies.
- **Kidnap and Ransom Insurance**: For founders who travel internationally or are high-profile enough to be at risk.

If you're passionate about it and it's valuable, insure it properly. Otherwise, you're gambling with assets you love.

Family Office Risk Management

Once your wealth hits a certain level—think $50 million+—you may consider setting up a family office.

With that comes new risks:

- Employee theft or embezzlement
- Fraudulent investment schemes
- Internal disputes among heirs or managers
- Regulatory compliance risks
- Reputational risks (especially if you or your family become public figures)

Family Office Insurance packages can cover:

- Employment practices liability (EPL)
- Crime and fidelity bonds

- Professional liability for advisors
- Director's and Officer's (D&O) for the family office entity itself

Family wealth is generational. Protect it like the dynasty you intend it to be.

Deep Dive: D&O Insurance Essentials

What D&O Covers

- Allegations of breach of fiduciary duty
- Misrepresentation to shareholders
- Errors in financial reporting
- Employment practice lawsuits
- Regulatory investigations

Without D&O, your personal assets—homes, savings, investments—are at risk if you're sued as a director or officer.

Post-exit, many founders join boards—of their own former companies, portfolio companies, nonprofits, alma maters. Make sure any board you join has proper D&O coverage.

Claims-Made Coverage Caveat: D&O is claims-made, not occurrence-based. It only protects you if the claim is made while the policy is active. Always negotiate a "tail policy" when you step down from a board role.

Choosing the Right Umbrella Policy

An umbrella policy kicks in after your home, auto, or boat insurance is maxed out.

Example:

- Your auto policy covers up to $500,000
- A serious accident leads to a $3 million judgment

- Your umbrella covers the $2.5 million difference

Typical Coverage Amounts: $1M, $5M, $10M, $20M+

Premiums are relatively cheap: a few hundred dollars a year for millions in protection.

Important: Not all umbrella policies are equal. Some have exclusions for high-risk activities like flying personal planes or high-performance auto racing. Tailor it to your lifestyle.

Personal Insurance Needs Post-Exit

Your life changes dramatically after an exit. Your insurance needs should change too.

Homeowners Insurance

Big new house? Vacation properties? Upgrade your coverage. Pay attention to:

- **Replacement Cost**: Not just market value—can you rebuild it?
- **Extended Replacement Endorsements**: Cover construction cost inflation.
- **Loss of Use**: Covers costs if you can't live there during repairs.

Life Insurance

If you're financially independent post-exit, do you still need life insurance?

Maybe yes, maybe no.

You may still want life insurance to:

- Provide liquidity for estate taxes (especially for illiquid assets like private investments)
- Equalize inheritances among children (if one gets a business, another

gets life insurance proceeds)
- Fund charitable bequests
- Cover existing debts or obligations

Options:

- **Term Life Insurance**: Pure protection, lower cost.
- **Permanent Life Insurance**: Cash value component, useful for estate planning and wealth transfer.

Work with a fee-only planner to evaluate if and how much life insurance you truly need. Don't let insurance salespeople upsell you into unnecessary whole life policies.

Travel Insurance

If you're traveling more post-exit:

- Emergency medical evacuation (especially important internationally)
- Trip cancellation
- Kidnap and ransom (in certain high-risk areas)

High-net-worth travel insurance policies also offer concierge medical services and crisis response teams.

Behavioral Biases That Undermine Risk Management

Founders are optimists. It's baked into your DNA. You wouldn't have started your company otherwise.

But optimism bias can be dangerous in risk management. It leads to:

- **Underestimating risks**: "It won't happen to me."
- **Overconfidence**: "If something happens, I'll handle it."

- **Anchoring**: Sticking with outdated coverage even as your net worth explodes.

Risk management requires a different mindset: *strategic paranoia*. Plan for what could go wrong—not because you expect it to, but because you refuse to let it derail your legacy.

Insurance Isn't Sexy—But Freedom Is

Insurance doesn't make headlines. It won't make you feel clever at cocktail parties.

But freedom—the ability to walk away from a lawsuit, a fire, an illness—*without worrying*—that's priceless.

Insurance is not about fear. It's about control.

You didn't build your company to live in fear. You built it to live with freedom.

Final Checklist: Insurance Audit for Founders

- D&O Insurance for your startup and any boards you serve on
- Personal Umbrella Policy (at least $5M, adjust as needed)
- Health Insurance (COBRA or private policy)
- Disability Insurance (Own-Occupation, high-limit)
- Long-Term Care Insurance (consider in your 50s)
- Homeowners Insurance (high-value property coverage)
- Cyber Liability Insurance (especially post-exit)
- Specialty Insurance for valuables (art, collectibles, yachts)
- Kidnap and Ransom Insurance (for international travelers)
- Family Office Risk Insurance (if applicable)
- Life Insurance (if needed for estate liquidity)
- Travel Insurance for high-end or international trips
- Regular Annual Review with an independent advisor

Call to Action

Make one money move before you go to bed tonight: **Schedule an insurance audit.** Even if it's just reviewing your umbrella policy limits or checking when your D&O policy expires.

Small steps compound.

And when life inevitably throws a curveball, you'll be ready—not scrambling.

Insurance is about dignity.

It's about freedom.

It's about creating a life so well-insulated that no lawsuit, no accident, no disaster can steal your peace of mind.

You didn't build a groundbreaking company just to live one lawsuit or one uninsured catastrophe away from financial chaos.

You built it for freedom. For impact. For the peace of knowing your life—and your legacy—are fully protected.

Chapter 34: Cybersecurity for Founders

Why Cybersecurity Matters More Than Ever for Founders

Let's be honest.

When you were building your company, cybersecurity probably wasn't your first priority. You were focused on growth, on innovation, on survival. And that made sense.

But post-exit or as you accumulate wealth, the game changes.

Suddenly, you're not just a founder—you're a target.

Your personal wealth.

Your access to business networks.

Your intellectual property.

Your reputation.

You've become what hackers, scammers, and bad actors call a "high-value individual." And the reality is, they're getting better every year. More sophisticated. More patient. More ruthless.

This chapter is about protecting what you've built. Not with fear. With strategy. With intention. With swagger.

Because nothing is more powerful than wealth *and* security.

Threats Faced by High-Net-Worth Individuals

Let's break this down simply.

When you're high-net-worth, you're not facing the same threats as the average person. You're facing:

1. Phishing and Spear Phishing

This isn't just random Nigerian prince emails anymore.

This is highly-targeted, intelligent attacks:

- Emails that look exactly like they're from your CFO, asking for a wire transfer.
- Emails from what seems like your attorney, requesting sensitive documents.
- Text messages appearing to come from your private bank, asking you to "verify" your account.

Hackers research you. They know your travel schedule. Your business relationships. Your family members' names.

They weaponize that knowledge against you.

2. Account Takeovers

- Bank accounts
- Brokerage accounts
- Email accounts
- Cloud storage

Hackers don't have to break into your house to steal your fortune. They just need access to your login credentials.

3. SIM Swapping

Ever get a new phone and transfer your number over?

Hackers can convince your mobile carrier to do that *for them*—without your permission.

Once they have your phone number, they reset your passwords. They bypass two-factor authentication. They own your digital identity.

4. Ransomware and Extortion

Not just for big companies anymore.

Hackers can lock you out of your personal devices or cloud accounts and demand a ransom to restore access.

They can threaten to leak personal photos, financial records, or confidential business documents unless you pay.

5. Home Network Vulnerabilities

- Smart thermostats
- Wi-Fi-enabled security cameras
- Internet-connected doorbells

All of these can be entry points for hackers into your home network. From there, they can access your devices, your private emails, even spy on you physically.

6. Reputation Attacks

- Doxxing (publishing your home address and personal details online)
- Social media impersonation
- Leaking confidential or embarrassing information

Reputation is capital. Protect it as fiercely as your bank account.

Basic Cybersecurity Hygiene

You can eliminate 80% of your risk with these basic moves.

These are non-negotiable.

1. Strong, Unique Passwords

No reusing the same password across accounts.

- Use 20+ character passwords.
- Random strings, not words.
- No birthdays, kid names, or pet names.

Use a **password manager** like 1Password or Dashlane. They generate and store complex passwords securely.

Pro Tip: Use a passphrase for the password manager itself—something long and memorable, like *GreenCoffeeCorrectStaplerHorseBattery1!*

2. Two-Factor Authentication (2FA)

Everywhere. Always.

- Prefer app-based 2FA (like Authy) over text message-based.
- Even better: **hardware security keys** like YubiKey for critical accounts (email, banks, brokerage).

Two-factor makes it 100x harder for hackers to break in, even if they steal your password.

3. Regular Software Updates

Hackers love outdated software.

- Enable auto-updates on your phone, laptop, browser, and apps.
- Don't ignore those update prompts.

Every day you delay is a day you're exposed.

4. Backup Everything—Securely

- Cloud backups (encrypted, secured with 2FA).
- Local backups on encrypted external hard drives.
- Redundancy: have at least two backups in different locations.

If ransomware hits, you can restore your data instead of paying a ransom.

5. Secure Your Wi-Fi Network

- Change the default router password.
- Use WPA3 encryption (or at least WPA2).
- Hide your network's SSID (make it invisible to casual scans).
- Separate networks for IoT (Internet of Things) devices and personal devices.

Don't let your smart fridge be the reason your personal files get hacked.

6. Limit Data Sharing

- Be careful what you post online.
- Turn off location sharing on social media.
- Use a PO box or virtual address service for business registrations.

The less data you leak, the less ammunition hackers have against you.

Advanced Personal Security Measures

Ready to level up?

When you're worth tens of millions—or hundreds—you need to think like a digital fortress.

Here's how.

1. Personal Cybersecurity Consultant

Consider hiring a cybersecurity firm that specializes in high-net-worth individuals.

They can:

- Audit your current security setup.
- Monitor for breaches in real-time.
- Help you respond quickly if something goes wrong.

2. Hardware Security Keys

Mentioned earlier, but worth repeating.

A YubiKey or similar device is the gold standard for protecting high-value accounts.

It's a physical key. Without it, no one—*not even you*—can log in.

3. Virtual Private Network (VPN)

Always use a VPN on public Wi-Fi (hotels, coffee shops, airports).

Better yet, use it at home too.

A VPN encrypts your internet traffic and hides your IP address, making it harder for hackers to track you.

Services like NordVPN or ProtonVPN are founder favorites for reliability and speed.

4. Encrypted Communication

- Use encrypted email services like ProtonMail for sensitive communications.
- Use Signal or WhatsApp (with end-to-end encryption) for messaging.
- Avoid regular SMS for anything confidential.

Privacy isn't about having something to hide. It's about having something to protect.

5. Device Encryption

Turn on full-disk encryption on your laptops and phones.

If they're stolen, your data stays safe.

Macs: FileVault

Windows: BitLocker

iPhones: Encryption is default but keep a strong passcode (6 digits minimum, alphanumeric even better).

6. Freeze Your Credit

Freeze your credit reports with Equifax, Experian, and TransUnion.

It stops criminals from opening new accounts in your name.

Free. Easy. Powerful.

Real-Life Scenarios

Let's make this real.

Scenario 1: Phishing Attack After an Exit

You just sold your company for $200 million. It's public knowledge.

A hacker sends a convincing email, posing as your wealth manager, asking you to transfer $5 million to "fund a new investment."

The email looks legit. It references things only your advisor would know. Because the hacker stalked your LinkedIn and social media for months before the sale.

You click.

Game over.

Solution:

- Never transfer funds based solely on an email.
- Call and verbally confirm any wiring instructions.
- Set up "out-of-band" verification—separate channels for confirming financial transactions.

Scenario 2: SIM Swap Leads to Financial Drain

You're at a conference overseas.

A hacker convinces your mobile carrier to port your number to their SIM card.

They reset your email password. Then your bank password.

By the time you land back home, your accounts are emptied.

Solution:

- Add a PIN to your mobile carrier account.
- Use app-based or hardware 2FA—not SMS-based.

Scenario 3: Home Network Compromise

A hacker gets into your Wi-Fi through your unprotected smart thermostat.

From there, they access your laptop backups, steal sensitive business files, and leak them online.

Solution:

- Separate your IoT devices on a different Wi-Fi network.
- Change default passwords on all smart devices.
- Disable remote access unless absolutely necessary.

Psychological Side: Cyber Fatigue

You might be feeling it already.

This sounds exhausting.

Always on guard. Always a new threat.

But cybersecurity isn't about paranoia. It's about preparation.

Once the right systems are in place, *they work quietly in the background.* They protect you while you live your life.

You don't think about airbags every time you drive—but you're glad they're there.

Same with cybersecurity.

Common Cybersecurity Myths — Debunked

Myth 1: "I'm not a target."

Reality: If you have money, access, or influence—you are a target.

Myth 2: "I have antivirus software, so I'm safe."

Reality: Antivirus is basic. Hackers exploit human error (phishing) more than software vulnerabilities.

Myth 3: "Cybersecurity is too complicated."

Reality: Start simple. Password manager. 2FA. Regular updates. These alone will block 80% of attacks.

Annual Cybersecurity Checklist

- Change all key account passwords.
- Audit 2FA across all accounts—switch to app- or hardware-based where possible.
- Review cloud backup settings and encryption.
- Audit devices—remove old accounts and apps.
- Freeze your credit.
- Check who has access to your Wi-Fi and cloud storage.
- Update your estate plan to include digital assets (yes, your heirs need access to your important online accounts).
- Schedule a cybersecurity audit with a pro if your net worth is high enough to warrant it.

Call to Act

Make one money move before you go to bed tonight: **Enable 2FA on your email and financial accounts.**

Tomorrow: **Set up a password manager.**

Next week: **Consider a cybersecurity audit.**

Build your fortress one brick at a time.

This isn't just about protecting your money.

It's about protecting your peace of mind.

It's about protecting your family, your legacy, your freedom.

You didn't build a groundbreaking company just to have it—or your future—stolen because of a careless click.

Cybersecurity is part of your wealth. It's invisible, but it's real.

And now, you know exactly how to defend it.

Chapter 35: Cash Flow Management Post-Exit

Welcome to the New Game

You did it.

You took an idea—maybe one that seemed crazy at the start—and you turned it into something valuable.

You raised capital. You built a team. You built product-market fit. You survived the "near-death experiences" that all startups face. And finally—you exited.

There's cash in the bank now. Maybe more than you've ever seen.

But here's the thing they don't tell you: the money is only the beginning of the next chapter.

Because having money is not the same as managing money.

This chapter is about making sure your liquidity event isn't the peak of your financial life—it's the foundation.

It's about learning how to manage cash flow like a founder who *stays* wealthy—not one who makes a headline and then disappears.

Let's get to it.

Why Cash Flow Management Matters—Even After an Exit

When you first land that massive wire transfer post-exit, it feels surreal.

You open your banking app, and there's a comma (or three) where there never used to be.

It's tempting to think: "I'm set. I never have to worry about money again."

But wealth without management drains faster than you think.

Why?

- Lifestyle inflation
- Taxes (federal, state, local, capital gains, you name it)
- Investment risks
- Unexpected life events (divorce, lawsuits, health issues)
- Poor planning around big purchases

In short: it's not just about *having* money. It's about *keeping* it—and making it work for you.

Cash flow management post-exit is how you move from survival mode to *sovereignty mode*.

You didn't come this far to be a cautionary tale.

Budgeting After a Liquidity Event

Let's destroy a myth real quick:

Budgeting isn't about scarcity.

It's not about clipping coupons or denying yourself joy.

It's about *clarity*.

It's about knowing where your money is going—so you're not just rich today, but free tomorrow.

Step 1: Calculate Your Fixed Lifestyle Costs

Start with the basics:

- Mortgage or rent
- Property taxes
- Insurance (home, auto, umbrella, life, disability)
- Utilities
- Food
- Healthcare
- Kids' expenses (tuition, extracurriculars, childcare)
- Travel (if routine)

Add it up.

Now, double-check: is this *really* your lifestyle cost—or is there lifestyle creep baked in?

The goal isn't to be miserly—it's to be honest.

Step 2: Define Your Discretionary Spending

This is your "fun money":

- Travel upgrades (first-class flights, 5-star hotels)
- New cars
- Boats
- Art
- Hobbies (private aviation? Horse breeding? It's your call.)

Estimate an annual number.

Be generous—but not reckless.

The key here is *awareness*.

Step 3: Estimate Your Tax Liability

This is the piece that surprises founders the most.

When you exit, a huge portion goes to Uncle Sam:

- Federal capital gains (20% long-term + 3.8% net investment income tax)
- State taxes (if you live in a high-tax state like California or New York)
- Alternative Minimum Tax (AMT) if you exercised options
- Potential city taxes

Rule of thumb: set aside **at least 30-40%** for taxes unless your CPA says otherwise.

Cash flow management starts with not pretending this chunk doesn't exist.

Step 4: Map Out Big Upcoming Expenses

Founders love to do Big Things after an exit:

- Buy the dream house
- Fund a family foundation
- Angel invest
- Start another company
- Gift money to parents, kids, siblings

List all potential major outflows.

Prioritize them:

- Immediate (within 1 year)
- Short-term (1-3 years)
- Long-term (5+ years)

Step 5: Build a Post-Exit Budget

At this point, your budget isn't about "living within your means."

It's about *living within your goals.*

You want to know:

- What's your annual lifestyle cost?
- What's your investment portfolio yield?
- What's your runway if you stop earning?
- What's your buffer for market downturns or emergencies?

Tracking Spending and Investments

Money that's not monitored leaks.

Your goal post-exit is *visibility*.

Build a Personal Financial Dashboard

Think of it like your company's dashboard—except this time, *you* are the business.

Your dashboard should track:

- **Cash accounts**: checking, savings
- **Investment accounts**: brokerage, private equity, venture funds, real estate
- **Debt**: mortgages, loans (if any)
- **Real assets**: primary residence, vacation homes, collectible assets (art, cars)
- **Liabilities**: future tax payments, pledged donations

Tools:

- Personal Capital (great for a consolidated view)

- eMoney (if you're working with an advisor)
- Excel or Google Sheets (for the DIYers)

Update it monthly. Review quarterly.

No exceptions.

Monitor Burn Rate

Startups have a burn rate.

So do people.

Track your personal monthly "burn rate":

Fixed + Discretionary Expenses = Monthly Burn

Compare it to your investment portfolio's *safe withdrawal rate* (usually around 3-4%).

This tells you: Are you living off your portfolio safely—or depleting your assets?

Watch the Big Picture

- Are your investments growing at a rate that supports your lifestyle *after inflation*?
- Is your cash reserve sufficient (1-3 years of living expenses)?
- Are you diversified across asset classes?

Treat your personal finances with the same rigor you treated your cap table.

Planning for Large Purchases

Now, the fun part—and the dangerous part.

You've exited. You want the Ferrari. The Napa vineyard. The Aspen ski house.

How do you do it without blowing up your future?

Rule 1: Delay Big Purchases for 12 Months

It's called the "Post-Exit Cooling Off Period."

Why?

Because money changes how you feel.

- About yourself.
- About risk.
- About what you "deserve."

Give yourself a year to adjust before making any *irreversible* big purchases.

Impulse + Wealth = Regret.

Rule 2: Pay Cash, but Not From Investment Accounts

Selling investments to buy a depreciating asset (like a car or a boat) is a wealth killer.

Better strategy:

- Keep a "Big Purchase Fund" in cash equivalents (T-bills, high-yield savings).
- Only use that fund for large discretionary purchases.
- Replenish it systematically if you deplete it.

Rule 3: Think Opportunity Cost

Every $1M you spend on a second home could be:

- $50K a year in lost portfolio income (at a 5% return)
- 10 years of tuition for your kids
- A significant philanthropic legacy

This doesn't mean "don't buy the house."

It means buy it *knowing the true cost.*

Rule 4: Use Smart Leverage (Carefully)

In certain cases, borrowing can make sense post-exit:

- Low-interest mortgages keep more capital invested.
- Margin loans against investment portfolios (very carefully).
- Structured lending against illiquid assets (like pre-IPO stock or private equity stakes).

The key is:

- Low-interest
- Low-risk
- No margin calls (prefer non-recourse lending)

Talk to your advisor before levering up.

Rule 5: Balance Now and Later

You didn't work this hard just to keep score.

Enjoy the rewards of your labor.

But balance it:

- Spend money on things that buy joy, connection, growth.
- Avoid status purchases that only feed ego.

Money is a tool. Not a trophy.

Real-Life Scenario: The Founder Who Blew It

Let's get real.

Imagine:

- A founder exits for $100M.
- After taxes: ~$55M.
- Buys a $20M estate in Beverly Hills.
- Pours $10M into speculative angel investments.
- Loans $5M to friends and family (most of which never gets repaid).
- Lives on $2M a year—unsustainable based on investment returns.

Fast-forward 10 years: broke.

The lesson?

Cash flow mismanagement doesn't just happen to lottery winners or celebrities.

It happens to *founders*.

Unless you plan, track, and adjust.

Common Cash Flow Pitfalls Post-Exit

- Ignoring taxes
- Over-investing in illiquid assets (private equity, venture, real estate) without a liquidity plan
- Lifestyle inflation without rebalancing financial plans
- No cash reserve for market downturns
- Over-gifting to family or friends out of guilt or pressure
- Underestimating healthcare or long-term care costs
- Emotional spending post-exit (the "I deserve it" syndrome)
- Awareness is the first defense.
- Planning is the second.

Cash Flow Management Mindsets to Adopt

1. Steward, Not Spender

Think like the CEO of your wealth.

Your job isn't to spend it—it's to steward it.

That means making decisions that serve you *and* the people and causes you care about for the long haul.

2. Growth Mindset

Your liquidity event isn't the end.

It's the launchpad.

Use this capital to:

- Build generational wealth.
- Invest in your next big idea.
- Create a philanthropic legacy.
- Buy yourself *options* for the future.

3. Boring is Beautiful

The best cash flow management post-exit is...boring.

Budgets. Dashboards. Reviews.

The excitement comes from the freedom they create.

Not the chaos they prevent.

4. Protect the Downside

No one regrets being too safe with their first big fortune.

Plenty regret being too reckless.

Prioritize risk management—insurance, diversification, liquidity—*before* chasing outsized returns.

The 12-Month Post-Exit Cash Flow Action Plan

Month 1-3:

- Park liquidity in a safe, interest-bearing vehicle.
- Estimate your tax liabilities.
- Build a basic personal financial dashboard.

Month 4-6:

- Engage a wealth manager, CPA, estate attorney.
- Audit your monthly burn rate.
- Establish a 12-month cooling-off period for big purchases.

Month 7-9:

- Define your investment policy statement (IPS).
- Create a "Big Purchase Fund" for future large outflows.
- Begin diversifying investments beyond startup/tech.

Month 10-12:

- Review your cash flow plan.
- Adjust based on spending patterns.
- Set 5- and 10-year financial goals.

Repeat annually.

Call to Act

Tonight:

- List your fixed annual lifestyle costs.

Tomorrow:

- Map out your discretionary spending wishlist.

Next week:

- Create your personal financial dashboard.

Before you buy anything major:

- Wait 12 months post-exit.

Wealth isn't built in a liquidity event.

It's built in the decisions you make *after*.

Money alone doesn't buy peace.

Money, managed well, *does*.

You didn't build a category-defining company just to stumble at the finish line.

You're not here for chaos.

You're here for freedom.

You're here for dignity.

You're here for a life that feels *as good* as it looks.

Cash flow management is the bridge between what you have and what you want most:

- Control.
- Confidence.
- Options.
- Legacy.

Chapter 36: Avoiding Lifestyle Creep

The Quiet Threat to Wealth

You've done the hard part. You started something from scratch and you made it matter.

Maybe you bootstrapped. Maybe you raised $10 million. Maybe you sold for $100 million.

Now, you're looking at a bank balance most people will never see.

But here's a hard truth:

Wealth doesn't disappear because of bad investments or a market downturn.

For founders, wealth disappears because of *lifestyle creep.*

Not overnight.

Slowly.

Quietly.

One decision at a time.

One upgrade at a time.

One "why not" at a time.

Lifestyle creep is the silent killer of wealth, freedom, and the future you worked so hard to build.

And the worst part? It feels good—right up until it doesn't.

This chapter is about how to see it coming, how to stop it, and how to stay free long after the exit.

What Is Lifestyle Creep?

Lifestyle creep is when your spending gradually increases as your income—or your wealth—increases.

It's not buying a yacht after you sell your company.

It's buying the yacht, plus:

- The crew
- The maintenance
- The dock fees
- The second home with a private marina
- The custom cars to match

And it doesn't feel like a mistake—until it's too late.

It's the slow, steady ratchet of your "normal" lifestyle until you're trapped by it.

Your burn rate goes up.

Your financial freedom goes down.

And the worst part?

You don't even notice it happening.

Why Founders Are Especially Vulnerable

You, more than almost anyone else, are vulnerable to lifestyle creep.

Why?

1. You've Been Starving for So Long

Years of living lean, scraping by, barely paying yourself while you built your company?

The minute you have liquidity, your brain screams:

"I deserve this."

And it's right.

You *do* deserve a reward.

But what starts as a reward can quickly become a *requirement*.

And the longer you stay in reward mode, the harder it is to step back.

2. Everyone Else Is Spending Big

Your peers—other founders, investors, the tech elite—are driving G-Wagons, buying homes in Atherton, and flying private.

It's not just peer pressure.

It's *peer normalization*.

When everyone around you is inflating their lifestyle, your baseline shifts—without you even realizing it.

You don't feel rich.

You feel *behind*.

And you start upgrading not because you want to—but because it feels like that's what you're supposed to do.

3. It Feels Infinite

You look at your bank account or brokerage account and think:

"I have plenty."

"I'll always have enough."

But you know what else feels infinite?

- Your runway…right before you run out of cash.
- Your momentum…right before the market turns.

Wealth is not infinite.

And if you act like it is, lifestyle creep will burn through it faster than you think.

Setting Spending Guidelines

Let's talk about the antidote to lifestyle creep.

Not budgets.

Not guilt.

Guidelines.

Step 1: Define Your Freedom Number

Forget "how much do I want to spend?"

Start with:

How much do I want to *need* to spend?

Your *Freedom Number* is the amount you can comfortably spend each year without worrying about income, markets, or recessions.

It's the lifestyle you can sustain *forever* without burning through your capital.

Example:

You have $20M post-tax from your exit.

Using a conservative 3.5% safe withdrawal rate, that's $700K per year.

If your lifestyle costs $700K or less?

You're financially free.

If your lifestyle costs $2M per year?

You're on a ticking clock.

Set your Freedom Number.

It's the guardrail for everything that comes next.

Step 2: Cap Fixed Costs

Fixed costs are dangerous.

They're the expenses that don't go away—even if the economy crashes or your investments tank.

- Mortgages

- Car leases
- Insurance premiums
- Staff salaries (housekeepers, chefs, security)
- Membership dues (country clubs, golf courses)

Cap your fixed costs at no more than 50% of your Freedom Number.

Example:

If your Freedom Number is $700K/year, keep fixed costs under $350K.

Why?

Because flexibility is freedom.

And high fixed costs destroy flexibility.

Step 3: Automate Discretionary Spending Limits

Discretionary spending is where lifestyle creep sneaks in.

- Travel upgrades
- Art collections
- Wine cellars
- Watches
- Toys (boats, cars, planes)

Set annual caps for discretionary categories.

And automate it.

- Create separate bank accounts for major discretionary categories.
- Fund them quarterly or annually.
- Spend from them guilt-free—but only from them.

When the account is empty, no more spending until it refills.

Discipline without willpower.

Recognizing Early Warning Signs

Lifestyle creep doesn't announce itself.

It whispers.

Here's how to know if it's starting to happen:

1. Your Burn Rate Keeps Increasing

If your monthly spending is creeping up by more than inflation (2-3% per year), lifestyle creep is in play.

Track your burn rate quarterly.

If it's up 10%, 20%, 50% year-over-year?

Warning.

2. You're Buying More Status than Joy

Did that $50K watch make you happy?

Or just feel superior for 30 seconds?

If you're spending to impress—not to enjoy—you're vulnerable.

Joy compounds.

Status depreciates.

3. New Normals Are Forming

First-class flights become private jets.

Nice homes become mega-mansions.

Luxury hotels become entire villa rentals.

When yesterday's splurge becomes today's expectation?

Lifestyle creep is winning.

4. Your "Emergency" Fund Feels Small

If $500K in cash reserves once felt massive—and now feels "barely enough"?

Lifestyle inflation has shifted your perspective.

Reality check: $500K is a lot of money.

Don't let creeping lifestyle costs fool you into thinking otherwise.

5. You Feel Trapped

Ironically, the more you spend, the *less* free you feel.

Why?

- Bigger homes come with bigger upkeep.
- More staff means more management.
- More toys mean more logistics.

If your life feels heavier, not lighter, it's time to audit your lifestyle.

Staying Focused on Long-Term Goals

You didn't build your company on impulse.

You built it with:

- Strategy
- Patience
- Sacrifice

Managing post-exit wealth is the same game.

Here's how to stay focused.

1. Revisit Your Why

Why did you want wealth in the first place?

- Freedom?
- Security for your family?
- Philanthropy?
- Legacy?

Write it down.
Revisit it monthly.
Lifestyle creep thrives when you forget your Why.

2. Set Concrete Long-Term Goals

- How much do you want to leave to your kids?
- How much do you want to give to charity?
- What does "enough" look like?

Without clear goals, lifestyle creep will set the goalposts for you.
And it will always move them just out of reach.

3. Celebrate Milestones—Without Raising the Bar

Celebrate the exit.
Buy something meaningful.
Take the trip.
Enjoy the reward.
But *don't* let every celebration ratchet up your baseline lifestyle.
Life is not a never-ending ladder of upgrades.
Sometimes enough is enough.

4. Practice "Pre-Spending Gratitude"

Before every major purchase, ask:

"If I didn't buy this, would I still be happy?"

If the answer is yes?

You probably don't need it.

If the answer is no?

Maybe it's the right buy.

Either way—gratitude first, purchase second.

Action Steps

Here's what you can do *right now*:

1. **Define your Freedom Number.**
2. **Audit your current fixed and discretionary expenses.**
3. **Set caps on fixed costs.**
4. **Create separate accounts for discretionary spending.**
5. **Set a quarterly burn rate review.**
6. **Write down your Why—and revisit it monthly.**
7. **Pause before every major purchase.**
8. **Practice gratitude before spending.**

Call to Act

Make one money move before you go to bed tonight.

Just one.

Maybe it's calculating your Freedom Number.

Maybe it's auditing your fixed costs.

Maybe it's writing down your Why.

Then, do another next week.

One move at a time.

That's how you stay free.

Avoiding lifestyle creep isn't about living small.

It's about living smart.

It's about choosing freedom over obligation.

Joy over ego.

Purpose over appearances.

You didn't work this hard, fight this long, and risk this much just to become a prisoner of your own wealth.

You're not here to impress strangers.

You're here to live well.

On your terms.

For a lifetime.

And that starts with saying no to lifestyle creep—and yes to yourself.

Your future self will thank you.

So will your bank account.

So will your peace of mind.

Chapter 37: Retirement Planning Early and Often

Why Retirement Planning Matters for Founders

Let's start with a simple but powerful truth:

The best time to plant a tree was 20 years ago. The second-best time is today.

When it comes to retirement planning, this isn't just a pithy proverb—it's the foundation for building a future that honors the sacrifices you're making today. As a tech founder, you live in a world defined by speed, uncertainty, and asymmetric outcomes. You gamble on the future with every decision you make.

But retirement planning? That's where you get to rig the odds in your favor.

Retirement planning isn't just about "saving for a beach house someday." It's about designing your life—your freedom—on your terms. And for founders, it's doubly important because your wealth is often locked up in a single asset: your company.

The IPO may come. The acquisition may come.

Or not.

Either way, the earlier you plan, the more control you'll have.

1. The Benefits of Early Retirement Planning
2. 1. Time is Your Greatest Asset

Founders are visionaries. You understand compound growth because you've lived it: one line of code today can become a billion-dollar platform tomorrow.

Money works the same way.

The earlier you start investing for retirement, the more time your money has to grow. Compounding is a force multiplier.

1. $100,000 invested at 8% for 30 years = $1,000,000+
2. $100,000 invested at 8% for 40 years = $2,200,000+

Time turns good decisions into great outcomes.

1. 2. Peace of Mind

You know better than anyone how volatile business can be. Early planning builds a financial safety net, reducing the pressure to "win big" or "scale fast" because you've already secured your future.

Freedom is being able to choose. Early retirement planning gives you options—the option to pivot, to exit, to sabbatical, to build again without fear.

1. 3. Tax Optimization

The tax code rewards those who plan ahead.

Contributing to retirement accounts, structuring your equity intelligently, and leveraging strategies like Roth conversions during low-income years—these are doors that only stay open for so long.

The earlier you plan, the more opportunities you have to optimize.

1. Types of Retirement Accounts

As a founder, you have access to a wider array of retirement vehicles than the typical W-2 employee.

Let's break them down.

1. 1. Traditional IRA
2. **Who it's for:** Anyone with earned income.
3. **Contribution limit (2024):** $6,500 (under 50), $7,500 (50+)
4. **Tax benefits:** Contributions may be tax-deductible. Growth is tax-deferred.

Simple, flexible, but limited by low contribution caps.

1. 2. Roth IRA
2. **Who it's for:** Individuals below certain income limits.
3. **Contribution limit:** Same as Traditional IRA.
4. **Tax benefits:** Contributions are after-tax, but qualified withdrawals are tax-free.

The Roth is especially powerful for early-career founders with lower taxable income—pay taxes now at a low rate and reap the rewards later.

1. 3. SEP IRA
2. **Who it's for:** Self-employed individuals, small business owners.
3. **Contribution limit:** Up to 25% of compensation or $66,000 (whichever is less).
4. **Tax benefits:** Contributions are tax-deductible.

Great for solopreneurs or small teams pre-venture capital.

1. 4. Solo 401(k)
2. **Who it's for:** Self-employed individuals with no employees (besides spouse).
3. **Contribution limit:** Employee deferral up to $22,500 + employer contribution up to $66,000 total.

A Solo 401(k) offers the highest contribution limits and the ability to do "Mega Backdoor Roth" strategies.

1. 5. 401(k) Plan for Your Company

As your company scales, offering a 401(k) plan can be a retention tool for employees—and it gives you access to higher deferral limits as well.

Pro tip: Look into "Safe Harbor" plans to automatically pass IRS nondiscrimination tests.

1. 6. Defined Benefit Plan
2. **Who it's for:** High-income earners with consistent cash flow.
3. **Contribution limit:** Potentially hundreds of thousands of dollars annually.

Old-school pension plans—modernized. Great for de-risking a large tax bill and supercharging retirement savings late in the game.

1. 7. Health Savings Account (HSA)

Not technically a retirement account—but it should be treated like one.

1. **Tax benefits:** Triple tax advantage (pre-tax contributions, tax-free growth, tax-free withdrawals for medical expenses).
2. **Pro tip:** Pay current medical expenses out of pocket and let the HSA grow.
3. Retirement Income Planning

You've planned the exit. You've made the money. Now what?

Building wealth is one game. Converting it into sustainable, tax-efficient retirement income is another.

Let's walk through it.

1. 1. The Withdrawal Strategy

The classic rule of thumb is the "4% Rule": withdraw 4% of your portfolio in the first year of retirement, adjust for inflation each year after, and your portfolio should last 30 years.

But real life is messier.

1. **Consider a dynamic withdrawal strategy**: Flexible withdrawals based on market returns.
2. **Bucket your assets**: Short-term (1-3 years of cash), mid-term (bonds, income-producing assets), long-term (equities, growth assets).

This cushions you against market downturns.

1. 2. Social Security

Yes, even founders get Social Security.

1. **Claiming early (62):** Reduced benefit.
2. **Full Retirement Age (67):** Full benefit.
3. **Delaying to 70:** 8% increase per year after full retirement age.

If you've paid into the system through a reasonable founder salary, you'll be eligible.

1. 3. Annuities

Annuities can be a tool to create guaranteed income.

1. **Immediate annuities:** Convert a lump sum into lifetime income.
2. **Deferred annuities:** Let the annuity grow before income starts.

Use carefully—they're complex and come with fees.

1. 4. Tax-Efficient Drawdown

Order of operations matters:

1. **Taxable accounts**
2. **Tax-deferred accounts** (Traditional IRA, 401(k))
3. **Tax-free accounts** (Roth IRA, HSA)

Drawing down in this order can minimize your lifetime tax liability.

1. 5. Required Minimum Distributions (RMDs)

Once you hit 73 (or 75 depending on law changes), the IRS requires you to start withdrawing from traditional retirement accounts.

Plan early. Roth IRAs don't have RMDs—another reason to convert early if appropriate.

1. Pros and Cons of Early Retirement Planning
2. Pros
3. **Compounding:** More time = more growth.
4. **Flexibility:** More time to adjust to changes.
5. **Tax Optimization:** More opportunities to reduce your tax burden.
6. **Peace of Mind:** Less pressure during economic downturns or life changes.
7. Cons
8. **Overconfidence:** Early success can create complacency.
9. **Illiquidity:** Retirement accounts have penalties for early withdrawals.
10. **Complexity:** Multiple account types = more planning required.
11. Action Steps
12. **Open a retirement account** if you haven't already.
13. **Max out contributions** to tax-advantaged accounts.
14. **Create a retirement income plan** now, even if you're 20 years away.
15. **Hire a wealth advisor** who understands founder dynamics.

16. **Review your retirement plan** at least annually.
17. Plain-Language Breakdowns
18. Roth IRA vs. Traditional IRA
19. **Traditional IRA:** Pay taxes later.
20. **Roth IRA:** Pay taxes now.

When you're young and your income is lower—Roth. When you're older and your income is high—Traditional.

Simple.

1. Solo 401(k) vs. SEP IRA
2. **Solo 401(k):** Higher contribution limits. Roth option.
3. **SEP IRA:** Easier to set up. Great if you have no employees.

If you plan to grow—Solo 401(k).

1. Backdoor Roth IRA

Too wealthy for a direct Roth IRA?

1. Contribute to a Traditional IRA.
2. Immediately convert it to a Roth IRA.

Tax magic, legally.

1. Safe Withdrawal Rate
2. **4% Rule:** Start with 4% of your portfolio.
3. **Dynamic withdrawal:** Adjust based on market performance.

Adapt or risk running out of money.

1. Real-Life Scenarios
2. Scenario 1: The 29-Year-Old Founder

You just closed your $2M seed round. Your salary is $75,000.

Now is the perfect time to max out a Roth IRA. $6,500 a year now will turn into hundreds of thousands by retirement.

You can also start a Solo 401(k) to defer even more and potentially contribute to a Roth 401(k) component.

1. Scenario 2: The 42-Year-Old Serial Entrepreneur

You've exited twice. You're sitting on $15M.

Time to:

1. Establish a deferred compensation plan.
2. Max out HSA contributions.
3. Build a tax-efficient drawdown strategy.

You're planning not just for your retirement, but potentially your children's future.

1. Scenario 3: The 55-Year-Old Founder

You just had a liquidity event. You're sitting on $50M.

Now the game is:

1. Set up a Charitable Remainder Trust (CRT) for philanthropy and tax benefits.
2. Use a defined benefit plan to defer more income.
3. Convert Traditional IRAs to Roth during low-income years.

It's about legacy now.

1. Call to Act

Make one money move before you go to bed tonight. Just one. Open an

IRA. Book a call with a financial advisor. Sketch out your retirement vision.

And then do another next week.

Brick by brick, you'll build the future you deserve.

This isn't just about budgeting and investing.

This is about dignity.

This is about freedom.

This is about the power to say no to burnout and yes to wealth, wellness, and peace of mind.

You didn't build a groundbreaking company just to feel trapped by money.

Tech Business Founders is your permission slip to build the financial life you actually want—and deserve.

Your future self will thank you.

So will your bank account.

So will your peace of mind.

Chapter 38: Deferred Compensation Strategies

Why Deferred Compensation Matters

When most founders think about wealth, they think in terms of big liquidity moments: the Series C, the IPO, the acquisition offer that lands like a thunderclap.

But what often gets overlooked is what happens after that thunderclap.

Because while one big exit can make headlines, it's *managing the aftermath* that determines whether you're wealthy for a year—or wealthy for a lifetime.

This is where deferred compensation strategies come in.

They aren't glamorous. You won't see them shouted from a stage at TechCrunch Disrupt or posted about on LinkedIn. But they are one of the most powerful, understated wealth-building tools available to founders who are thinking ten steps ahead.

Deferred compensation is about smoothing out your income so that your wealth grows quietly, efficiently, and—most importantly—with an eye toward minimizing taxes and maximizing freedom.

It's about understanding that liquidity events are only half the game.

Managing the windfall is the other half.

And that's the half where real financial freedom is built.

What Is Deferred Compensation, Anyway?

Deferred compensation is exactly what it sounds like: compensation you've earned but chosen to delay receiving.

Instead of taking a big bonus or cash payout now (and taking the immediate tax hit), you elect to push the income into the future, strategically timing it to align with lower tax years or specific personal milestones.

Deferred compensation can be formal or informal.

Formal plans—like Non-Qualified Deferred Compensation (NQDC) plans—are structured through your company and regulated under IRS rules, particularly Section 409A.

Informal deferral might look more like equity that vests later, but formal plans offer much greater customization for cash flow planning.

The goal?

To match your income to your needs, not the IRS's calendar.

Think of it as *retirement account logic*, but on steroids—and without the rigid age restrictions.

The Key Benefits of Deferred Compensation

Let's break this down simply.

1. **Tax Deferral**
2. By deferring income, you delay the associated taxes. This can help you stay in a lower tax bracket now and potentially receive the income when your tax rate is lower—say, after you exit the startup grind and no longer have massive W-2 or bonus income.
3. **Tax Bracket Management**
4. Deferred compensation allows you to smooth your income over time instead of getting hit with a massive one-year windfall that vaults you into the highest federal (and possibly state) tax brackets.
5. **Customized Timing**
6. You can align income with life events: buying a house, funding your

next venture, or just ensuring you have a steady income stream without needing to liquidate investments at the wrong time.

7. **Compounding Advantages**
8. In many plans, the deferred amount can be invested and grow tax-deferred. That means you earn returns on money that hasn't been taxed yet—a powerful force for compounding.
9. **Psychological Benefits**
10. Big liquidity moments can create enormous pressure to spend—or to panic. Deferred compensation creates built-in patience, helping you act strategically rather than emotionally.

Deferred compensation isn't just about taxes.

It's about control.

And when you're managing newfound wealth, *control* is the most valuable currency you can have.

Common Types of Deferred Compensation Plans

Founders, especially those with complex compensation packages, can tap into several types of deferral vehicles. Let's explore them.

1. Non-Qualified Deferred Compensation (NQDC) Plans

NQDC plans are agreements between an employer and employee to defer receipt of income to a future date.

These plans don't have contribution limits like 401(k)s do. That means you can defer a significant portion of your income if structured properly.

However, NQDC plans are subject to strict IRS rules under Section 409A. These rules dictate:

- When you can elect to defer (generally before the year the income is earned).
- When you can receive the deferred income (usually only upon certain

trigger events like retirement, death, disability, or a change in company ownership).

The downside? These plans are considered unsecured promises to pay. If your company goes bankrupt, your deferred comp could be at risk.

Pro Tip: Founders who are still active in the business (and thus, insiders) need to tread carefully with NQDC plans, ensuring they don't create unwanted financial or reputational exposure.

2. 457 Plans (For Certain Nonprofit or Government Roles)

Less common for founders but worth mentioning: 457 plans offer similar tax deferral benefits without the same 409A restrictions. If you ever transition to a nonprofit or government role later in life, keep 457 plans on your radar.

3. Equity Deferral (Stock Options and RSUs)

Equity compensation can also function as a type of deferred compensation—if managed strategically.

For example:

- Incentive Stock Options (ISOs) can be held post-exercise to defer gains.
- Restricted Stock Units (RSUs) typically vest over time, deferring taxation until vesting and settlement.

Key Point: Understanding the nuances of equity deferral is critical, especially around timing exercises, managing Alternative Minimum Tax (AMT), and aligning vesting schedules with life goals.

Deferred equity requires different tax strategies than cash deferral—but the end goal is the same: control the timing of your income and your tax exposure.

Would you like me to continue from here and fully develop this into a

10,000+ word deep dive?

I can expand into:

- **The 409A risk and how to navigate it**
- **How to build a deferred comp strategy post-exit**
- **Real founder stories of doing it right—and wrong**
- **Pros and cons of different timing strategies**
- **Detailed action steps to implement deferred comp today**
- **A "Deferred Comp Readiness Checklist"**
- **Long-term simulations of deferred vs. non-deferred income**

The Hidden Risks: Why Deferred Compensation Isn't Always Easy

Deferred compensation is a powerful tool—but it's not without risk.

Let's talk about the fine print.

409A Compliance – What You Must Understand

Section 409A of the IRS code is the rulebook for non-qualified deferred compensation.

And it's not just fine print—it's serious.

409A sets out strict guidelines for when you can defer compensation, how you can structure your payouts, and what penalties you face if you violate the rules.

Penalties for noncompliance are brutal:

- Immediate taxation of the deferred amount.
- A 20% federal tax penalty.
- Potential state penalties.
- Interest charges back to the year the compensation was earned.

In other words, mess this up, and the IRS isn't just taking a bigger bite—

they're coming back for back taxes and fines.

Here's what you have to get right:

- **Election Timing**: You must elect to defer *before* the year the compensation is earned. If you're getting a bonus for 2026, you must elect deferral before 2025 ends.
- **Distribution Triggers**: You must specify the events that trigger payment—retirement, separation from service, death, disability, or an unforeseeable emergency.
- **Payout Schedules**: You need to commit to a payout schedule upfront. Once locked, you can't just change it on a whim without resetting the 409A clock (which adds a five-year delay).

Action Step: Before you even *think* about signing up for a deferred compensation plan, get an expert (CPA, tax attorney) to walk you through 409A compliance.

Company Solvency Risk — The Quiet Killer

Deferred compensation is technically an unsecured promise.

It's not in a trust.

It's not ring-fenced.

It's a corporate IOU.

If the company tanks, your deferred money is at risk.

This risk is usually acceptable at massive Fortune 500 firms with bulletproof balance sheets. But for startup founders—especially those post-exit still serving on boards—it's real.

If you're deferring compensation from a company that's not publicly traded or that's in an unstable industry, think twice.

Reality Check: Deferred comp is only as good as the company's ability—and willingness—to pay it later.

Building a Deferred Compensation Strategy Post-Exit

Let's imagine a scenario:

You've just exited your company for $100M.

You're sitting on a $10M payout after taxes.

You could stop reading here and ride into the sunset, right?

Not so fast.

Because what you do next—especially with future income streams from board seats, advisory roles, speaking engagements, or angel investing gigs—matters.

You're not done earning.

And deferred comp can be a key lever in building a second (or third) fortune.

Here's how.

Step 1: Identify Future Income Streams

Post-exit, many founders earn income from:

- Serving on corporate boards (cash and equity).
- Consulting or fractional CxO gigs.
- Investing (angel, venture partner roles).

Action Step: List out all expected (and potential) income sources over the next 5–10 years.

Step 2: Forecast Tax Brackets

The goal of deferred compensation is tax *arbitrage*.

You want to:

- Defer income when your tax bracket is high.
- Receive income when your tax bracket is lower.

Example:

- 2025–2027: You expect $1M+ income annually from board seats.
- 2028–2032: You plan to semi-retire, dropping income to $200K/year.

You want to defer as much of that $1M+ now to the 2028–2032 window when your tax bracket will be lower.

Action Step: Work with a CPA to model your future income and projected tax brackets.

Step 3: Structure Deferral Elections Carefully

You'll usually have to elect:

- What percentage of salary, bonus, or fees to defer.
- When the income will be paid out (date or event).
- How the payout will occur (lump sum, installments).

Most NQDC plans allow lump sum or periodic payouts (e.g., 5 annual installments).

Pro Tip: Installments can be better than lump sums for tax smoothing and cash flow management.

Caution: Once you pick the schedule, it's locked under 409A rules. Choose carefully.

Step 4: Align Deferral With Investment Opportunities

Deferred compensation plans often let you allocate the deferred funds to investment choices—think mutual funds, ETFs, or fixed income portfolios.

Your deferred dollars can grow *tax-deferred* inside the plan.

Action Step: Treat your deferred comp like a mini-retirement plan. Diversify it.

If you're taking risks elsewhere (venture investments, real estate), this is a place to be more conservative.

Step 5: Create a Liquidity Plan

Deferred comp isn't just a tax tool—it's a liquidity management tool.

You don't want to defer *everything* and find yourself cash-strapped.

Remember:

- Taxes.
- Lifestyle spending.
- Health insurance premiums.
- Travel, kids' education, new ventures.

Action Step: Map out a personal liquidity plan—when will you need cash, and how much?

This will help you choose appropriate deferral amounts and payout timelines.

Real-Life Founder Stories: Deferred Compensation Done Right (and Wrong)

Case Study #1: The Cautious Planner

Sara sold her SaaS company at 39.

She stayed on the acquiring company's board for five years, earning $500K annually in cash comp.

She deferred 50% of her board fees into an NQDC plan, scheduled for payout over 10 years starting at age 45.

Why it worked:

- She was still in the highest federal tax bracket while on the board.
- When her board service ended, her taxable income dropped dramatically.

- The deferred amounts grew at 6% annually inside the plan.
- She paid lower marginal rates on the distributions.

Result? She saved over $1M in taxes versus taking the income immediately.

Case Study #2: The Illiquid Mistake

David founded a biotech startup and exited in a stock-for-stock merger.

Post-exit, he deferred 80% of his board fees into an NQDC plan at the acquiring company.

Two years later, the acquirer went bankrupt.

David's deferred comp? Gone.

Why it failed:

- He underestimated the acquiring company's financial health.
- He deferred too much, leaving himself cash-poor.
- No bankruptcy protection for NQDC.

Lesson: Don't over-defer at a company that isn't rock-solid.

Pros and Cons of Deferred Compensation Strategies

Let's put it in simple, founder-speak terms.

ProsCons

Tax deferral

Company solvency risk

Tax bracket management

409A compliance risk

Investment growth pre-tax

No access to funds until payout

Customized payout timing

Payout timing is inflexible

Psychological separation from wealth

Lack of liquidity during deferral

Deferred comp is powerful, but it's not a hammer for every nail.
It's one tool in a larger wealth strategy.

Action Steps: Building Your Deferred Compensation Playbook

Ready to put this into action?
Here's your founder-specific playbook.

1. Assemble Your Team

- Tax attorney (409A expert)
- Wealth advisor
- CPA

2. Model Future Income Scenarios

- Board seats
- Consulting gigs
- New ventures
- Speaking, teaching, writing

3. Forecast Future Tax Brackets

- High-income years vs. low-income years
- Retirement years
- Residency changes (moving from high- to low-tax states)

4. Design a Deferral Strategy

- Percentage of income to defer
- Payout trigger events
- Lump sum vs. installments

5. Allocate Investment Choices

- Diversified, conservative
- Match risk to your broader portfolio

6. Document Everything

409A compliance is about *paperwork*. No shortcuts.

7. Revisit Annually

- Income changes.
- Tax law changes.
- Life changes.

Your plan should adapt.

Deferred Comp Readiness Checklist

- Understand 409A compliance.
- Assess company solvency risk.
- Model income and tax brackets for the next 10–20 years.
- Design a liquidity plan to avoid being cash-poor.
- Work with qualified professionals—no DIY here.
- Choose investment allocations aligned with your risk tolerance.
- Document and revisit your elections annually.

The Bigger Picture: Deferred Comp Is About Control

As a founder, you're used to controlling your company's destiny.

Deferred comp gives you a way to control your financial destiny.

It's about:

- *Smoothing* volatile income streams.
- *Strategically* managing taxes.
- *Aligning* cash flow with your life plans.
- *Growing* wealth patiently and purposefully.

It's not sexy.

It won't be the cocktail party story.

But it will quietly, steadily, power your freedom.

And that's what wealth is really about.

Not bragging rights.

Not Twitter followers.

Freedom.

Freedom to say yes to what matters—and no to what doesn't.

Freedom to build again—or to walk away.

Freedom to live life on your terms.

Deferred compensation is one piece of the puzzle.

But used wisely, it's a powerful piece.

A Call to Act

Make one money move before you go to bed tonight.

Just one.

Maybe it's:

- Emailing your CPA about deferred comp modeling.
- Scheduling a call with a wealth advisor.
- Starting a list of future income streams.

Then do another move next week.

Tiny, consistent action builds financial freedom faster than any exit ever could.

This isn't just about taxes.

This is about dignity.

This is about freedom.

This is about the power to say no to burnout—and yes to wealth, wellness, and peace of mind.

You didn't build a groundbreaking company just to feel trapped by money.

Tech Business Founders is your permission slip to build the financial life you actually want—and deserve.

Chapter 39: Succession Planning for Founders

Why Succession Planning Is Non-Negotiable

If you're reading this, you're a builder. A creator. A founder. You've poured sweat, sleepless nights, and maybe a few tears into something that matters.

And yet, for so many founders, succession planning feels like the furthest thing from urgent.

You're too busy building.

Or you believe succession is something you'll figure out "someday."

Or you think if you exit, you'll exit clean—and the company will be someone else's problem.

But here's the truth: ignoring succession doesn't delay it; it invites chaos.

Succession is not just a business issue—it's a *legacy* issue.

Succession planning is how you protect:

- Your employees' futures.
- Your customers' trust.
- Your investors' capital.
- Your own reputation.

And frankly, it's how you sleep at night knowing your life's work doesn't collapse the day you leave the corner office.

If you don't plan succession, succession will plan you—and it usually won't be pretty.

Illness. Burnout. Acquisition. Unexpected opportunities. Family obligations. The list goes on.

No matter how young, healthy, or hungry you are, life happens.

And when it does, you'll be grateful you didn't leave your company—and your legacy—rudderless.

Succession planning isn't a luxury.

It's a duty.

It's leadership.

And if you want to win not just at the game of startups but at the game of life, you must start now.

What Succession Planning Really Means

Let's demystify it.

Succession planning isn't just about naming the next CEO.

It's about designing a *system* that ensures the company thrives without you at the helm.

It's not just about choosing who's next.

It's about answering:

- *What skills and values will the next leader need?*
- *What timeline makes sense for transition?*
- *How do we prepare the team, customers, and investors for change?*
- *How does succession fit into our overall strategic plan?*

At its best, succession planning isn't a single plan.

It's a *playbook* for continuity, growth, and stability.

It gives your team clarity.

It gives investors confidence.

And it gives you the ultimate founder superpower: optionality.

You get to leave—or stay—on your terms.

The Hidden Wealth in Succession Planning

There's another reason to take succession seriously: it makes your company *worth more.*

Buyers, private equity firms, and public markets all care deeply about one thing: stability.

If the business can't survive without you, it's not valuable.

If it thrives without you, it's priceless.

Founders who can point to a clear, documented, and rehearsed succession plan often:

- Attract higher valuations.
- Close exits faster.
- Reduce earnout risk.
- Enjoy smoother IPO transitions.

Succession isn't just a feel-good leadership thing.

It's a wealth builder.

It's financial engineering for your cap table—and your legacy.

Identifying and Grooming Your Successors

Let's get tactical.

How do you find the right successor?

Here's the honest answer: you don't find them.

You *build* them.

The right successor is usually not the flashiest executive.

It's not always the one with the longest resume.

And it's rarely someone from outside who swoops in and "saves" the company.

The best successors often:

- Understand the mission at a cellular level.
- Have earned internal credibility.
- Possess leadership potential, even if it's still raw.
- Are coachable and humble enough to learn.

Your job? Identify them early.

Then invest in them relentlessly.

Here's a blueprint:

1. Define Success

Get crystal clear on what the company will need in the next phase.

Will it need:

- A builder or a scaler?
- A visionary or an operator?
- A stabilizer or a disruptor?

Succession isn't about cloning yourself.

It's about finding someone who fits the company's *future*—not just its *past*.

2. Look Beyond the Obvious

Sometimes your successor is not the person with the flashiest title.

Look deeper:

- Who shows leadership in crises?
- Who earns trust across departments?
- Who can think three moves ahead?

Create a short list of 3–5 internal candidates.

Then have the courage to be honest about their gaps.

3. Build a Development Plan

Once you've identified high-potential successors, start grooming them.

That might mean:

- Giving them P&L responsibility.
- Exposing them to board meetings.
- Coaching them on strategic thinking.
- Encouraging external executive education.

Leadership isn't a gift.

It's a craft.

And it's your responsibility to help them sharpen it.

The Founder's Dilemma: Letting Go

Here's the hardest part of succession planning:

You.

You are the biggest risk to a smooth succession.

Not because you don't care.

But because founders struggle with:

- Letting go of control.
- Trusting others with "their baby."
- Redefining their identity post-transition.

It's normal.

You didn't build this company to hand it over lightly.

But if you grip it too tightly, you'll choke its future.

You must be willing to:

- Delegate before you're desperate.
- Teach before you leave.

- Empower before you exit.

Succession is an *act of generosity*.

It's giving your creation a future bigger than yourself.

It's leadership at its highest level.

Transitioning Leadership Smoothly

Let's get even more tactical.

How do you make the actual leadership transition?

Here's the playbook:

1. Communicate Early and Often

Silence breeds fear.

Rumors kill morale.

As soon as you have a plan, communicate it internally—clearly and transparently.

Explain:

- Why you're planning succession.
- How the process will work.
- What the timeline looks like.

Transparency calms nerves.

It builds trust.

It keeps the company focused on the mission, not on hallway gossip.

2. Stage the Transition

Don't just announce a successor and disappear.

Design a runway.

Typical stages:

- **Announcement**: Publicly introduce the successor and transition plan.
- **Shadowing**: Let the successor gradually take over responsibilities with you as a mentor.
- **Authority Handoff**: Publicly—and symbolically—hand over decision-making power.
- **Exit**: Step away completely to give the new leader space.

3. Support, Don't Hover

After the transition, resist the urge to meddle.

Your successor needs:

- Space to lead.
- Authority to make mistakes.
- Confidence that you trust them.

Stay available—but stay out of the way.

Real-Life Succession Stories

Case Study #1: The Reluctant Founder

Jen built a $200M fintech company from scratch.

She was beloved by the team.

When she started thinking about succession, she quietly promoted her COO to President, giving him more authority over day-to-day operations.

For two years, she slowly shifted more responsibility to him—without fanfare.

By the time she officially stepped down, it wasn't a shock.

It felt natural.

The result?

The company kept growing.

Investors cheered.

And Jen got to exit gracefully—knowing her life's work was in good hands.

Case Study #2: The Trainwreck

Tom ran a fast-scaling SaaS company.

He assumed he was irreplaceable.

He didn't groom anyone internally.

When a health crisis forced him to step down, the board scrambled to find an external CEO.

Culture crumbled.

Top talent fled.

Revenue dipped.

The company was sold at a discount just two years later.

Lesson: Succession planning isn't optional.

It's insurance for your legacy.

Pros and Cons of Different Succession Approaches

Let's break it down.

ApproachProsCons

Internal Grooming

Cultural continuity, employee trust

Takes time, may have skill gaps

External Hire

Fresh perspective, new skills

Cultural mismatch risk, longer ramp-up

Acquisition by Larger Firm

Liquidity, risk offloading

Loss of independence, integration risk

Employee Stock Ownership Plan (ESOP)

Motivates employees, founder exits gradually

Complex, requires careful structuring

Action Steps: Building Your Succession Plan

Ready to get real about succession?

Here's your founder-specific checklist.

1. Start Now

Succession planning takes 2–5 years.

Start before you "need" to.

2. Define the Future CEO Profile

Based on where your company is going—not where it's been.

3. Identify High-Potential Leaders

Look for capability and character.

Not just title and tenure.

4. Build a Development Pipeline

Give them real responsibility—and coaching.

5. Create a Transition Timeline

Stage it.

Communicate it.

Commit to it.

6. Get Your Board and Investors on Board

They need to be part of the process early.

7. Design Your Next Act

Whether it's a new venture, a sabbatical, or a board role—know what's next for *you*.

Succession is easier when you're excited about the next chapter.

Succession Planning Is Freedom Planning

Founders often fear succession because they think it's the end.

It's not.

It's the beginning of something even bigger.

Succession is about:

- Building a company that outlasts you.
- Creating a leadership legacy.
- Protecting your people.
- Unlocking your next adventure.

And the best part?

A well-planned succession lets you leave when you're *ready*—not when you're *forced*.

It's not just smart business.

It's freedom.

A Call to Act

Make one money move before you go to bed tonight.

Just one.

Maybe it's:

- Making a list of potential successors.
- Scheduling a lunch with your COO to discuss leadership development.
- Talking to your board about succession planning.

Then do another move next week.

Tiny, consistent action builds the future faster than any funding round ever could.

This isn't just about you stepping down.

This is about dignity.

This is about freedom.

This is about the power to say no to burnout—and yes to legacy, leadership, and peace of mind.

You didn't build a groundbreaking company just to have it crumble when you leave.

Tech Business Founders is your permission slip to build the leadership bench, the succession plan, and the enduring company you—and the world—deserve.

Chapter 40: Building a Financial Legacy

You didn't build a company to sell it. You didn't accumulate wealth to flash it. You built. You earned. You fought battles no one saw. And now, you have something bigger staring at you from across the horizon: legacy.

Legacy is the reason you're even considering this conversation. It's not estate taxes. It's not market returns. It's not asset allocation. It's not even "generational wealth" in the Instagram sense. It's the deeper, quieter, far more difficult work of building something that will outlast you — something that matters long after the money itself has moved or multiplied.

Legacy is the real impact you leave behind — on your family, your community, your society. It's the difference between your story ending with you, and your story starting a ripple effect that carries across generations.

Founders like you — founders with grit, foresight, and audacity — understand this instinctively: true success isn't measured by what you build, but by what survives you. And yet, too many founders let that survival become an afterthought.

They assume wealth will naturally translate into security. They assume the next generation will "figure it out." They assume the story will continue without a script. But wealth without intentionality is a house built on sand. The statistics are sobering: over 70% of wealthy families lose their wealth by the second generation. 90% by the third.

It's not because the markets collapse. It's not because assets vanish. It's because leadership disappears. Values disappear. Stewardship disappears.

Wealth transfer without legacy transfer is a gift wrapped in chaos. If you want to build a real financial legacy, you need more than a well-funded trust account and a stack of legal documents. You need a philosophy. You need a system. You need education. You need governance. And most importantly — you need to start before it feels necessary.

Educating the Next Generation

Let's start where it matters most — your heirs. Whether it's your children, nieces and nephews, godchildren, or the next layer of leadership you envision, one thing is universal: if they're next in line for your story, they need preparation.

Most founders' first instinct is to shield their heirs from money. Keep the balances secret. Avoid "spoiling" them. Hope that if you don't talk about money, they'll somehow learn to respect it. But silence is not stewardship.

If you don't teach them about wealth, the world will. And the world's lessons aren't always the ones you want shaping your heirs. Instagram will. TikTok will. Entitlement will. And none of those forces have your family's best interests at heart.

Wealth without wisdom is a grenade without a pin. So how do you prepare them for stewardship without breeding entitlement?

1. Normalize Money Conversations Early

Money shouldn't be taboo. It should be as everyday as talking about school, health, or careers. Start young. Teach basic lessons early: how a bank works. Why saving matters. The difference between earning and spending.

As they grow, layer in complexity: how compound interest works. Why taxes exist. The concept of investing. What entrepreneurship means. Don't just teach them how to make money — teach them how to understand and respect it.

The goal isn't to raise kids obsessed with money. It's to raise kids comfortable around money — but not defined by it.

2. Teach Values Before Valuations

Before you dive into balance sheets, teach balance. Before you talk about inheritance, talk about impact. The most successful legacy builders focus on instilling:

- Work ethic
- Humility
- Gratitude
- Responsibility
- Service

Teach them that money is a tool — not an identity. If they internalize the right values, they'll handle the money well. If they don't, no amount of legal structuring will save them from self-sabotage.

3. Expose Them to Real-World Financial Decisions

Education without application is incomplete. Involve them — don't just lecture them.

Bring them to board meetings (when appropriate). Introduce them to your financial advisors. Let them sit in on meetings about charitable donations. Walk them through investment decisions. Let them see the real work that goes into stewardship.

When mistakes happen — and they will — turn them into debriefs, not shame sessions. The goal is to let them experience decision-making under pressure — with a mentor standing next to them, not rescuing them.

Real financial education happens in real time, guided by someone who cares enough to teach patiently.

Family Governance Frameworks

Philosophy is important. But philosophy without structure is hope without architecture. Legacy that survives generational shifts needs governance.

Family governance isn't about turning your family into a boardroom. It's about creating a system — structures, agreements, processes — that help the family manage wealth, make decisions, resolve conflicts, and stay aligned on values.

Without governance, even the strongest families drift. With governance, even imperfect families endure.

1. Create a Family Mission Statement

Every business you built had a mission statement. Your family should have one too.

A good family mission statement answers questions like:

- What do we believe in?
- Why do we exist as a family unit?
- What kind of impact do we want to make on the world?
- What are our shared values?

It's not about control. It's about clarity. It's not about dictating behavior. It's about defining identity. And just like your business plan, it's not a one-and-done document. Review it annually. Let every big decision be filtered through its lens.

2. Set Up a Family Council

Think of the family council as your family's board of directors.

Typically composed of family leaders, representatives from the next generation, and sometimes outside advisors, the council manages:

- Strategic financial priorities
- Education initiatives
- Conflict mediation
- Philanthropic strategies

It brings clarity to chaos. It turns one-off conversations into coordinated strategy. It's not bureaucracy — it's breathing room. When people know how decisions are made, they fight less and focus more.

3. Draft a Family Constitution

A family constitution is not a legal document. It's a living one.

It formalizes the mission, the governance structures, and the rules of engagement:

- Decision-making processes
- Roles and responsibilities
- Succession plans
- Conflict resolution protocols

It evolves with the family. It doesn't guarantee unity, but it gives the family a roadmap for finding its way back when conflict arises. Think of it as your family's operating manual — for when things are good, and for when they're not.

Sustaining Wealth Across Generations

Education and governance are necessary. But sustaining wealth through generations requires more.

Markets change. People change. Mistakes happen. Even with preparation, wealth can evaporate. So how do you create not just a financial legacy — but a resilient one?

1. Prioritize Sustainability Over Size

Chasing bigger isn't the goal. Protecting resilience is.

A $500 million estate with no risk management can collapse faster than a $50 million estate with cautious stewardship. Focus on:

- Long-term investing principles
- Prudent diversification
- Reasonable, sustainable lifestyles
- Disciplined risk management

Teach your heirs that preserving wealth is step one. Growing it can come later. Humility sustains more fortunes than aggression.

2. Leverage Multi-Generational Trusts

Trusts aren't just for tax avoidance — they're for stewardship.

- Incentive trusts can release funds when beneficiaries hit life milestones.
- Generation-skipping trusts can bypass layers of estate tax, preserving wealth longer.
- Silent trusts can delay disclosure until heirs reach an age or level of maturity.

Trusts allow you to guide behavior without suffocating autonomy. They allow structure without control. The best trusts protect not just the assets — but the intent behind them.

3. Invest in Financial Literacy Continuously

Education isn't one-and-done.

Financial literacy must evolve as markets, tools, and risks evolve. Make it a tradition:

- Annual retreats with guest speakers
- Investment workshops
- Family book clubs on financial topics
- Mentoring programs within the family

Financial education should be part of the family culture — not an emergency response to a wealth event.

Real-Life Legacy Builders

The Pritzker Family: Founders of the Hyatt empire, they nearly destroyed their wealth through infighting. Once they realized the risk, they restructured their governance — splitting the fortune, clarifying leadership, and investing in next-gen education. Today, multiple Pritzkers lead significant ventures and philanthropic causes.

The Rothschilds: They understood early on that wealth preservation required strategic marriages, rigorous financial education, and meticulous governance. Their wealth lasted across centuries, through wars and upheaval — because they understood that money without mission decays.

Pros and Cons of Different Legacy Structures

StructureProsCons

Family Trusts

Asset protection, tax efficiency

Complexity, legal costs

Family Constitution

Cultural continuity, conflict resolution

Requires ongoing commitment

Family Council

Clear decision-making, shared governance

Needs genuine buy-in

Direct Education

Builds capability, promotes leadership
Success depends on engagement
Philanthropic Foundations
Public legacy, significant tax advantages
Complex management, regulatory hurdles

Action Steps: Building Your Financial Legacy

Here's where you start:

1. **Write your family mission statement.** Pen and paper. No consultants needed. Just honest conversation.
2. **Start one money conversation.** This week. With one family member. Budgeting. Saving. Giving. Start normalizing.
3. **Create a governance outline.** Even if it's messy. Even if it's simple. Get a starting point.
4. **Commit to education.** One initiative this year. A retreat. A speaker. A workshop. Set the tone.

This isn't just about money.

This is about dignity. About autonomy. About the freedom to say no to the forces that erode generational wealth — and yes to the forces that build generational strength.

You didn't fight to build your company just to watch your wealth evaporate two generations later. You didn't create innovation only to let disorganization destroy your legacy.

You are the architect not just of success — but of significance.

Make one move before you go to bed tonight. Just one. Then another next week. Tiny moves compound. Tiny moves build dynasties.

Your future self will thank you.

So will your children.

So will your grandchildren.

So will your great-grandchildren — whether they ever know your name or not.

Conclusion: Wealth is Only the Beginning

You didn't build your company just to make money. Money was never the goal — it was a byproduct. It was the applause after the performance. The scoreboard after the game. The residue of something far more powerful: your vision.

You built because you believed you could change something — an industry, a life, the world itself. You built because you had a truth inside you that was too big to stay there. Now you stand at a crossroads few ever reach. Perhaps the wealth is already in your hands, tucked away in brokerage accounts, real estate holdings, private equity deals. Or maybe it's just over the next ridge — the IPO, the acquisition, the long-awaited liquidity event. Either way, here you are — closer to the summit than most ever get.

The world will tell you that wealth is the finish line. They are wrong. Wealth isn't the end of the story — it's the prologue to a much richer one. It's only the beginning.

Money Is the Fuel, Not the Destination

Wealth is not the destination. It's a tool. A powerful, dangerous, liberating tool. But just that — a tool. Not a trophy. Not an identity. Not a guaranteed ticket to happiness or peace or purpose.

Money can buy you time. It can amplify your voice. It can multiply your impact. It can secure your family's future. It can fund revolutions — of thought, of industry, of community. But it can also isolate you. It can confuse you. It can trap you. It can dilute your values. It can erode your drive. It can leave you lonelier at the top than you ever imagined at the bottom.

It all depends on how you use it.

The most successful founders — the ones who not only make wealth but master it — know a secret that sounds obvious but feels radical: money is fuel. It's not the car. It's not the road. It's not the driver. It's the fuel.

Fuel for freedom. Fuel for dreams. Fuel for a life of deep intentionality and relentless meaning. The goal isn't more fuel. It's better driving.

Financial Freedom Enables New Ventures

One of the most persistent myths in entrepreneurship is that the story ends with the exit. You build. You sell. You retire. You disappear onto a yacht or a private island.

But that story doesn't fit you, does it?

Founders like you aren't built for idle retirement. You're wired to build. To innovate. To push. Financial freedom doesn't end the game — it unlocks a whole new one.

With wealth, you have the freedom to start businesses not because you have to — but because you want to. You can back entrepreneurs you believe in. You can invest in causes that ignite you. You can launch a foundation. Write the book. Fund the documentary. Teach the next generation.

Financial freedom buys you resilience. It allows you to take swings without fear of striking out. It lets you build from a place of abundance, not scarcity. It enables you to design a life aligned not with your net worth, but with your deepest values.

Freedom isn't a lack of responsibility. It's the freedom to choose the responsibilities that matter most.

Your Wealth Can Empower Your Legacy

Money alone doesn't build a legacy. It buys headlines, not history. It creates data points, not dynasties.

Legacy isn't about dollars. It's about values, actions, impact, relationships. It's about the business you built, yes — but also the lives you touched, the values you lived, the lessons you passed down.

Wealth can be a force-multiplier for your legacy — if you design it to be.

It can fund scholarships that reshape families. It can back ventures that reimagine industries. It can support nonprofits that solve the problems that governments ignore. It can give your family the freedom to dream bigger, build bolder, and give more generously.

Legacy isn't what you leave behind. Legacy is what you set in motion.

Real-Life Founder Journeys

Let's step away from theory. Here's how real founders — founders like you — moved from wealth to legacy.

Case Study #1: The Serial Creator

Jason built and sold his first company at 35 for $50 million. For a year, he tried the "retirement" thing. Golf. Travel. Angel investing. But he felt restless. Unfulfilled. Like an athlete benched in the prime of his career.

So he started a venture studio. He funded and mentored first-time founders, not to get rich — but to pass the baton. He didn't chase unicorns. He chased impact. Today, he's helped launch 27 companies, backed dozens of social enterprises, and sits on the boards of four nonprofits. His wealth didn't retire him. It freed him.

Case Study #2: The Legacy Architect

Nina sold her e-commerce company for $150 million. After the initial rush, she realized that what she wanted wasn't luxury — it was legacy. She set her sights on ending generational poverty in her hometown. Scholarships. Business grants. Affordable housing.

But she didn't stop there. She brought her children into the process. She taught them about philanthropy, entrepreneurship, stewardship. Today, she runs a $500 million family foundation — with her children on the board, and her grandchildren in training. Nina didn't just make money. She made change.

Pros and Cons of Financial Freedom

ProsCons

Freedom to choose your next venture

Risk of losing focus or sense of purpose

Ability to take bigger swings without fear

Potential to overextend or chase distractions

Time for family, health, passions

Risk of isolation or boredom

Opportunity for deeper impact

Possible dilution of hunger and drive

Financial freedom is a blank canvas. But blank canvases can be paralyzing without vision and intention.

Action Steps: Your Next Move

You don't have to figure it all out today. You just have to take the first step.

1. Define Your Personal Mission

Ask yourself: What do I want my wealth to do? Not just for me — but through me. Write it down. No edits. No filters. Fill a page.

This is the first draft of your Wealth Mission Statement.

2. Map Your Next Venture

Financial freedom gives you optionality. What do you want to build next?

- A new business?
- A venture fund?

- A nonprofit?
- A family foundation?
- A memoir?

Choose one project. Commit to one small action this month. A phone call. A meeting. A brainstorm. A journal entry. Start.

3. Craft Your Legacy Plan

Legacy isn't "someday." Legacy is built now.

- Who do you want to mentor?
- What causes matter to you?
- What traditions do you want to pass down?

Start documenting. Start conversations with your family. Start living your legacy — today.

Make one money move before you go to bed tonight. Just one.

Maybe it's:

- Sending an email to your wealth advisor.
- Researching donor-advised funds.
- Writing the first line of your mission statement.
- Scheduling a family money meeting.

Tiny moves compound. Tiny moves build dynasties. Tiny moves build legacies.

This isn't about money. It's about leadership. It's about designing not just a life, but a legacy. It's about building a future where your impact outlives your income, where your influence outlasts your ownership.

You didn't build your company just to feel trapped by the money it created. You built it to build something bigger.

Ultra Affluent isn't just about wealth. It's about freedom. It's about stewardship. It's about the life you were born to live — and the legacy you were born to leave.

Here's a list of questions you should ask financial advisors, CPAs, estate planning attorneys.

Questions to Ask a Financial Advisor (For Tech Founders)

- **Are you a fiduciary 100% of the time?**
- Fiduciaries are legally obligated to put your interests first—no commissions, no hidden agendas.
- **Do you have experience working with tech founders, startup executives, or equity-compensated clients?**
- Your world includes stock options, RSUs, liquidity events, and complex tax considerations. Make sure they understand the landscape.
- **How do you get paid?**
- Fee-only, fee-based, or commission? Transparency matters. Know if they earn money from selling products or strictly from advising.
- **Can you help with equity compensation planning, including stock options, RSUs, and pre-IPO shares?**
- Equity is a critical part of your wealth strategy. You need someone who knows how to optimize it.
- **Will you coordinate with my CPA, estate attorney, and other professionals?**
- Great advisors collaborate. Your financial, tax, and legal strategies should be integrated.
- **What's your investment philosophy?**

- Look for clear, evidence-based strategies. Avoid hype and high-risk speculation disguised as advice.
- **How do you help founders prepare for liquidity events, acquisitions, or IPOs?**
- Life-changing events require sophisticated planning for taxes, diversification, and long-term security.
- **Can you advise on risk management, including asset protection and liability insurance?**
- As a founder, your personal and business risks often overlap. Make sure they understand how to protect you.
- **Are you familiar with retirement planning for entrepreneurs, including SEP IRAs, Solo 401(k)s, and defined benefit plans?**
- Startup founders have different retirement needs compared to traditional employees.
- **Do you provide scenario planning and financial modeling?**
- You need clear projections for different outcomes—whether that's an acquisition offer or taking a year off post-exit.

Questions to Ask a CPA (Certified Public Accountant)

- **Do you specialize in working with tech entrepreneurs, founders, or VC-backed companies?**
- Your income streams, deductions, and tax strategies are not one-size-fits-all.
- **Do you provide proactive tax planning—or just file returns?**
- You need year-round strategy, not just an annual tax prep session.
- **Are you experienced with QSBS (Qualified Small Business Stock) rules and Section 1202 exclusions?**
- These can be major tax savers for founders during an exit—don't miss out due to inexperience.
- **Can you advise on optimizing retirement contributions and tax-efficient charitable giving?**
- Smart CPAs help you grow wealth and give back—efficiently.

- **Do you handle multi-state income, international tax issues, or complex entity structures?**
- Founders often work across borders and states; your CPA should know how to navigate that.
- **Will you represent me in the event of an IRS audit?**
- Audit protection is crucial, especially with complex financials.
- **Do you consult on real estate investments or other passive income strategies?**
- Founders often diversify post-exit; make sure your CPA can guide you.

Questions to Ask an Estate Planning Attorney

- **Do you have experience working with founders and business owners?**
- Your estate plan must reflect company ownership, stock options, and liquidity events.
- **What core documents should I have in place?**
- Will, trust, durable power of attorney, and healthcare directives are essential.
- **Can you advise on asset protection strategies to shield personal wealth?**
- Lawsuits happen. Protect your gains early.
- **How do you handle estate planning for business owners and investors?**
- Company shares and investments require strategic estate planning.
- **Should I set up a revocable living trust or more advanced structures like GRATs or IDGTs?**
- High-net-worth founders often benefit from advanced strategies.
- **Can you help with succession planning for business continuity?**
- If you're still involved in your company, plan ahead.
- **How often should I update my estate plan?**
- Life moves fast—your estate plan should keep pace.

Questions to Ask a Business Attorney (For Founders Who Own or Are Scaling Companies)

- **Do you specialize in startups, venture-backed businesses, or tech firms?**
- Startup law isn't traditional business law.
- **Can you advise on entity formation—C-Corp vs. LLC, Delaware incorporation, etc.?**
- The right setup has long-term implications for fundraising and taxes.
- **Will you review or draft shareholder agreements, IP assignments, employment agreements, and funding documents?**
- Founders sign complex contracts; don't do it blind.
- **Do you help with IP protection—patents, trademarks, software licensing?**
- Your IP is often your most valuable asset.
- **Can you advise on exit strategies, mergers, or acquisitions?**
- Your lawyer should be an asset from launch to exit.
- **Do you charge hourly, on retainer, or offer flat fees for standard documents?**
- Know your costs upfront.

Bonus: Questions to Ask Other Key Professionals

Insurance Agent (Life, Disability, Umbrella, Key Person)

- Are you independent or captive?
- Can you tailor coverage to protect both personal and business risks?
- Should I consider key person insurance for my startup?
- Can you explain the pros and cons of term versus permanent life insurance for a founder?

Real Estate Advisor or Investment Specialist

- Can you help evaluate real estate investments based on cash flow and long-term ROI?
- Are you experienced with 1031 exchanges or Opportunity Zones for tax advantages?

Career Coach or Executive Consultant

- Can you guide founders through burnout, life after exit, or transitioning to VC, angel investing, or other next chapters?
- Can you model the financial impact of career pivots or startup advisory roles?

Final Thought

Choosing the right financial team is one of the highest-return decisions you'll ever make as a founder.

Ask smart questions.

Expect straight, transparent answers.

You wouldn't ship code without a QA process.

Treat your financial life with the same discipline—build a team worthy of your vision.

Important Disclaimer

Financial Literacy for Tech Business Founders is written to educate, empower, and encourage tech entrepreneurs at every stage of their journey—from startup launch to scaling, exiting, and beyond—to take control of their financial lives. The insights in this book are based on the author's personal experience, professional training, and over two decades of work in financial services, personal finance education, and advising clients in technology, innovation, and entrepreneurship.

That said, it's important to be clear about what this book is—and what it is not.

Educational Purpose Only

All content in this book is provided for general educational and informational purposes. It is intended to introduce tech founders—whether pre-seed, venture-backed, bootstrapped, or post-exit—to essential financial concepts, strategic tools, and a deeper awareness of the financial opportunities and challenges unique to the startup world.

While this book offers frameworks, strategies, case studies, and real-world examples, it is not personalized financial advice. Every founder's situation is unique. Your goals, equity structure (stock options, RSUs, founder's shares), ownership interests, fundraising rounds, tax position, and risk tolerance must all be considered individually.

Before making significant financial, legal, or business decisions, you should work with licensed professionals who understand your specific needs and goals.

No Legal Advice

Although founders routinely deal with contracts, cap tables, stock option plans, intellectual property protections, and M&A deals, this book does not provide legal advice. It is not a replacement for working with a qualified attorney.

If you are:

- Drafting or negotiating shareholder agreements
- Setting up a corporate structure (LLC, C-Corp, S-Corp)
- Protecting intellectual property like patents, software, or trademarks
- Structuring business succession or exit plans
- Managing fundraising rounds or term sheets

...you should seek the counsel of an attorney who specializes in startup law, corporate law, intellectual property, or M&A. Legal frameworks vary by jurisdiction and individual circumstances. You are responsible for ensuring compliance with all applicable laws and regulations.

No Financial or Investment Advice

This book covers important topics like budgeting for startups, managing personal and business finances, retirement planning, investing after a liquidity event, and long-term wealth-building—but from an educational perspective, not an advisory one.

This book is not written by a Certified Financial Planner™, Registered Investment Advisor, or broker-dealer. The strategies, sample models, and examples are general and may not directly apply to your situation.

Before executing any financial strategy, reallocating investments, exercising stock options, or planning a liquidity event, consult a licensed financial professional who understands the nuances of tech entrepreneurship and equity compensation.

Your business equity, personal investments, and long-term financial health are too important to leave to generalized advice.

No Accounting or Tax Advice

Taxes are a central part of wealth-building and preservation for tech founders—especially those navigating QSBS, 83(b) elections, fundraising structures, or multiple exits. However, this book is not written by a CPA, Enrolled Agent, or licensed tax preparer. Any discussions around tax deductions, equity compensation, or IRS rules are for general educational purposes only.

If you:

- Exercise or sell stock options (ISOs, NSOs, RSUs)
- Qualify for QSBS exemptions or 83(b) elections
- Earn income internationally or hold ownership across multiple entities
- Need help with business deductions, entity taxation, or advanced tax strategies

...you should hire a qualified tax professional. Only a licensed tax advisor can analyze your situation and help you comply with current laws while optimizing your tax outcomes.

No Guarantees or Promises

Reading this book does not guarantee startup success, favorable investment returns, a successful exit, or financial independence. Financial literacy, much like entrepreneurship, is not a one-time accomplishment—it's an ongoing discipline that demands learning, practice, and strategic action over time.

The case studies and examples are for illustrative purposes only. They are not guarantees or predictors of future performance. Your financial results will depend on many factors—your decisions, market dynamics, economic conditions, company performance, and sometimes luck.

Limitation of Liability

By reading this book, you agree that the author, Pat Brown, MBA, and all affiliated websites and brands—such as FinancialLiteracyForTechFounders.com and FinancialLiteracyForNIL.com—are not responsible for your financial outcomes, legal challenges, tax liabilities, or business consequences.

Neither the author nor any associated entity shall be liable for financial losses, legal actions, tax penalties, or other negative outcomes associated with your use of the information presented here. You are fully responsible for your financial, legal, and business decisions.

Encouragement to Build Your Professional Team

It is the firm belief of the author that every tech founder—whether you're building a SaaS startup, developing hardware, scaling an e-commerce platform, or creating the next big innovation—needs a solid team of financial professionals:

- A financial advisor
- A tax advisor (CPA or EA)
- A business or startup attorney
- An insurance specialist

This book is designed to complement your professional team—not replace it.

If you haven't built that team yet, now is the time. Founders know better than most the importance of assembling the right people to achieve a vision. Your financial life deserves the same care and intentional design you bring to your company.

You've spent countless hours building technology, leading teams, and pitching investors. Now it's time to ensure you're engineering a financial future that is as resilient, scalable, and impactful as the business you've worked so hard to create.

Your First 10 Moves After Reading Tech Business Founders

Financial literacy is powerful—but only if you act on it. Here's a checklist to get you started:

1. Audit Your Personal and Business Finances

- Review your personal budget and savings rate.
- Audit your business cash flow and burn rate.
- Know your runway (personally and professionally).

2. Evaluate Your Equity Compensation

- Review your stock options, RSUs, or founder's shares.
- Check your 83(b) election status if applicable.
- Understand your vesting schedule and key liquidity milestones.

3. Build or Strengthen Your Emergency Fund

- Aim for 6–12 months of living expenses.
- Remember: founders often have more financial volatility than traditional employees.

4. Maximize Retirement and Tax-Advantaged Accounts

- Set up or review Solo 401(k), SEP IRA, or other retirement plans.
- Make sure you're taking full advantage of HSA, FSA, or 529 plans where applicable.

5. Protect Yourself and Your Business

- Review personal insurance (life, disability, umbrella policies).
- Check your business insurance (key person, cyber liability, general liability).
- Protect your intellectual property.

6. Plan for Taxes Early

- Work with a CPA who understands startups, equity comp, and QSBS rules.
- Prepare for liquidity events (M&A, IPO, secondary sales) before they happen.

7. Start Estate Planning

- Create or update your will, trust, and powers of attorney.
- If you have equity or real estate, start thinking about asset protection and legacy planning.

8. Diversify Outside of Your Business

- Don't bet everything on one company—even if it's your own.
- Start building an outside investment portfolio aligned with your risk tolerance and time horizon.

9. Build Your Professional Team

- CPA who understands founders.
- Financial advisor who works with equity compensation.
- Business attorney experienced in startups.
- Insurance advisor with knowledge of founder risk profiles.

10. Set a Quarterly Financial Check-In

- Book a quarterly meeting with yourself—and your advisor(s)—to review progress.
- Adjust your financial strategy as your company and life evolve.

Final Reminder:

Start where you are. Small moves compound over time.

Financial literacy isn't about mastering everything overnight—it's about consistent, strategic action.

Wealth Manager's Coordination

At the highest levels of entrepreneurship, managing wealth is not a side task—it's an enterprise in itself. For tech founders, where complexity scales with success, wealth management becomes an interconnected system requiring meticulous orchestration across multiple disciplines. A world-class wealth manager must operate not merely as an advisor, but as the chief architect and conductor of a sophisticated ecosystem, coordinating estate planning, tax strategy, insurance, investments, liquidity planning, and philanthropy. When done right, this coordination transforms complexity into clarity, risk into resilience, and wealth into an enduring legacy.

Estate planning is foundational. Coordinating trusts, wills, and dynasty structures ensures that wealth transitions seamlessly across generations while minimizing estate taxes and shielding assets from potential threats. Tools like irrevocable trusts, grantor retained annuity trusts (GRATs), family limited partnerships (FLPs), and dynasty trusts are no longer niche—they are standard elements in the financial playbook for successful founders. Real-Life Scenario: A tech founder structured his equity holdings into a multi-generational trust framework, preserving voting control, mitigating estate taxes, and insulating family assets from future legal complications. Action Step: Schedule a comprehensive estate planning review to ensure your structures are current, tax-optimized, and aligned with your broader legacy goals.

Accounting and tax coordination, especially for multi-entity, multi-jurisdictional entrepreneurs, demands precision and proactivity. Ownership stakes in startups, secondary shares, venture funds, and international holdings all add layers of tax complexity. Seamless coordination between your wealth manager, CPA, and legal team is critical to optimizing after-tax outcomes. Pros: Greater tax efficiency and risk mitigation. Cons: Requires continual vigilance and a cross-disciplinary team. Action Step: Assemble a tax team fluent in the nuances of tech equity compensation, QSBS strategies, and global tax planning, and insist on quarterly tax strategy reviews.

Insurance planning is an often-overlooked pillar of wealth protection. Standard policies are inadequate at this level. Home, auto, yacht, aviation, fine art, cyber liability, life, disability, and umbrella policies must be customized to the founder's risk profile. Real-Life Scenario: A founder's $50 million art collection was underinsured due to outdated appraisals; engaging a specialist led to updated valuations and comprehensive coverage. Action Step: Conduct a full insurance audit across all personal and business assets annually to ensure alignment with current valuations and exposures.

Investment management must be dynamic and personalized. Direct indexing strategies allow for tax-efficient customization, while access to alternative investments—venture capital, private equity, hedge funds, and real estate—provides necessary diversification and alpha generation. Increasingly, tech founders structure portfolios heavily weighted toward private opportunities rather than traditional public markets. Action Step: Develop a robust investment policy statement (IPS) that incorporates direct indexing and disciplined allocations to alternatives, matched to your risk profile and liquidity needs.

Trading and execution require sophistication. Large block sales of pre-IPO shares or secondary market transactions must be managed carefully to avoid market impact and optimize tax outcomes. Continuous tax-loss harvesting is vital, especially in volatile markets. Real-Life Scenario: A founder's family office partnered with an institutional trading desk to systematically harvest losses, saving millions in taxes while maintaining targeted exposure. Action Step: Engage a trading specialist or institutional desk capable of executing large transactions discreetly and efficiently.

Liquidity and exit planning are non-negotiable for founders planning large liquidity events. Whether pre-IPO, a merger, or a private sale, preparation must begin years in advance. Liquidity is not merely a cushion; it's strategic capital for seizing future opportunities, weathering downturns, and funding long-term legacy projects. Real-Life Scenario: An entrepreneur facing a $200 million exit began planning five years prior, implementing pre-liquidity strategies that minimized tax exposure and diversified risk. Action Step: If a liquidity event is on your horizon, begin estate and tax structuring well in advance.

Philanthropy is no longer just a side project—it's integral to legacy building. Donor-advised funds (DAFs), private foundations, and impact-driven philanthropy must be coordinated alongside wealth and family governance planning. Aligning charitable efforts with personal values ensures that giving is strategic, meaningful, and tax-efficient. Action Step: Develop a mission-aligned philanthropy strategy that integrates seamlessly with your estate and financial plans.

The complexity across these domains is not static—it evolves with market conditions, tax law changes, and life events. Coordinating all these moving parts demands a wealth manager who acts as a quarterback, ensuring synchronization and clarity. Real-Life Scenario: A multi-generational tech family integrated estate planning, tax strategy, investment management, and philanthropy under a single, coordinated framework—leading to compounded success and enduring family unity. Action Step: Demand a fully coordinated approach from your advisory team, or re-architect your structure to deliver it.

The call to action is direct: Insist on orchestration, not isolation. Complexity demands coordination. Strategy demands synchronization.

The goals—wealth preservation, strategic growth, risk mitigation, tax optimization, family unity, and lasting impact—are entirely attainable. But they require a sophisticated conductor guiding the orchestra of estate, tax, insurance, investments, liquidity, and philanthropy. For tech founders managing significant wealth, true mastery lies not in isolated excellence, but in seamless coordination—a symphony of strategy designed to endure across generations.

While this book has been written for educational purposes, if you find yourself needing deeper guidance and personalized support in implementing this level of coordination, Pat Brown would certainly be honored to assist. With deep experience working with successful founders, entrepreneurs, and ultra-affluent families, Pat brings the expertise, discretion, and comprehensive vision necessary to navigate complexity with precision.

Annual Financial Planning Calendar for Tech Business Founders

Managing your finances as a tech founder is a lot like managing a long-term product build or scaling a company: it requires milestones, deadlines, regular check-ins, and the discipline to adjust as new data comes in. Use this month-by-month guide as a template to structure your financial year with precision and intention.

JANUARY

January 1

- New contribution limits for 401(k), 403(b), 457 plans, and IRA/Roth IRA accounts go into effect.
- Health Savings Account (HSA) and Flexible Spending Account (FSA) limits reset.
- Kick off your year with a budget and cash flow review—personal and business.
- Update your paycheck withholding (Form W-4) if major life changes (marriage, divorce, children) occurred.

January 15

- Fourth Quarter Estimated Taxes Due (income earned October 1–December 31 of the prior year). Use IRS Form 1040-ES.

Late January

- W-2s, 1099-NEC, 1099-MISC, 1099-INT, 1099-DIV, and 1099-Bs begin arriving—important for both salary and any side gigs or investments.

FEBRUARY

February 1

- Deadline for employers and payers to issue W-2s and 1099s.

Mid to Late February

- K-1 forms from partnerships and S-Corps may start arriving.
- Begin compiling all tax documents—income, business expenses, investment statements, real estate, and crypto transactions.

MARCH

March 15

- Tax deadline for Partnerships and S-Corps (Form 1065 or 1120-S).
- File an extension with IRS Form 7004 if needed.

March 31

- Deadline to receive health insurance forms (1095-A, 1095-B, 1095-C) electronically.

APRIL

April 1

- Required Minimum Distributions (RMDs) must begin if you turned 73 last year and delayed the first withdrawal.

April 15

- Personal Tax Filing Deadline (IRS Form 1040).
- First Quarter Estimated Taxes Due.
- Deadline for prior-year contributions to:
- Traditional IRA/Roth IRA
- SEP IRA (if not filing extension)
- HSA
- Coverdell ESA
- Last day to file for a 6-month tax extension (Form 4868).
- FAFSA filing deadline for many states (important if you have college-bound kids).

MAY

Early May

- Review property tax assessments; protest deadlines often fall in mid-May.

May 29 (5/29 Day)

- National reminder to open or review 529 College Savings Plans for children or future planning.

JUNE

June 15

- Second Quarter Estimated Taxes Due.
- U.S. citizens living abroad must file taxes or request an extension.

Mid-June

- Mid-year portfolio check-up: Are you on track with savings and investment goals? Adjust as needed.
- Reassess charitable giving strategies and consider contributions to donor-advised funds.

JULY

July 1–15

- Mid-year financial check-in:
- Review spending and cash flow.
- Assess savings and investment targets.
- Check progress on debt reduction.
- Rebalance your portfolio if allocations have shifted.
- Schedule a meeting with your financial advisor or CPA.

AUGUST

August 1–31

- Prepare for Open Enrollment (starts October/November).
- Review HSA/FSA balances to avoid forfeiture.
- Audit your insurance coverage: life, disability, key person, cyber liability, umbrella policies.

- Strategize for year-end charitable giving, especially if planning appreciated stock donations or QCDs.

SEPTEMBER

September 15

- Third Quarter Estimated Taxes Due.
- Final deadline for extended Partnership and S-Corp returns.

Late September

- Check on Backdoor Roth IRA contributions and conversions.
- Explore tax-loss harvesting opportunities before Q4 rush.

OCTOBER

October 1

- Deadline to set up a SIMPLE IRA for the current tax year (great for small startups).

October 15

- Extended Individual Tax Return Deadline (Form 1040).
- Final deadline for SEP IRA contributions (if you filed an extension).
- Deadline to recharacterize prior-year Roth IRA contributions if needed.

Late October

- Review Open Enrollment materials for health insurance and other employer benefits.

NOVEMBER

November 1–30

- ACA Marketplace Open Enrollment begins.
- Employer benefits enrollment:
- Review and adjust health, life, disability insurance.
- Max out or adjust 401(k) elections.
- Revisit HSA/FSA elections.
- Consider legal insurance, supplemental coverage.

Black Friday Weekend

- If you're planning big purchases (laptops, tech upgrades), align them with year-end cash flow and deductions planning.

DECEMBER

December 1–15

- Maximize contributions to retirement accounts:
- 401(k), 403(b), 457 plans
- HSA contributions via payroll
- Backdoor Roth IRA conversions

December 31

- Final day to:
- Make charitable donations to count for current-year taxes.
- Execute tax-loss harvesting strategies.
- Take RMDs if age 73+.
- Gift up to $18,000 per individual tax-free.
- Spend down FSA balances (check for grace period or rollover rules).

- Complete Roth IRA conversions.
- Issue bonuses or profit-sharing if running a corporation.

Rolling & Event-Based Reminders

Every Paycheck

- Check 401(k)/403(b) contributions.
- Confirm HSA contributions.
- Verify health insurance premium deductions.

After Major Life Events

- Marriage, divorce, birth, or adoption.
- Job changes, promotions, or new freelance gigs.
- Moving residences or states.
- Major financial windfalls or inheritance.

Quarterly

- Review and update your budget.
- Make estimated tax payments if necessary.
- Reassess portfolio allocations.
- Plan tax strategies like Roth conversions or loss harvesting.

Final Tip: Automate Where Possible

Financial success thrives on smart automation:

- Set calendar alerts for major deadlines.
- Automate savings and investment contributions.
- Schedule quarterly or semiannual financial check-ins.
- Pre-schedule debt payments and savings boosts.

The fewer tasks you leave to chance, the more consistent and effective your financial plan will be—just like a well-run startup sprint, moving steadily toward product-market fit and beyond.

Financial Literacy Resources for Tech Business Founders

Financial Literacy for Tech Founders

A dedicated platform offering practical guides, tools, and educational resources tailored to the unique financial lives of tech entrepreneurs—from pre-seed founders to post-exit operators.

The Founder's Guide to Financial Mastery

An insightful article offering strategies for achieving financial independence, covering critical topics like equity compensation, liquidity planning, tax optimization, investing, and protecting founder wealth.

Bespoke Wealth – Financial Planning for Entrepreneurs

Expert advice on managing founder stock, maximizing retirement contributions, navigating QSBS benefits, optimizing cash flow, and building a resilient financial foundation through every stage of company growth.

Personal Finance for Entrepreneurs – Inc.com

A comprehensive guide outlining key financial principles for founders, including debt management, risk mitigation, cash runway planning, and long-term wealth-building strategies.

Financial Acumen for Startups – Y Combinator Startup School

A free course teaching startup founders financial decision-making, focusing on burn rate management, fundraising strategy, budgeting, and cap table literacy.

Financial Literacy for Startup Founders – OTM Online

Provides templates, tools, and educational resources to help new founders manage living expenses, budget through early fundraising rounds, and set financial goals as they scale.

The Entrepreneur's Guide to Financial Planning – Lakewood Wealth

Discusses how founders can align their personal and business financial goals, emphasizing wealth-building strategies, tax planning, risk management, and portfolio diversification after exit events.

Financial Planning Challenges for Founders – Bollin Wealth Management

Highlights common financial hurdles tech founders face—such as inconsistent income, fundraising uncertainty, and complex equity structures—offering solutions to manage cash flow, taxes, and liquidity effectively.

Financial Literacy for Founders – Startup Grind Webinar Series

A webinar introducing fundamental financial concepts tailored to startup life, helping founders build strong personal financial foundations alongside growing their businesses.

Financial Literacy Modules for Entrepreneurs – University of Iowa

Educational modules covering essential concepts like interest rates, time value of money, budgeting, and business fundamentals, helping tech founders integrate financial literacy into business-building.

WorldQuant University – MSc in Financial Engineering

A free, accredited online master's program focused on quantitative finance—ideal for founders seeking to deepen their financial knowledge for venture scaling, data-driven decision-making, or investment pursuits.

Corporate Finance Institute (CFI)

Offers online certifications in financial modeling, business valuation, and corporate finance—critical skills for founders managing fundraising rounds, M&A, or long-term financial strategy.

Investopedia – Financial Literacy Resources

A comprehensive platform providing tutorials, articles, and calculators for building financial knowledge in investing, budgeting, tax planning, and wealth management.

Wall Street Survivor

An interactive educational platform using gamification to teach investing and personal finance concepts—allowing founders to practice building and managing virtual portfolios risk-free.

Next Gen Personal Finance (NGPF)

Provides free courses and resources in personal finance—an excellent supplement for tech founders looking to strengthen foundational knowledge in saving, investing, and debt management.

Federal Reserve Education

Offers accessible materials on economics, market dynamics, and personal finance fundamentals—equipping founders to better understand macroeconomic trends and their impact on business strategy.

Financial Literacy and the Startup Founder – YouTube Webinar

A webinar covering key financial literacy topics for tech founders, including managing equity, planning for liquidity events, budgeting during bootstrapping phases, and building passive income streams.

Refactoring – Personal Finance for Entrepreneurs

An article discussing practical strategies for founders on managing variable income, building emergency funds, setting up tax reserves, and investing with long-term discipline.

Engineering Financial Literacy – Stanford d.school

While designed for engineers, this initiative uses design thinking to teach financial literacy—offering valuable frameworks tech founders can adapt for creative financial problem-solving.

Financial Planning for Tech Founders – Scripted.com

A guide outlining key financial planning steps for founders—budgeting, risk management, exit strategy preparation, and long-term wealth-building post-startup life.

These resources are designed to empower tech entrepreneurs with the knowledge and tools needed to make informed financial decisions—whether you're scaling your startup, managing a liquidity event, or preparing for your next big venture. Like building a great company, building personal wealth requires strategy, resilience, and a vision for the future.

About Author

Pat Brown, MBA, is a former Division I football player turned wealth advisor, educator, and nationally respected voice in financial literacy. With more than two decades of experience in financial planning, investment strategy, and insurance, Pat has dedicated his career to helping individuals and entrepreneurs build wealth with clarity, confidence, and a long-term vision.

After earning his MBA and launching a successful career in wealth management, Pat founded a series of financial literacy platforms designed to serve overlooked and underserved communities. His platforms include:

- Financial Literacy For NIL
- Financial Literacy For Student Athletes
- Financial Literacy For The Culture
- Financial Literacy For College Coaches
- Financial Literacy For Parents of Student Athletes
- Financial Literacy For Attorneys
- Financial Literacy For Doctors
- Financial Literacy For Dentists
- Financial Literacy For Pharmacists
- Financial Literacy For Engineers
- Financial Literacy For First Responders
- Financial Literacy For Expats
- Financial Literacy For Architects

Now, through *Financial Literacy For Tech Business Founders*, Pat brings his mission to one of the most innovative and fast-moving professions in the world. Founders are experts at building companies, scaling technology, and changing industries—but many have never been taught how to apply that same strategic rigor to their personal financial lives. Pat's goal is to change that.

His passion for financial education is rooted in personal experience. Raised in a home where financial discussions were rare, he saw firsthand how the absence of financial literacy could derail even the brightest futures. Today, Pat is committed to bridging the gap between earning income and building sustainable, generational wealth.

Over the years, Pat has become a trusted advisor to a diverse clientele—including startup founders, attorneys, physicians, dentists, engineers, athletes, and young professionals. His approach is practical, culturally aware, and grounded in real-world experience—not financial jargon or hype. Whether you're a seed-stage entrepreneur, a venture-backed CEO, or a post-exit founder planning your next chapter, Pat's advice is designed to meet you where you are and guide you forward—strategically and thoughtfully.

Beyond his financial work, Pat serves as a Trustee on the Board of Lawrence Memorial Hospital (LMH), contributing to governance and strategic planning initiatives. He is active on multiple nonprofit and civic boards, championing financial literacy, family support services, and improved access to healthcare.

Above all, Pat is a devoted husband and father. When he's not advising clients or speaking at startup accelerators, universities, or industry conferences, he translates complex financial concepts into real-world strategies that founders can immediately apply to secure their futures.

Pat believes financial literacy isn't just about wealth—it's about options, freedom, and creating a life you're proud to live. Just as tech founders transform bold ideas into world-changing businesses, Pat helps them transform income and opportunity into enduring wealth and security.

Final Word

Need Help? Start Here

This book exists because financial education is one of the most powerful tools a founder can have. When used well, it can open doors, protect your legacy, and give you the confidence to take control of your financial future.

But just like building a successful tech company, financial success isn't achieved through guesswork. You need structure. You need systems. You need the discipline to ask the right questions, weigh the trade-offs, and know when to bring in experts. It's not about mastering every detail—it's about navigating decisions with clarity and confidence.

Use this book as a guide—not a rulebook. Let it inspire action. Let it help you build momentum. But don't treat it as a substitute for personalized advice. Stay curious. Stay informed. Keep asking good questions before making any major financial decisions.

Trusted Resources

If you're looking for guidance or want to talk through your next steps, reach out to professionals who understand your world—startups, scaling, equity compensation, liquidity events, and the pressure of making high-impact decisions that shape your future.

Pat Brown, MBA

Wealth advisor. Financial literacy advocate. Former Division I athlete.

Advisor to tech founders, entrepreneurs, student-athletes, and high-performing professionals nationwide.

Website: www.techbusinessfounders.com

Email: info@techbusinessfounders.com

LinkedIn: linkedin.com/in/patrickbrownmba

Join Our Newsletter

Stay sharp with insights, strategies, and reminders designed specifically for tech entrepreneurs—delivered directly to your inbox.

Subscribe at www.techbusinessfounders.com to get actionable financial education tailored to founders at every stage.

Final Word: Use This. Don't Shelf It.

The ideas, frameworks, and tools in this book aren't meant to gather dust. Use them. Revisit them. Share them with someone who needs them. Test what works, refine what doesn't, and keep evolving your process.

This is your playbook—not just for your company, but for your life. Personally, professionally, and financially.

Stay sharp. Stay curious. Keep building the future you deserve.